To

I love you !

"Molly Knight Forde has created a living memoir that explores Fourth Way work practices applied in the midst of life. These practices are required for the development of inner life. Forde's clear examples and application of Gurdjieff's Fourth Way are not theoretical, but experiential and provide the reader examples of integrating inner and outer life."

–Dr. Russell Schreiber, author of *Gurdjieff's Transformational Psychology: The Art of Compassionate Self-Study*

———————

"Molly Knight Forde muses on life and consciousness from the perspective of Gurdjieff's 'Fourth Way'. She says: "The Fourth Way has everything to do with maintaining presence as I go about life." This explains much of the charm of this collection of articles. They connect with real life rather than unreal ideals and are written with a modesty and freshness that is rare. Molly takes the reader along with her; does not preach, but shares the meaning she has discovered in her search and makes contact with as she writes. Dip into the book anywhere and one finds the sparkle of jewels of insight and compassion. There are no heavy explanations but the sense of a friendly conversation one is invited to be part of."

–A.G.E. Blake, author of *The Intelligent Enneagram*

"With the present, repair the past, and prepare the future."

–Gurdjieff

To Manny

BE PRESENT

REFLECTIONS ON THE WAY

MOLLY KNIGHT FORDE

Be Present: Reflections On The Way

Copyright © 2017 Molly Knight Forde

www.mollyknightforde.com

ISBN 978-1975775384

Edited by Dawn Wakefield and Sean Forde

Printed in the United States of America

First Edition: September 2017
1 3 5 7 9 10 8 6 4 2

Set in Georgia font
Designed by Jason Storey
Illustrations by Vanessa Couto

TABLE OF
CONTENTS

———————

PREFACE

A few years ago, I set an aim to write an article every week. At first it was merely to gain more visibility for my meditation school, but it soon morphed into a much larger task. This aim became threefold.

It became obvious that I needed to improve my writing skills. I have known for a while that I have more than a few books to write; some of which I have already started. For most of my life, I have written a journal, but never for other people to read. It was high time I started to practice the craft intentionally. As a professional classical pianist and avid meditator, I believe in practicing and understanding first hand how discipline yields big results. Once I set this aim to produce an article every week, I started writing almost every morning after I meditated.

My aim also became a need to further understand the ideas of Gurdjieff and the Fourth Way, which I have been practicing and then teaching for over twenty years. Besides my initial six year intense practice of Zen Buddhism, Hatha yoga and Irano Egyptian yoga, the Fourth Way ideas and practices, known as The Work, have been my core guidance system and my spiritual sustenance. With these influences in place, I set out to clarify in writing what I had experienced over the years.

The Fourth Way has everything to do with maintaining presence as I go about life. I don't need to go to a monastery or an ashram to experience a deep spiritual process within myself. It is the awareness of my awareness within, while simultaneously living out in the world that has been my main practice. I learned to do it in the trenches as a parent, on stages as a musician, as a citizen of the world, and as a modern day seeker.

A more detailed explanation of Gurdjieff and the Fourth Way is in order since most of the ideas and terminology I use are from that tradition. G. I. Gurdjieff was a mystic who brought esoteric ideas of the East and West together. He formulated a system of transformation using unique and unorthodox methods to help individuals become free from their inherent mechanical nature. His main premise was that we are asleep, but through inner work we can harmonize the "three brains" - our thinking, our emotions, and our body - to develop our Essence and potentially access Higher Levels of Understanding. His cosmology included the belief that our inner transformation contributes to the maintenance and evolution of the planet, while at the same time developing the distinct possibility for our eternal life. He introduced the idea that we are not automatically born with a soul, but that we must develop a soul through right inner work.

The third aim was to serve the purpose of explaining these ideas from my own experience and in my own words to my students and the groups I have been facilitating. Many of the essays were inspired by retreats and movements seminars over the last five years. I was often provided with the material as a direct result of our group work. There was an unending stream of things to write about. I wanted to explain ideas as we went along by way of these articles. I am not sure it always served its purpose well. I have had people tell me they cannot understand what I am writing about.

My disclaimer, therefore, is that I am not really a writer yet. I am a mystic and a sincere seeker. I have known that from a very early age. I am an eternal student and I am in deep gratitude to my teachers for ferrying me to the other side. I am a musician and a teacher, so somehow things have converged to this point.

Perhaps what you are holding in your hand is a testimony to my own process as a writer.

You may notice the evolution of the writing because I have chosen to keep the essays in chronological order. Feel free to skip around and open the book randomly. Use it as a daily read or a weekly theme. There is no rhyme or reason to the order other than that is how it happened. Perhaps you will forgive my clumsiness in the beginning of the book. I believe it gets better as you go.

Some of the essays are purely personal. Some are born out of experiences with my everyday life and my own inner struggle. Some are channeled messages. Some are students' struggles. Some are merely to explain different Fourth Way ideas as a reference. They were all present in my Being, so I have included them all despite whether they segway correctly or not.

The ideas that run throughout the material may seem somewhat repetitive, but I have found that one cannot hear them enough in order to understand their complexity. We need to hear them in many different ways many times before it all sinks in..

Finally, the significance of the bee in my logo and in the illustrations represents the search for truth. The idea is not mine of course. I have always had an affinity for bees and honey. I am busy as a bee and I am always searching for the truth in spiritual disciplines of all sorts. I was stunned to learn that Gurdjieff also likened an ancient and secret society of seekers of the truth to bees gathering sacred nectar from many teachings. The bee serves as a symbol for the incredible alchemy required to transform nectar into sweet honey.

My wish is that these essays inspire you in your own search toward freedom and to spur you on to greater platitudes of presence. Spiritual things can take on a life of their own as a means to an end. For me, however, it must be an end unto itself. It serves a greater purpose than just our own personal transformation. I cannot live life without this connection to the divine within me and within others. Music has played a huge part in that but equally so has my inner spiritual quest.

The greatest gift of all has been the community of seekers that has formed as a result of my participation in this Great Work. The classes and regular meetings, the retreats, the Sacred Dances and the resulting transformation has affected all of us. Our individual process becomes service to humanity. Together we have experienced accelerated transformation in a most extraordinary way. These writings are partly an expression of those experiences.

I continue to seek deeper levels of Objective Reason and Conscience within myself. I will always put myself at risk to establish this.

This book is one such risk.

MANIFESTING

Lately I have been doing work with manifestation and have vowed to accept that things can come easily to me. I don't want to believe that it is only hard work that gives good results. For example, I am dedicated and committed to my business, contributing to its growth every day. This is one of the joys and the pitfalls of having my own business with no one to tell me when or how to do it. There are no deadlines and no pressure to achieve anything except from my own desire to make it happen.

If I believe it has to be hard, then it will be.

Do you find yourself believing that to get good results, it is going to take a long time or that it is a hard road? Did your parents instill in you a "good work ethic" meaning, if you don't work hard, you will not succeed. What about the idea that things can come easily and you deserve that! Doesn't that sound wonderful?

I believe in balance. I believe there has to be both effort and reception: two forces colliding to create a fused third force. If I start with a belief that it can be easy - that the right people will be presented to me in the right timing, then I can begin to take action toward that belief. There has to be the conviction that it is true, then action can be taken toward the manifested result.

The result may not take the form I thought it would, but I will leave that up to the universe to figure out how and what. I just know that I must make a certain kind of effort, the right effort, and allow the Universe to work with me. I must use my intuition as part of these tools so that I don't get in the way of the manifestation.

If my intuition says, "speak to this person about my classes" and I ignore that impulse, then I have missed something that already exists in the realm of possibility. If I follow my intuition, I will either get a "no" and learn something about the situation, or I will find a new student. It is my prejudgement that gets in the way, especially if I am holding a certain image of what a perfect student is.

Another example is timing. If I can muster the feeling that something has already happened, I tell my subconscious mind that it has already happened. I don't focus on it not happening fast enough. I don't focus on what is not working. I focus on something as if it has already happened, for somewhere out there outside of time and space, it has happened. There is an unmanifested pattern in the invisible world. I am affecting it with my intention to let it be.

There can be no room for doubt.

At one point, I decided I would have an all expense paid trip to an International Convention in Thailand. I saw myself having a reason to go to Thailand. I put this as a reminder in my phone and I suspended my disbelief.

In the next month, I won a free ticket to the convention and I knew that the Universe was bending to meet my expectation. I looked for enough frequent flyer miles to get there, but didn't have enough. It didn't look likely that I could go. When I got off the phone, my husband had overheard the conversation, looked in an old account for United, and found enough miles there for me to go for free.

When things start to manifest, my belief begins to soar. It gets easier and easier to see that what I believe and feel is what I manifest in my life. I believe my work can be easy, productive and fulfilling and so it is.

TRIBUTE TO A WELL LOVED DOG

Today, Tula, I give you a well deserved tribute. You showed up in our lives during a very intense retreat. It was a time of conscious creative propulsion toward lifelong wishes and goals. It was a week where many had gathered with a common purpose and aim. Some had not come together in this capacity for a very long time; some had been meeting regularly, but everyone that week was touched by a force greater than the sum of its parts. For this, in some way you represent a high point of our group's momentum.

You will always remind me of the Power of the Pack.

You, a wise and weary old traveller, wandered in to say these are my people, and so it was decided that our family would take you from a life in the wild and bring you home. The only one flustered by this was one territorial Tom, the Maine Coon Cat. Your wagging gratitude was apparent and we fattened you up like a Christmas goose.

One thing that impressed me about our entire time together was how well mannered you were, except when a little white furry bonbon would cross our path on a walk. You sent our hearts racing many times in pursuit of a helpless comrade. Other than that, you conducted yourself with the utmost decorum. You didn't feel compelled to sniff any human derriere or disturb the peace and quiet when visitors arrived. You were not a glutton for love, but a faithful bystander, ready and willing to please. As a solid family member, your motto remained, "others come first."

You endured a car accident in our absence and, with a weakened constitution, still gave birth to ten beautiful puppies in our home; an old pro, and probably a breeder of many Pit fighters in the past. You were a very good Mama indeed.

Your uncanny ability to transmit and reflect our feelings was intrinsic. I will never forget how you left the room at the detection of any tension or anger in someone's voice. Thanks for reminding us that there is no need for that kind of interaction. We would usually end up in laughter due to your departure. Through your eyes, we could communicate in a world outside of our own, wordless, boundless and free; a world where hearts blend to reach understanding. We have learned so much from this telepathic connection.

You have touched the lives of three children, many piano students, and your dog whisperer caretakers who appreciated the enlightened eyes through which you greeted the world. The smallest acts of kindness went a long way with you. Our walks brought us out of our own selfish needs and into just Being, simplicity, rhythm, nature, rain or shine. Your wholehearted appreciation for such small gifts taught us to take nothing for granted.

You have endured the coming and going of many a spiritual seeker on Monday nights over the years. It is no surprise that you chose to leave as a new group structure was born: a new octave, a change of format, the influx of new leaders. You were telling us all is well with these efforts, wishes and goals. The group Work will live on in strength and numbers. We can do this if we do it together.

There is a special place in our hearts that has been touched and you will remain there for eternity. You loved us without question and without promise, unconditionally. For us that is often a difficult thing, but for you Tula, Dog of Wonder and Teacher of Many, it was the most natural thing in the world.

Run Free Now.

FORGIVENESS

Forgiveness leads me to gratitude and peace.

Initially, when I forgive someone or myself, I strive for empathy. I try to understand from someone else's perspective the reasons for their actions. I also strive to not take things so personally. Even if someone's actions are not justifiable and feel hurtful, they are what they are. Understanding their origin is my way of reaching for more empathy. I learn to accept limitations, including my own.

This does not mean that I am making excuses for my actions. It means that I am pushing against self justification and entering a frequency outside of old habitual patterns. Those patterns appear as beating myself up for not being perfect, or always needing to be right. Finding this place of deep forgiveness is stepping outside of a mechanism which traps me emotionally, energetically and even physically.

Holding a grudge means that I am blaming someone else for my unhappiness. I am not seeing my part in the matter nor my lack of boundary. My reluctance to see outside of my own story becomes my gross inability to understand. If I can forgive, it means I can allow myself or someone else to make mistakes. If I cannot forgive someone, including myself, I choose to give power to the part of me that is identified with perfection and what I think should be. This prevents solid relationships and stagnates an energetic flow from my Being.

If I am only able to have negative thoughts and feelings around a particular situation or past incident, then I am not in sync with the God Essence within me.

This is what I mean by the flow of Being. If I do not have access to this, my behavior will most likely be reactive toward that person or situation when it is not to my liking. My behavior also becomes reactive to situations that I associate with unresolved issues. Someone may act the way my mother acted with me long ago and if that has not been forgiven and resolved, it triggers something within me. A build up of unforgiven actions and continual resentment creates even more reactive interaction and sensitivity within me. I will have a harder time releasing resentment and blame.

How then do I actually forgive myself and others so that I can experience freedom from reaction?

First of all, I must learn not to take things personally even if I have experienced harm and sadness. Secondly, I must see the person I am trying to forgive as an innocent child, or victim of their own circumstances. None of us are exempt from our conditioning. I cannot help what formed my conditioning and personality as a child, but I can work toward releasing those patterns by observing them.

I must strive to understand the chain of events from generation to generation and break the chain for myself by seeing the pattern within me, not by changing someone else's patterns. I cannot continue to wish things were different. I must try to accept that my parents were not perfect no matter how much it has affected me. I can only choose how I feel and not how someone else should act. That acceptance comes from knowing that there is no difference between us. I am looking in the mirror.

I must learn to feel this in a place within myself that is not analytical, not self righteous, not superior, but in a whole, loving, vulnerable place of empathy. I must be willing to feel this no matter how scary it may be. I attempt to see into the object of my forgiveness and allow myself to feel the pain of that person. I let my guard down... Wrong action and hurtful action comes from pain that resides within. We all have it, and to expect someone else not to have it is showing very little empathy for the human condition. To forgive myself and others is to accept that I don't know everything, that I don't know how to have proper boundaries, that I am still learning through life's trial and errors, that I don't have to take on the pain of others.

Finally, to feel this release means to let emotion come forward that perhaps has been held back by blaming others. I can accept my pain as a result of unmet expectations. This makes room for me to release those expectations I have of myself and others. When I no longer expect someone else to be perfect or to make me happy, I regain my own power and my own happiness.

I am then able to attract stability, love and abundance of all sorts instead of engendering negative emotion and reaction every time a situation triggers the old wound. In fact, the trigger will be gone. It is replaced with understanding from the heart and no expectation to be fulfilled from the outside.

To forgive is to release the wounds I carried along for so long that generated an endless fountain of associated anger and resentment. To forgive unravels the woven mesh of conditioned patterns making me believe I must be completed by someone else's behavior. To forgive will dissipate my anger. To forgive from my heart allows me to accept myself and others just as we are.

THE ZEN OF ROOFING

Having just finished a week long retreat, I have been reflecting on the practical work aspect of our practice and how effective it is. It is an integral part of our program that puts people in a physical mode and takes them perhaps way out of their comfort zone. It allows them to learn new skills. Most importantly, the participants learn how to be present while doing regular ordinary things.

Creating special conditions in which we do practical things allows us to experience being present.

Let me give you a concrete example. Our amazing practical work leader must find the right job for us as a group on these retreats. Ideally we are all working together on a project in which there are no assigned jobs. We must see how the process works or come to know the pattern and rhythm of things via chaos and mistakes. He must gauge the scope and difficulty of the project with the finite amount of time we have on the retreat, also keeping in mind that he has unskilled workers. Often we have people who don't even know how to hammer a nail properly. His role creates ways for him to work internally as well.

This week we are putting a new roof on a work shed and extending the building on either end. That means, we are taking off the old roof, digging holes for new posts, building and framing the extensions, leveling the ground underneath, papering the top, and then putting the new flashing and roof on the entire building. As we begin, no one knows who will do what. Our practice is to see the need and begin to do it. Through trial and error, a way emerges.

Our leader will often show us a correct method with safety in mind, but our aim is to find the way ourselves through our own effort. Sometimes this task can seem daunting and impossible or at least very unpalatable to an unskilled person. Removing the old roof with tools I have never even seen before offers me a chance to experience how my body works to pry off nails and shingles without messing up my back if I am to last the rest of the week. I know the people next to me are thinking the same thing. Each one of us is experimenting with which tool works best. Later on in the week, I laugh hard as I am looking at a nurse, a yoga teacher, a classical pianist, a social worker and a legislative aide gearing up with nail guns, cutters, and flashing scissors.

We must layer shingles in a staircase fashion all the while making sure that things stay parallel with our lines on the paper. From time to time, we step back from measuring each shingle with the previous one and just look at the work to get a different perspective. Any slight variance in alignment will gradually screw it all up. The shingles are each nailed five times in an overlap with the previous shingle. We quickly realize that it is good to have a nailer and an assistant who gets the next shingle ready and holds it in place once it has been measured and placed properly. We work in pairs.

For someone who has never used a nail gun, there is some trial and error that occurs. If you tap it to the surface with hesitation or lack of confidence, the nail goes in a little askew. If you use too much force, more than one nail comes out. Judging the distance of the nails is also a procedure to discover.

We learn this as we go, turning what looks like a hopeless situation into empowerment and focus. Like other work projects in the past, I notice that I find a rhythm, a pattern, a sequence, and a oneness with the activity and the others. There is always a phenomenon which occurs amongst the workers involving co-operation, leadership, teamwork, and individual attention and effort. Skills are acquired and things move along much more efficiently.

When we stop on the hour, each hour, I sense the oneness of the group in their efforts to be present, in their effort to engage in the activity, and in their willingness to dare to try. Stopping like this helps us gain perspective on how identified and invested we are with a result, goal, or deadline.

This kind of identification creates stress and discordant interaction amongst people during any kind of project in all aspects of life.

As the stop occurs, people settle into a stillness and remember the purpose, the real purpose of the practical work as a vehicle for transformation. Sometimes this brings me to tears to feel the concerted effort of many and our collected stillness. It is meaningful and determines for me that there is a way for us all to work together in harmony. That presence and cohesion spreads from one member of the group to another as the project moves on from day to day.

This is when roofing becomes a way to freedom.

DAILY DISCIPLINE

Daily discipline creates great results. What may seem insurmountable becomes possible through small consistent effort. The prisoner digging the tunnel with a spoon over years and years from "The Shawshank Redemption" comes to mind. It is a perfect example of how to get things done. He was determined, consistent and patient.

I myself know this from being a classical pianist and a spiritual practitioner of meditation. I could look at a piece of music and think I don't know if I could ever play that, but with microvision of daily practice, isolating small runs and passages, not caring about big results, I am able to eventually master the piece. My focus must be to do the smallest of tasks on a daily basis even if I don't want to. This is the biggest battle of all.

If I set something in motion with intention, I know that the only way to achieve it is to work on it consistently. Anyone can accomplish their dreams with these parameters in place, no matter how unskilled or untalented they are.

There are key factors involved. There must be a strong belief that it is possible. Without this, we will find many ways to sabotage our work. There also must be a keen wish driving the momentum to accomplish the task. Without this wish, the first sign of difficulty will send us running.

If I have emotion behind my wish to achieve a goal, and if I feel as if the outcome has already happened, then there is a better chance of overcoming things that get in my way. I see myself on the stage playing those pieces. I see myself traveling and emotionally experience what it feels like to be there.

The wish must be emotionally fixed in me by seeing and feeling the final outcome as if it were real. This emotional energy is the driving force behind this wish!

Part of me will have fear, resistance or doubt (whether I am conscious of it or not) and that part of me will always sabotage the daily goals unless I push against it with a certain kind of effort. In achieving the tiniest daily goal, I learn to override that sabotaging mechanism within me by tapping into the emotion that desires the outcome. That will then give me more energy to push in the moment of resistance.

In a given day, I might not feel like doing it, but my desire overcomes this, and so I go practice. Each day becomes a drop in the bucket. As the bucket gets more full, it gets easier to push against the "laziness." I get more positive because results are happening. the scale begins to tip from doubt to resignation.

If you have ever dieted, quit smoking, gone on an exercise program, started meditating, you know what I am talking about. Even if I falter after a few weeks, I have felt the ease with which it began to happen, compared to the first few days. That recollection can lead me to try again.

If I can continue on for at least 28 days, it becomes a solid habit and though I might miss a day here and there after that, I know it takes less effort to get back in the game. When I do fall off the horse, a key element is to understand and accept that I will make mistakes and waiver in my consistency. I learn self compassion by feeling good about all the other efforts I have made toward this goal. It is so easy to exaggerate a small failure and make that an excuse to give up.

With any goal, there will always be push back. That is a universal law, so part of achieving what I may think is impossible is to know that I must face the things that get in my way. The more prepared I am to stand up to the obstacles, the easier they are when they show up.

My expectations about challenges carry a lot of weight in the matter. If I know that there will be resistance somewhere in some form, then I set my expectation to know that it too is supposed to be there as a learning curve, a stepping stone, a character builder.

I accept the small stumbles as part of the process so that I am not thrown by them. If I can see them as progress instead of setback, I will not be deterred from actualizing my goal. My emotional desire keeps my laser focus: my self compassion allows me to fail.

Many of us do not even attempt to achieve what we think is impossible because it involves failing and experiencing difficulty. We are taught as children that it is not ok to fail. In fact, now the school system is reluctant to hold people back in school or even fail them on a test. No wonder we can't achieve our goals. We have not learned how to fail! Knowing that I will encounter some resistance and failure along the way and recognizing it as part of the plan will help the discipline. "Feeling the vision" will help get it done daily!

You can do this!

ANGER

I have been doing a lot of research on anger. For myself, I have worked many years toward getting to the root cause of my own anger and what is called in Fourth Way terms: identification. The identification is what causes the anger. No amount of anger expression gets rid of that seed. Without understanding identification, our anger is an endless strand of unskillful expression or perilous suppression. If one does not address the real causes of the anger, then there is a need to have to express it somehow somewhere. One will always feel wronged, cheated, and hurt, if there is identification with the way things "should be."

I found that my anger decreased immensely when I experienced it in all of my centers (body, mind and emotions) simultaneously. I began to understand my own conditioning in regard to the way things should be. If things were not a certain way according to my likes and dislikes, then it would bring up a state of anger.

Meditation can relieve some of these feelings, but there is no substitute for daily self-observation to catch ourselves in a state of identification. If a situation is highly charged and negative emotions abound, then one can rest assured that one is in a state of identification. Also, associated anger occurs because one has triggers lodged within from the past that are activated through present situations. Our anger then is not actually occurring from the things at hand but from unresolved past events that have formed our view of things. It is re-ignited by current events that remind our "system" of the initial response. We however cannot focus on healing the past. We must focus on healing the now.

Our ego, (parasite as it is called in the book, Mastery of Awareness by Dona Bernadette Vigil) feeds off of anger. If one fights the outward expression of anger in a struggle with one's own ego, a higher energy is produced. I am saying that one can find one's way to freedom from anger, not by suppressing it or expressing it, but by questioning its existence in the first place and studying it through experience in the moment. Keeping it in front of us as it happens is going to make a huge difference. We don't have to fix it, change it, or suppress it. We must observe it from a new perspective.

In my study of anger, I have also observed small children. Tiny babies up to age 2 or so do not have anger. They simply have a crying response that is for survival and a call for comfort. Once a child's ego develops around age 3, their conditioning creates and solidifies their likes and dislikes. When they don't get what they want, it causes an anger response. At this point, a parent will usually try to make that child suppress the anger or they will convey the message that what the child is feeling is not legitimate.

Unfortunately most of us raise children to develop their likes and dislikes. When they don't get what they like, anger ensues. If we are not consistent with clear boundaries, we feed these likes and dislikes. We can help our children by trying not to encourage these likes and dislikes. When they get angry, they learn that they can't always get what they want or deserve. They see that people don't act the way they want them to act. They learn to accept the way it is.

We need to acknowledge children's angry feelings and try to see what they are really asking for. If they have an expectation that they only get what they want and never have to do what they don't like, imagine the problems later in life. This is not about not giving into their whims. Life itself will provide many injustices that they must learn to accept and forgive. If children are protected from making mistakes or feeling pain, they have a very low threshold for dealing with reality.

The trend lately has been all about giving children choices, but I am not in agreement with that. Serving dinner, as a simple example, with no other options, has taught my children to eat what they thought they didn't like. I don't make deals. If instead I try to please my child with what they like and avoid what they don't like, I am developing someone who experiences negative emotion when things don't go their way.

Anger is manifested outwardly in our society because it is utterly suppressed. We are not encouraged to look at the dark side. We are taught in religion that the shadow part of us is bad. Our collective anger is emerging in most unhealthy ways; it is pervasive in all cultures from media violence, war, discrimination, domination, isolation, to bullying and self mutilation. We must find a way to look at our anger when it arises, with a struggle to not act it out, but to acknowledge that it is there and discover what it is. We cannot continue to suppress it through distraction, self improvement and "positive thinking."

To do this, we must come to have enough attention and inner presence to be on the lookout for impending volcanic eruptions. At that moment, we attempt to notice our body, our feelings and our thoughts simultaneously. This type of inner vigilance comes from daily practice so that we are ready before the cat gets out of the bag. Sitting with those feelings without acting upon them will reveal the truth about what they are and where they may be coming from.

"A great exercise the next time you feel angry is to notice your body between your throat and your pelvis. Notice where there is tension, rapid heart rate, shortness of breath, pressure in your chest, a tightened stomach perhaps. Sit with these physical sensations and notice this anger within your body, not defining it, not stopping it and not expressing it. Let it remind you of past bodily sensations that have felt the same way. Perhaps you will have a memory of this same physical feeling that will lead you to more information about what is really causing your anger." - from Gurdjieff's Transformational Psychology by Russell Schreiber

You don't have to relieve the anger, you simply need to see what your body has to say to you. Are you able to hold your attention on your body and your thoughts at the same time? If you are inundated with anger and cannot extricate yourself, remember you have the power to watch it, like it is a movie. You create space around it. You may begin to realize the anger is not you.

THE MOVEMENTS

The first time I was exposed to The Gurdjieff Movements I was transported to another time and place, perhaps even another dimension. The combination of gestures and music created a sense of deep reverence in me. I could hardly believe something so profound existed. I felt I was part of a lineage just by being in the room, like some sort of transmission was happening.

The irony of this is that my first exposure was not as a participant in the class but as the pianist. I had an infant on my back, was new in town, and had been hired by a friend to play for a class. I did not know what I was in for, and my friend was unaware that I had been an avid participant in a Zen Dojo, meditating daily for 9 years.

The second irony is that I had been living in Paris where Gurdjieff had lived for many years and had choreographed some of his best movements. "Work" groups had formed in places very near to my arrondissement and I had no idea.

The third irony is that I took Martha Graham dance classes twice a week in a studio where the Movements were being taught next door. I can remember passing by a closed door late one evening after my class, hearing a hauntingly exotic middle eastern melody wafting through the cracks. I was stunned by the feeling that overtook me. The music actually called to me and I did not realize until much later after I had devoted my life to work with the Movements that it had been the very same Movements music written by Thomas de Hartmann.

The only way to really know what the Movements can offer is to experience them for yourself. The first time I was a participant in a class, I struggled to keep track of the different patterns, often irregular ones, and the interplay between my arms and legs. Adding the head took me into an emotional tailspin, inner self bashing, and somehow anger. Part of me wrestled with the fact that as an amateur dancer, I should have been getting this pretty easily. After many classes I began to see a process that was occurring within me. I realized the only way to do the correct gestures was to calm down the emotional hystrionics occurring on the inside.

It would be countless classes later before I made the correlation between my reactions to the Movements and how I dealt with real life. They had revealed to me an aspect of my automatic behavior in a flash, and with full participation, I could learn to be present, enter into the dance, and replace that behavior. This revelation was a life changing extraordinary moment for me. From then on, I treated these Sacred Dances as a means to my own transformation and I am deeply grateful to my Teacher John MacPherson for leading me to places within my Being that I would never have known otherwise.

Through The Movements, I have come to understand the concept that Gurdjieff taught so often, "With the present moment, repair the past and prepare the future." I learned to do this not just in the Movements class but out in regular life. That is the valuable gift they can offer to everyone.

The power of the movements cannot be underestimated, for they transmit certain energies that work within our bodies to create change. As a pianist, a participant, and a teacher of the Movements, I can unquestionably say that I have seen countless people make breakthroughs in their life when the movement unlocked patterns that resided in the body on a cellular level and were otherwise inaccessible.

I have touched realms that I am unable to see through my mind alone. With struggle and intention to synthesize the body, the emotions and the mind, I have found a vehicle and method that creates real and permanent results. When I am finally able to actually dance the dance, feel the dance and be the dance, I know certain patterns have been replaced and I can fully participate. This is the true value and purpose of Sacred Dance.

SOUTHERN FRIED PREJUDICE

I have been reflecting on my own experience of race and prejudice. I am a white woman who grew up in the southern United States. My experiences as a young girl in the South have formed my view of African Americans, and it is not all black and white. Do I see things objectively, or am I tainted with automatic reaction from learned behavior and initial imprinting? In order to study this question, I have given myself the task to intentionally notice impressions that I receive in regard to race; real impressions, not those based on opinion, memory, or subjective feeling. You will forgive me, at the risk of being politically incorrect, if some of my past impressions may seem to stereotype black folks. It was what I took in as a child.

I grew up in the Deep South eating soul food, listening to exquisite jazz and R&B, dancing, working and singing to old spirituals. I fell deeply in love with music, storytelling, passion, conviction and superstition. I learned what service really meant and how to tuck my confusion and misery into my back pocket. I witnessed true injustice first hand and cringed with embarrassment around the plethora of bigots who were my kin. For them, servants were a status symbol, for me, they were a saving grace.

From the early age of two, I remember sitting in my maid Maddie's lap laughing and laughing as she jiggled me up and down while I tried to balance on her knees. However, her song was a sad song, a creole song and sometimes with words I magically understood though I knew it wasn't exactly English. I remember her drawing circles of protection around me to ward off the evils in this world. I felt safe with her, but I knew even at that early age that something was terribly wrong.

As the years went by, Janie Banks replaced Maddie in our new city far away from New Orleans and Alabama, but just as backward, just as southern, and just as crazy-ass as it gets. Janie taught me how to tie my shoes, brush my hair and wash my hands before lunch. When I hid in a tree or raced off on my get-away bike, Janie would seek me out, round me up and send me home with a whoop and a holler. No one else seemed to care. In her ragged way, she read to me each day before my nap which I vehemently refused to take until she took me in her arms. I would furrow right into that nappy black hair and inhaled brown skin with hints of chestnut, cinnamon, and chocolate. What it really smelled like was heaven on earth, the comfort of love, and it made me fall right to sleep.

In the afternoons, we sang song after song while she folded laundry or cooked dinner. I would sit on the counter, legs dangling to the beat, taking in the amazing aromas as she made the best fried chicken I ever had. I was watching every move she made and every step she took. I knew her gold toothed smile like the back of my hand and when that image wells up inside me today I feel only gratitude for the joy I experienced as a child. Somebody loved me. It helped me forget the pain of my own family, the absence of my mother and father, their sense of entitlement and status, and the role of the black woman in our home. It helped me forget and also reinforced the horrible atrocities we grew up with as people living in hypocrisy and delusion.

Some evenings I would dance to great records that my dad bought and I noticed then that most of the best musicians were the black ones. Voices like Sam and Dave's "Soul Man" and Gladys Knight stirred my soul and put goosebumps on my legs. One evening, I stood behind a crowd of adults with their martinis and cigarettes, trying to maneuver my way to the front to see the commotion from the TV. All I could hear was, "it was probably a nigga who did it" and I knew that once again someone had been shot; this time exiting from the kitchen door of a hotel. In my lifetime so far, I was aware of Dr. King, President Kennedy and now his brother being killed out in public, but where I came from, not many talked about Martin Luther King, his assassination and the importance of his speech. We were not allowed to hear his speech in school, nor did we celebrate anything close to MLK day. The first time I heard that speech, I was moved to tears because I could feel his passion. His words rang out like a beacon in the night. What I understood when I heard his voice was that he was black, so he must be on the good side.

The more I was loved and cared for by a black woman, the more pronounced the people's prejudice became. My experience did not match up to what was seeping into my tiny system from parents, my white private school and the media. I watched my world as an outsider, a non believer, and a sceptic. The people who I was taught were an indignant, inferior race, were in fact the very ones that fed my soul like no other white person had.

Back then, I could never have imagined that in my lifetime we would elect a black man to the highest office of this nation. Today, my children have black friends and go to integrated schools (well, kind of in Seattle), one of my close friends is in an interracial marriage, and there are positive black female role models in society. Though the childhood impressions that rest so deeply within me may form my opinions and make me assume automatically that people like Trayvon Martin and Troy Davis must be innocent, it doesn't take too much objectivity to see that we still have a long way to go.

STIRRING THE HORNET'S NEST

Relationships can be eye opening if one is committed to the long haul. Risk-taking, I am beginning to see, is a key factor to a healthy marriage. If we are to continue to grow and evolve with one another, we must be willing to challenge the status quo, the repetitive patterns, the familiarity, and the daily grind. That is difficult to say the least!

How can we put our own discomfort and dissatisfaction into question?

With enough love and commitment, we will be able to deepen our ties and understand ourselves better when we challenge what is in front of us. We need brutal honesty. No matter what the outcome, things will be better on the other side.

Sometimes, we have to stir the hornet's nest at the risk of losing everything. The shock that comes along with that can be a frightening endeavor, but if there is a true aim to improve the situation, then there is never a loss. The real risk is learning more about ourselves and each other. Just when we think everything is OK, a question like, "What do I really want for myself and my life?" can turn our world upside down. Communicating more effectively and striving to see the deeper issues does not necessarily end up in divorce.

We often settle for less in one area of our marriage as a trade off for the other things that work. No union is ever perfect. We also do not change and grow at the same rate. However, our personal transformation does have an effect on our partner. This can lead to one person realizing that they are no longer willing to tolerate certain behaviors.

What a shocker for the partner who is now confronted with something that has been accepted for so long. All of a sudden, one of us has had it with the way things have been. This can be a result of newfound boundaries that one never had as a child. This can be the result of new found courage to set things right for oneself. This can be an "I have had enough" moment.

Communication about this is a slippery slope because so much blame and hurt can ensue. A third party can be absolutely key in gaining some objectivity. It may take many sessions and sometimes it can feel like being on TV. Give a therapist a chance before giving up on him or her. They stand as an outside observer and can offer food for thought. Therapy can keep us from acting like complete jerks to one another. Communication can miraculously improve.

If we find ourselves blaming a partner for our unhappiness, we know that there are things within our own being that we do not yet understand. First, If we are not satisfied with the way things are, something must change. Secondly, we are usually finding fault and blame not within ourselves but with our partners. When it comes to blame, we can assume we are projecting.

There is also a phenomenon called gatekeeping at play. This is our way of filtering information due to our conditioning. We see what we want to see and cannot really have an objective perspective. So why don't we skip a couple of steps and assume that what we are blaming them for is really our own stuff... mmm, hard to fathom, but worth the attempt.

We expect our partners to fulfill unmet childhood needs all the time and that is an untenable situation. When we blame them for not satisfying these unmet needs, they essentially become "bad partners." Let's compound matters by knowing that we marry people who have qualities like our parents, in good ways and in very bad ways, We have found them, perhaps unconsciously, to assist in our healing journey. We perpetuate the conditions in which we grew up, so we can work out freedom from those patterns. The very thing we thought we had avoided in choosing them slowly creeps into the picture as a recurring theme in our lives.

Of course, abuse of any kind, be it physical, drug/alcohol or infidelity has been offered up to strengthen boundaries. Are we strong enough to say, "I won't tolerate this"? No one is expected to remain in a truly abusive relationship, so demanding better for ourselves will either be a wake up call for the abuser or our ticket out of there. I always believe in a second chance, but only one...

When we aren't psychologists, it sometimes feels like putting together a 10,000 piece puzzle. Is it something we are not seeing in ourselves? Does our lack of boundary hinder us from accepting their issues and from taking care of our own issues? Isn't taking their behavior personally also a result of poor boundaries?

Is our inner work revealing our deepest wounds and offering solutions, so that our partners do not have to do that? Can we find the way to meet each other as two mature adults instead of 3-year-olds in adult bodies who now substitute sex for the attention we never got from our parents? Can we connect in that intimate spiritual realm without tons of baggage? Do we have a means for dumping that baggage?

Doesn't avoidance of each other, living side by side in parallel lives without a snitch of romance or deep connection deserve a big stir of the pot? Doesn't obsession with being oversexed or solving our arguments with a great romp in the bed deserve a second look? Do we stay like this because we are afraid of change? Do we continue in the same old way because we are afraid of being alone? The irony lies in the fact that we are alone in most of these scenarios.

I ask these questions to stimulate thought about relationships. If we can ask questions and not assume anything, then we are in a better position to see what is happening. One thing we can be sure of is, if we begin to blame someone for our unhappiness, the gatekeeper is at work. We must, like scientists, try to objectively observe our feelings to understand where they are really coming from.

One glimpse of that true deep feeling can change everything.

We have to put the details of the present situation aside and simply try to experience our feelings regardless of the actual circumstances we think are causing it. If we can do this, we can connect the dots of our lives and find the root causes of our unhappiness. It never turns out to be the result of someone else's behavior.

If we stir the hornet's nest, we risk not being alone.

Perhaps that is what scares us most of all.

EMPATHY

I was asked recently "How do you have empathy?" and in answering this question, I had the realization that the only true way for one to have empathy with others is to know the suffering and grief in one's own heart. This pain is felt from the great depths within us and can be found through surrender, trust and faith. Guidance from another with experience of this is essential.

First, let us examine what empathy really means. The Oxford English dictionary states that empathy is "the ability to understand and share the feelings of others." This is not an intellectual understanding, but one that can be discovered in the World of Being, also known as the Heart Mind or the Higher Emotional Center in Gurdjieff's terminology. When one begins to experience some degree of freedom, there is a space and a realm in which the unity and diversity of all things is understood. We are all made of the same thing. We are all one. Each individual is a human expression of the Divine and that Divinity is the higher consciousness in which we are all connected. The Masters of Wisdom of Central Asia referred to this as the Unity of Being.

This is the place in which we are all the same.

To have empathy with others, one is aided by a path that will facilitate the opening of the Heart Mind through specific gradations of Energies. When one is able to surrender, there has been support and strength built from the practices of this path. There is a container and foundation built to support the surrender. This comes from a disciplined spiritual practice of stillness and self-observation on the functional level. It comes from meditation and prayer.

As this practice advances, one begins to "see" certain mechanical buffers that keep us from experiencing reality, and more importantly from feeling the pain. When one allows the true feelings of love to enter through surrender, the pain that has been pushed back usually for the majority of one's life floods in as well.

As these buffers are broken down, one begins to see a pattern emerging and this becomes the key to freedom. The surrender involves seeing, feeling and understanding one's own suffering. At this point, one can begin to see and accept "the terror of the situation."

With most people, the surrender is the difficult part and it requires the utmost trust and faith in God. Trust and faith in a guide or someone more experienced than ourselves is also helpful because it means our ego is willing to submit to another. We are required to make our reluctant ego step aside. This breakdown can feel like we have been living our lives in a most meaningless way, a total lie, and a mechanical wasteland in which feelings, Real Feelings, have been avoided, both the blissful and the most painful. Because there is no distinction in this emotional world, if one avoids feeling the pain, love is shut out as well.

Jesus taught "Love Thy Neighbor As Thyself." This is a key. We must learn to love ourselves and this entails forgiveness, trust, faith and above all, surrender. If we have no trust in something higher, then our lives are reduced to the mechanisms of our own ego. Gaining that trust comes from this beautiful inner work of awareness in order to surrender. If we can experience our own pain, we will understand the pain of others.

The problem is not the neighbor, it is thyself.

AT THE RISK OF BEING AUTHENTIC

At the risk of being authentic, I break the rules around writing. I am sick of trying to do the right thing with the right amount of words, paragraphs with less than five sentences, big headlines and the like.

I need to write the way my creative self wants to do it. I don't have to cater to people's lost attention span to be able to make a point. Inspiration comes in many forms and originality can only be that when it is unlike other.

I don't need to go out and get the latest thing in order to fit in. I don't need to be politically correct. I don't need to conform to be accepted.

At the risk of being authentic, I will not sacrifice who I am and what I love in order to make money. I can make money doing what I love.

At the risk of being authentic, I will rise to the occasion and speak my mind after years of being worried about hurting someone's feelings or disappointing someone, so if you don't like the article, go read something that conforms to standards and sounds like everyone else.

At the risk of being authentic, I ignore my ego's distorted perception of not being successful, not being accepted, not being professional, not being good enough, not measuring up, not being heard, not receiving recognition, not being supported and will do it my way.

What if Beethoven had changed the way he composed to please the people? Did Van Gogh succumb to the desires of his public? Why did Mozart die a pauper?

No great artist, thinker, musician or philosopher ever really worried about what someone else thought. If they had, they may never have become their great creative selves.

At the risk of being authentic, I can tap into my own power, use my own voice, and believe that I have something of value to say even if society does not agree.

I give myself permission to be totally creative.

I am not going to keep up with the Joneses.

I am not going to blindly follow because I can't hear my own intuition which tells me that that isn't my way. That isn't me.

At the risk of being authentic, I don't need to want to be like someone else or wish I had their success or their looks or their talent because more than likely I have just as much if not more. The issue is recognizing my own power, using my intuition, and staying true to self. I don't need to copy someone's style because they have financial success.

I don't have to maintain the status quo.

I can take the risk to teach my children to quit following like sheep and to listen to their own intuition. I can resist giving in when they say "but everyone else's parents are letting them do it."

At the risk of being authentic, I will no longer override what I feel in my heart in order to not make waves or deny myself of what I truly deserve.

At the risk of being authentic, I will tap into my creative flow and trust that all is well.

STILLNESS

I am in such gratitude for the stillness in me which I find each day in the depths of my body, mind and soul. The practice of meditation is an important one for bringing about stillness in our lives. The evolution of this practice brings stillness even amongst the most frenetic of environments. It can calm stormy waters and brings absolute peace.

As I sit in stillness, or even experience stillness not sitting, my body becomes heavy with a sensation that is much much bigger than my physical body. I am aware of a greater body and this greater body is the necessary grounding for my Higher Understanding and Perception. The extreme sensation in the lower body is a precursor to this very large opening. An opening like this must be accompanied by this depth of sensation. Without it, higher energies have no foundation and can cause damage to the physical body.

Besides sensation of substantial proportion, my mind must remain focused and this is a result of practice. It is like a muscle that must be strengthened. Once this muscle is in top shape, the focus remains constant no matter what the environment. I am able to meditate "in a cage of monkeys" so to speak.

We all must learn to turn off the distractions that we have created as a society, if true learning is to take place. These distractions come in myriad forms and nearly everyone has some kind of electronic device in their hands these days. The ease of such access to distraction means that even more discipline is needed to seek out stillness and singleness of mind. We are so used to having background input from the tv, the radio, and even the tv running with no sound.

Now a phone is a lifeline to the internet, so that we don't have to go far without it. We become always available and always subject to multitasking. All of these distractions keep us away from Work on Oneself.

What are we trying to avoid?

Even before all the electronic devices, there were plenty of distractions, so it is not just an issue of today. Now the issue just requires even more discipline. We are immune to all the noise and stimulation. Remove ourselves from it for a week or two, and the reality may appear before us. In our group, there is often an assignment to turn everything off, read nothing, no radio, no tv, no internet for a couple of weeks. This can be a very revealing exercise.

If we allow the stillness to come over us, avoided feelings will surface. Things that we were unconscious of can come to the light of day.

The stillness can allow us to see within ourselves, and that is half the battle.

NECESSITY IS THE MOTHER OF INVENTION

I want to take the time to enjoy the summer.

Allowing myself to do nothing sometimes sparks the most amazing ideas.

I recently hosted a French 13-year-old for four weeks in my home. I love bringing people of different cultures into the house. Being in close quarters allows me to get to know someone, their character, their preferences and their habits. It gives me perspective. I get to be someone else's Mom for a short period.

This is the second time I have done it. The first was an eleventh grader from Germany who stayed for six months. She was a very different character from the boy this summer. Both were a joy to have in my home.

I noticed something this time that got me wondering about children in relation to technology, adventure, and boredom.

Summer is a great time to relax for children. It could be a time for space from the hectic schedules to which they are subjected. The weather offers great opportunities for swimming, biking, walking around and even getting into trouble. It is often the time to travel and explore new places.

It is the perfect time to schedule nothing.

Boredom can offer an impetus to dream, to imagine, to create and to take action from a need to fulfill some longing. For an adult, boredom just doesn't happen. That time space is usually superseded with the need to get things done. It gets filled with stuff.

When children have the space to be bored, they invent and create out of necessity to fill the void. They rally up friends to hang out with or go make friends with the neighbor for lack of someone else. They bake something, make something or start messing around on the piano.

They walk out the door to go get ice cream or walk to the park. They get the skateboard out, jump on the trampoline or play with the dog.

They create neighborhood businesses, make lemonade stands or try to sew something.

They have time to think. They have time to ponder. They have time to notice the clouds drifting by or the sound of Aspen trees fluttering in the wind. They can lay by the river and start to understand motion, physics, and light.

They can experience nature and the vibration it has to offer in and of itself.

My God, this sounds like the 1970's.

For a foreign kid, they can take in a totally different culture just by walking around, looking at the people, the cars, the plants and the architecture. Just by getting out, taking the bus, running an errand where they might have to practice their English can be an eye opening experience.

I may not have been a pianist if it weren't for boredom. I wouldn't have felt the freedom of going off on the bike with no plan. I wouldn't have wondered why coquinas bury themselves in the sand once I dug them up. I wouldn't have learned how to play tennis or taught myself to sail a boat. I may not have gotten into so much trouble...

The bottom line is if I had had that damn phone in my hand twenty four seven I may never have left my room. Everything that it offers takes away the void and the necessity. It fills every second with something and it is tantalizing. It is instant gratification. It requires no patience. It substitutes human interaction.

When left to their own discretion, children won't put it down.

I realized that I wasn't hearing, "I'm bored. What can I do?" from the French kid or my daughter.

And then, I blinked and blinked and I got very quiet and I got very sad.

I then took action and took away the phone for extended periods and at bedtime altogether,

He may hate me now, but at least he got bored and he saw America.

Enjoy your downtime!!!

FUNCTION, BEING AND WILL

If we examine the Gurdjieff structure of Function, Being and Will, we have the chance to understand and experience the universe in terms of dimensions, vibratory light, and our place within each of these worlds. We are able to experience these worlds simultaneously because we live in all of these Worlds whether we are aware of them or not. John Bennett so clearly referred to the four worlds and terms them Function, Relative Being, Being and Will. He elucidates the formal construction of Gurdjieff's ideas of the Higher Centers and the interrelatedness of all things in terms of systematics and vibration.

Certainly when looking at the physical world we can see absolute parallels between matter and the greater universe, solar systems, galaxies and black holes. Superstring theory may have everything to do with the very smallest foundational element found in all vibratory experience no matter how dense or refined. Gravity is another force which plays into these worlds and our ability to experience more subtle and finer vibrations in the air and in people and things. Our world moves from a solid earth core to Infinite Space, so clearly delineated by Barbara Hand Clow in her book The Alchemy of Nine Dimensions. Gurdjieff's system corresponds perfectly to these nine dimensions. The aspects of Function operate under certain Laws or Energies. These correspond with the automatic functioning of the body and manifestation of Nature in our 3D world. The Instinctual Self fits into this scenario as well as our three brains , the moving center, the emotional center and the thinking center.

Relative Being refers to the 4th Dimension and includes the collective archetypes and emotional ether shared by all within a framework of the time space continuum. This is where people get trapped, functioning under Laws that govern a much more dense vibratory level than our

Higher Nature and Absolute Value. As Barbara Hand Clow points out, this realm is where religion comes from as well as systems that keep us from having our own good mind. It is how the Elite can control the masses.

Gurdjieff purported that "man cannot do " and in light of the history of mankind, his statement is true. His teaching offered a way of working on oneself to enable the development of higher bodies other than our physical bodies, bodies that could encode and comprehend the higher dimensions of Love and The Great Void. He referred to the Kesdjan Body as a vehicle for the Higher Emotional Center, something I have mentioned in my other writings, a center which has really nothing to do with emotions as we know them in ordinary life.

As this kesdjan body is formed, it becomes the means for our permanent transformation and the vehicle to greater awareness and opening to the vibration of Love. This represents the Fifth Dimension or Heart Realm. We have glimpses of this world of Being when we experience a beautiful sunset, connection with nature, but deeper understanding of this world is the experience of the Unity of All Things.

The complete formation of the Kesdjan Body enables us to become volitionally open to this Higher World in which we can experience the connection we all have. This Realm of Love is the Heart Mind which opens our consciousness to the Bliss of Existence. It is how the present can repair the past and prepare the future.

There is another body which Gurdjieff referred to as the Higher Being Body which accesses The Great Void outside of time and space in which an utter stillness emerges for the Infinite Light to penetrate our consciousness. The established Higher Being Body enables one to cocreate with the universe, free from the tethers of lower vibrational fields. One is able to live by revelation from the Absolute and manifest in the lower dimensions in a way that demonstrates freedom and choice.

This is the World of Will, the seventh through ninth dimensions. We are all vibrating in all of these fields. The development of these higher bodies through transformation of energies allows us to experience these Higher Worlds. We are able to experience all dimensions simultaneously and various information comes from different vibrational fields expanding our Awareness and Consciousness.

When looking at Transformation in this way, we can begin to see that we are already part of the Light, in fact, we are made of it and manifest at certain vibrations according to codes found in higher dimensions. When we open ourselves by Right Work, we are able to heal the trauma of our lives and our collective lives, creating a void for something higher to come in. It is a Sacred Law which states the higher works on the lower to activate the middle. This law can be seen in our physical World, the World of Quantum and in String Theory. Gurdjieff found the representation of this law in the triangle as part of the Enneagram. It must follow that the higher vibrational world can be accessed through work that raises our vibratory functioning. This intake of subtle finer substance creates strength to assimilate what we could not see before, creating a void and opening us to Higher Worlds, Greater Insight, and the ability to truly love.

With these vibratory transformations in place by more and more people, the collective vibration will resonate with the Earth. More and more will have access to the higher vibrational field. This is what is happening with the Earth now as we have come to the end of this particular Epoch. It is the time that was to mark the awakening of a Higher Consciousness on the planet.

Those who are attuning to what is happening will activate a higher vibration in themselves so that humans will finally be able "to do."

GOJI GRATITUDE

As I picked the goji berries growing in my parking strip on this beautiful August morning, an overwhelming feeling of peace and gratitude came over me. I was quick to realize that this was a deeper and much more profound feeling that practically brought tears to my eyes. Was it the fact that I was in awe of actual goji berries, a tropical exotic bright orange berry, growing in the Northwest? Was it the realization that the care I had given this plant was part of its being able to thrive outside of its normal habitat? Was it the synchronicity of an amazingly hot summer in Seattle?

Each berry that I picked somehow reinforced my connection with nature, with color, with the energy of this plant and with the whole process; one in which the sun, the plant, the rain, and I myself all came together to produce a succulent vitamin packed gift. I not only have a few, I have a copious crop.

I think about my dedication to making sure it was watered through this dry season. I think about staking this wiry vine like bush so that it was strong enough to bear children in a free floating non clingy world of a parking strip. I think about the gift that keeps on giving each day as I pick these things. It is connecting me to the energy of nature. It is making me aware of the choreography of my role with these plants, sun and water. I begin to feel an overwhelming sense of gratitude that takes over my senses and feelings.

As I pick these berries, I am also aware of my awareness of being present and take a breath with each pick. This then fills me with some inexplicable joy of being here and being alive and part of it all. Once that happens, I am brought back to the goji berries which started this whole process inside me and how grateful I am to them for helping me realize how profound and fulfilling the most simple things in life can be.

BEND

Two weeks ago I spent a weekend in Bend with an intentional group that has been together 20 plus years under the leadership of Cari, a wise 91-year-old woman totally devoted to helping others. They have a beautiful tradition of gathering after Easter for a Women's Movements Weekend in which women come from all around to do the Movements created by Gurdjieff specifically for women. Movements like The Sacred Goose, the Women's Prayer and the Assyrian Women Mourners encompass softer more ballet like gestures than the Dervish dances for men which are very precise and linear. I have learned many Movements in my lifetime but I have seldom had the occasion to do the Women's Movements exclusively with women.

Bend is in the high desert and a welcome respite from the wet, rainy Seattle Spring. Two of the members have a lovely home which transforms into a Movements hall if you move the tables, chairs and gorgeous oriental rugs. The night my friend Barbara and I arrived, a dinner was being served and cooked by the men in the group. In fact, they cooked all weekend in honor of the women. I met people who had come from The Farm, started by Mrs. Staveley, an astounding student of Gurdjieff with a method of her own, and others coming from Sisters Oregon and surrounding small towns.

We all came with an intention and an aim.

My host that night spoke of years past in the group, the group dynamics and her personal history in The Work. Many who are attracted to this particular path are serious seekers and have found great use in the extraordinary unorthodox methods of Mr. Gurdjieff. However, the Bend group I was told does not call themselves a Gurdjieff group per se.

They are gathered around their founder's premise that all comes from Love. Cari's teacher, Nan, died shortly after they started their school, and so Cari was left to carry on the traditions and beliefs of her beloved guide. Nan had discovered the commentaries of Nicoll who wrote about the ideas of Gurdjieff. This is how they came to weave the Gurdjieff Work into their practices.

They are most certainly loving and welcoming.

The day of Movements was very meaningful for me as a participant because I am usually teaching or playing the piano for Movements classes. I allowed myself to be a student, a dancer, a mystic, and a woman. Most of all, the very reverent and sensuous qualities of a woman were brought forth in me, not only because of the gestures themselves, but because we were women gathered in Sacred Dance. The poignancy of this can hardly be expressed, but I can give you some reference points.

Rarely do we have chances to gather in Sacred Ceremony as women in our culture. I have also been part of a group with a Native American lineage that has proven to be a vehicle for intentional ceremony. Doing these particular movements in ceremony with the women had visceral and emotional effects on my Soul, yet there was more.

The quality of the music, influenced by Central Asian melodies and harmonies, combined with ancient gestures being done by many women with unified attention, in synchronistic motion, was nothing less than profound. I was carried to ancient times of healers when women embodied their full energetic power. I was plugged into my body acting as a current of refined energy which moved through me and everyone else. The efforts of the many, the care and attention to each arm twirl or hip sway created an atmosphere of awe. It created something that we rarely get to experience in our usual daily life. It was Sacred Ritual of the highest order even if it was our meager selves that initiated the activity.

At the end of the day, we understood as Sacred Dancers how to serve humanity.

The evening ended with a dinner in which I could taste care in every bite. We as a ragtag group had created something from our hearts because of our sincere intention. We ate with the men in joy and appreciation, talking amongst ourselves, when suddenly a wave of Understanding, manifesting in an Absolute Silence washed over the table. Each one of us caught the wave and was able to participate in a deep communal experience where no words were necessary. In fact, words would have been a stone dropped into the still pond of our Beings that were clearly united in that Present Moment. We all took part in it. We were all aware of it. We will all remember it.

DEPRESSION

I am deeply saddened by the suicide of Robin Williams, one of my favorite actors of all time. When I first saw him as a child, I was struck by his passion, his spontaneity and his wit. His performances combining humor, depth, and calculated jabs never ceased to amaze me. As Mork, he convinced me that there really were aliens here on this planet. His improvisatory outbursts only proved that. I don't think he ever stuck to a script.

It isn't hard to pinpoint what I loved about him. He was filled with passion. He was an unfettered and original artist; a selfless clown capable of making anyone and everyone laugh.

I could feel the enormous level of Being in every role, and they were exemplary roles from the teacher, John Keating in Dead Poet's Society, Patch Adams, Mrs. Doubtfire, radio host in Good Morning Vietnam to the quirky doctor who took a risk with his patients in Awakenings. His choice of roles were always someone fighting for the cause of truth and justice in a world of intolerance.

He embodied the modern day clown expertly masking his inner state which in the end truncated his life.

Could this very dark side have only been balanced by an effervescent stream of consciousness humor and passion? Manic, bi-polar, mentally ill... ??? Manic or not, he was a genius and a force to reckon with on this planet.

His death has affected everyone all over the globe not just because we lost this genius but because it was a suicide. It brings up the question of depression and how our society addresses it.

It certainly makes us question the present human condition, the shadow, and the horrible effects of depression. What caused the depression, an inherent chemical condition or a caged bird syndrome? Is that kind of creativity, energy and Essence unable to thrive in conditions such as ours?

It is tragic in ways that break our heart.

He was a prisoner of his ego's distorted views of self and unable to get out from under its vice grip. I am of the understanding that our identified states can create false beliefs of the way things are, and when it is chronic depression, fighting the demons becomes life's daily agenda. This state compounds as time goes on if not addressed.

I wonder about the details around medication and antidepressants. I am saddened mostly because he clearly did not get the kind of help that addresses depression from an angle that can diminish if not obliterate its effects. My question is: was he seeking help to relieve this depression apart from pharmaceuticals? Could his prescription have caused him to do this?

Who am I to judge whether someone chooses to take their lives, but I believe no one really wants to take their life. They want relief from the pain they are experiencing on a daily basis. Death looks more promising than facing the pain and suffering.

I have seen Work with awareness and attention, meditation and Self-observation relieve this kind of pain in many people including myself. I have devoted my life to helping people uncover the veil the ego wraps around us and what makes us go to great lengths to guard the pain within. Our identification with certain thoughts consumes our attention and feeds the depression. With the development of presence, we can become free of this.

I believe at the present time on this planet, things are recalibrating. It is intense. It will require a swift exit for many who cannot find their way to the Opening. We are required to make decisions based on Truth. We are asked to stand in Integrity and act from Essence. The more we can bear, the more our Being develops. If this is not possible, life becomes increasingly difficult.

RIP Robin Williams. You will be missed by many.

CHOIR CAMP

Every summer I teach at choir camp as a member the faculty of the Seattle Girls' Choir. It is a chance to gather as an organization, a system with all of its moving parts in a beautiful setting on the Puget Sound.

The purpose of camp is to work consecutively over many days culminating in a small concert, and the other purpose is to bond with each other, both students, faculty, and chaperones. I am always amazed at what happens to a group in 6 days. I experience this bonding of a group in meditation retreats as well.

Not only do we sing, have campfires and walks, make crafts, but we have electives for smaller groups. I teach rhythm and Movement. This is a chance for me to work directly with 10-12 girls ages 10-15 on some very specific features of music. In the end, we work on much more than that.

They are hungry for the teaching: a much bigger teaching, a way of Being, an approach to learning and a standard of excellence. For me and for them, it is not about the end result. That is a by product of the process we go through.

This year, I set out to have them analyse the rhythm segment of a hip hop song, and choose which instruments, from drain pipes and trash can lids to traditional drums, cowbells and claves, would be appropriate for the sounds. Once that was done, we would set a form to follow which requires real focus and attention. The patterns are extremely repetitive; something a produced track usually does nowadays. When I played the song for them, they looked at me like deer in headlights.

The process became perfecting the execution of each part and then keeping track of where we were. By the end, they were chomping at the bit to integrate the sounds, implement their new skills, and produce our creation together as one.

They themselves were motivated to make it better, but it was light hearted and full of laughter. Without prompting, the older ones showed the way by helping the younger ones stay on track when they got off. The desire to stay late and do it one more time was indicative of something very healthy.

When it was not good enough, I told them so with the utmost diplomacy and they willingly picked up their sticks again. I was teaching them a standard of excellence that will translate into everything they do. They learned that letting themselves off the hook never produces the right result.

They proved to themselves that anything is possible.

PASSION PAYS OFF

How many of us are running around doing what we don't love?

Are you doing a job just because it pays the bills? Are you longing to get creative, open that dream store, run your own restaurant, sell your creations or teach sailing?

In working with people to help them become still and gain greater awareness of their Inner Voice, I have found that certain issues come up around following their passion. Once we uncover, for example, an identification with being the good guy, we unleash unfulfilled desires and regret for pleasing others instead of self. Working with regret uncovers the ceaseless demands we make on ourselves to be perfect.

Sometimes we uncover a strong fear of failure or... .the strong fear of success which is simply another side of the same coin. This sincere desire to not make mistakes keeps us from trying anything that seems like a risk. No risk, no reward. That goes for any endeavor from improving a skill to spiritual enlightenment.

In other cases, a lack of self esteem comes barreling through and until we access the True Nature of Self and heal wounding, we continue to sabotage our passion and believe that we are not good enough.

Sometimes it is an identification with being a victim, and blame is spewed out in all directions. In this case, we may be doing what we love but can't make money or have success. Until we can reach a sense of forgiveness with others and self, that identification cannot be released. We will always blame other people and circumstances for our failures.

It is a process of unraveling these identifications, one that takes awareness, grounding and then release.

So what is stopping us from doing what we want?

What if I said we can make money from anything, our passion especially! In fact, the stronger the passion, the more successful we will be.

When we believe in something with all of our Being and love what we are doing, we will have no problem telling others about it. When we get total satisfaction from anything from creating, organizing, assisting, parenting, nutrition, exercise, cooking, to teaching whatever it may be, we can market that skill.

The next step is uncovering the limiting beliefs and identification with false roles.

As a musician and meditation mentor, I have found enriching people's lives to be very satisfying work. Both skills are my creative outlets, and both have changed my life in ways I could never have imagined. I have been a loyal student of both disciplines for many many years. The key here is being a true student. Doing that keeps the juices flowing and brings meaning, renewal and understanding to life.

I did not drop either mission even when I got diverted by "making money." When that happened, I put my whole self into making money for money's sake, but something did not sit right with me. When I returned to my two passions, both fields successfully expanded like never before.

Somewhere somehow I had it lodged in me that we can't make adequate money in music or in spiritual endeavors. That was just my limited belief system in full swing.

Everyone deserves to be paid for their time and services no matter what they are offering.

Does anyone expect someone to work for free? If I am an expert in my field and yield excellent results, then the price must be accurate and reflect that. There are always people willing to invest in excellence.

Are you charging your worth?

Are you working just to make money or are you following your passion?

If you feel you aren't excellent due to lack of experience, your passion will make up for it. You will gain the needed experience faster if you love what you are doing and become an excellent student. The very nature of passion means we love it which means we have a natural propensity toward it. It means we have a natural knack for it or a desire to really improve our skills in that area.

If you want to be of service in the world, you need to offer up your passion. Things will flow. It will be easier to make money. You will find your work satisfying and not an uphill battle.

Obstacles will become mere setbacks.

Satisfaction and fulfillment will become the name of the game.

Things will work out because you believe in what you are doing.

Here are some questions:

Do you wake up excited to do your work?

Are you making money at what you love?

Do you feel creative and inspired?

Do you wish you were doing something else?

Are you trying to do one thing to get something totally different?

Do you find great purpose in what you are doing?

LOSING CONTROL

"I don't think we need hope. I think we need imagination. We need to imagine a future which can't be planned for and can't be controlled. I find that people who talk about hope are often really talking about control. They hope desperately that they can keep control of the way things are panning out. Keep the lights on, keep the emails flowing, keep the nice bits of civilisation and lose the nasty ones; keep control of their narrative, the world they understand. Giving up hope, to me, means giving up the illusion of control and accepting that the future is going to be improvised, messy, difficult."

—Paul Kingsnorth

I was astounded to read the perspective of Paul Kingsnorth in his most recent interview with Wen Stephenson. He is an English writer, founder of The Dark Mountain Project and once an "erstwhile green activist." He is basically giving up on "saving the planet."

"He's looked into the abyss of planetary collapse, and he's more or less fine with it: Collapse? Sure. Bring it on." (Stephenson)

I have never heard of this more fatalistic and intriguing approach but I have been *very open* to facing the chaos and destruction of our current way of living. I did not say the destruction of our planet because I do believe that Nature will prevail as it always does. It is us as a surviving species that is in question.

I am fine with our way of life as we know it today not surviving. I see adults and children all around me disconnected from nature, from each other and from themselves...

I don't participate in arguments about whether climate change exists. There is too much evidence supporting that fact and willful blindness is a curious phenomenon. I, as one human, can make choices to support a new way of life, but it feels futile sometimes.

People thought I was crazy to pay so much for organic back in the day. I have been out in the streets vehemently protesting against Monsanto. Family members think it would be so much easier if we had two cars. I am going to put up solar panels on my roof. My yard is a food forest and doesn't look pristine like everyone else's.

Am I doing it to relieve my conscience? Am I identified with doing the right thing? In my heart, I believe as one person it is my responsibility to contribute to the whole by living consciously. I will never give up my efforts. I am ready for the change.

There are systems in place to keep us consuming and destroying. No one would disagree with me on that. The interesting point in this article; the crux of Kingsnorth's idea lies in the quote above.

Giving up control and accepting that things will be messy reminds me of what I do on a daily basis. However, I refuse to accept that it will be difficult. It will be an adventure. It will mean going with the flow. It will mean greeting the day and improvising with love in my heart, trusting that all will be as it should be.

That doesn't mean that I won't make an effort to live in a way that is sustainable. I am in agreement with him in regard to his comments about what we all think sustainable means. Nature will force us to change.

"The end of the world as we know it is not the end of the world full stop." (Kingsnorth)

I would be fine with darning my socks and picking my carrots.

HEALING

We are in a time of great change. Our consciousness is expanding beyond the limits of the three dimensions in which we live. The collective archetypes are changing. Our collective consciousness is changing. Epochs and eras are simultaneously coming to a close. Time is accelerating and the earth is showing signs of a new birth.

We are entering into an era in which people can heal on a grand scale. We are finally opening to what has been available to us for a very long time. The convergence of so many factors is having a dramatic effect on us. Our transformational work in this world is evolving and we have a chance to participate in an expansion as has never been seen. We are moving toward this together.

We are one. We are one in our Spirits, in our Hearts and as One Mind moving toward a greater Unity. Our conscious awareness of this and our experience of this is changing the planet. Our Work depends both on taking action and receiving help from above. Daily attunements and sittings, observing ourselves, struggling against our usual mode of doing things, and ever striving to resist the urge to prove ourselves or be right, are all actions conducive to this opening.

The hard part is allowing the healing to occur. Some of us make it all happen ourselves. We are conditioned to be that way. Some of us wait around for someone or something else to change life for us. We are conditioned to be that way too. Neither approach will work. You can't beat down the doors of heaven, and you can't sit around on your ass waiting for God to help you.

I often hear people say "it is God's will," and accept what is really the result of their own resistance to Love and Harmony. Recognition of our part in the Great Dilemma will unlock certain doors. There is a balance of acting and receiving.

With inner work, we prepare for the necessary shocks to propel us forward in our transformation. We have to build strength in order to weather the blow of "seeing." Acceptance of what is, as we begin to see, will open our hearts. This enables a floodgate of feelings that have been shut back our whole lives. They are individual and collective. In fact, we do many things to insure that we do not feel what has been pushed back for thousands of years.

The healing is in the feeling.

It is time that we lay down all our weapons and unite as one humanity with nature. We are returning to a knowledge that has been with us all along. There is evidence of it from ancient cultures. There is evidence of this from Distant Intelligences. Many messengers have come to elucidate this for us throughout history. The Mayans have predicted this time of Awakening. It is the end of their calendar and the beginning of a New Universe. The Living Christ is entering our hearts and minds.

This is not the time of an Apocalypse. This is not the time for fear. Those aspects are the opposing force, "the priests and kings," the Elite making a last ditch effort to hold onto their power in the old patriarchal system.

It is not the time of the end of the world.

We as common loving people, men and women, can take responsibility for our own transformation and have freedom from this oppressive life. We can allow ourselves to open to the Emanating Eternal Source of Love. There is a call to Wake Up.

Do you hear it?

444: A SIGN FROM THE ANGELS

A few months ago, I woke up two nights in a row for 3 minutes or so only to look up at the clock and see 4:44. I happened across an analysis of angel numbers on Facebook yesterday seeing 444 across the screen. I have seen two license plates in the last 4 days with 444 on them.

Yesterday I had asked the Universe for a sign about some investments and the following day I awoke at 444, my grocery bill was $88.88, my tank fill up was $55.55 and my subscriber list hit 333.

It is said that 444 means you are totally backed by your Angels and that you are doing the right thing. 333 means the Ascended Masters are watching over you..

Now I am always seeing signs in things. I believe in messages from the Universe. I know my Angels and Spirit Guides, but I usually focus on my own efforts toward making progress in life, in all things spiritual and in business. I often take for granted that there is help from so many other-worldly sources, enlightened masters, and Ancient Records without my asking or needing a sign.

I have accessed this help in amazing ways throughout my life.

However, my radar is not on this realm of angels and guides because I was taught by a Master teacher that this is the imaginal world where so many people are attracted and then get distracted from their own efforts.

Imaginal in this case does not mean imaginary, but the world of Archetypes, Angels and Images. This world is an integral part of the whole, but there is so much beyond it.

Anyway, I have been struggling with an income opportunity I thought was leading me to my vision and serving my greater purpose. It was something extra that I took on seven years ago to make money. I worked very very hard at this job, for that is what it became, in order to create residual income. I have developed wonderful friendships in that job. I have learned about entrepreneurship, money, law of attraction and staying persistent.

When I took on this endeavor, I shifted my focus away from going more pro with the things I do best; playing classical music and teaching meditation and self-awareness through some very special and extraordinary means. These professions of mine are part of my ultimate vision. Somehow, somewhere I acquired the belief that I couldn't make good money doing that.

I endeavored to learn something totally new, something totally outside of my field. I vowed to give it everything I had: my time, energy, effort and resources. I became a perfect student of the entrepreneurial world.

I vowed to give it seven years.

In recent months, I changed gears out of sheer exhaustion and decided to focus solely on my actual professions, promoting the skills I have worked many, many years to refine. It has been exciting and exhilarating, but I never could have done it with this much precision and knowledge if it weren't for the other outside experience. What I learned as an entrepreneur is priceless.

The big question in my mind has been: "Is it ok for me to let go of an endeavor that would bring me a huge residual income?"

Putting it on the back burner has made life easier. I am pursuing my passion with different eyes and with more skill. I would rather take the risk to fail at what I love than do what I don't love.

In some way, I have been asking the Universe for signs to give myself permission to do what I love the most and make good money at it.

Sign #1: In the last month, I am having clients and students walk into my life that are of a much higher caliber. More people are flocking to my newsletter and online mentoring.

Sign #2: I get a very resounding yes from folks when promoting my services. I don't procrastinate. I feel creative, competent, excited, passionate, inspired and really really FREE.

Sign #3: The financial success I was seeking in the other business is falling into my lap with outstanding ease as I go completely and utterly pro with my passion.

Sign #4: 444

RECEIVING LOVE

As I focus on the Divine Feminine in my life, my attention turns to receiving. Do I really know how to receive? Do I push away love, support and help? If my answer is yes, then why would I want to do that?

My experience of love as a child came with big strings attached, and so somewhere along the way, I believed love happened this way. If there was real love out there being given freely, without conditions, I was not a recipient.

Many of us believe we have experienced unconditional love when in fact it was shrouded in expectation and conditions.

This brings us to the question of how we develop a sense of deserving something. If there is a belief that love is reciprocal or conditional, then we develop the sense that we shouldn't get anything for free. There are conditions around our behavior and giving something back in order to be loved. We have all experienced this as children when our parents served up shame when we exerted our own will or expressed ourselves honestly and freely.

We also experience guilt and shame when we hear the words, "I have sacrificed so much for you." or "I have fed and clothed you, this is the least you could do" or "after all I have done for you, how could you be so selfish." The underlying message is the love we have received means we have to behave in a certain way or we will not be loved. If we can't give back, then we should feel guilty.

This brings up the question of our motives when we are doing something for someone. If we grew up receiving conditional love, then we learned to serve it up that way too. Giving may not be giving for giving's sake. It may be to relieve our own guilt. It may be to relieve jealousy or loneliness. If we give to someone, then there may be a secret hope that they must give back, or pay attention to us, or do what we want them to do.

Is this how we believe love works?

It is not enough to say "let's get out there and receive love," because in actuality we don't know how.

We cannot change things unless we notice them. Here are things to notice in order to learn to receive without believing we don't deserve it, without mistrusting someone's motives, or without thinking we must reciprocate.

1. Begin to notice on a daily basis the ways you push help, love, and support away.

2. Notice if you feel resentful or angry or experience adverse circumstances from not saying no.

3. Notice how often you automatically give without question because it is "the right thing to do."

4. Notice if you feel guilty if you don't say yes.

5. Notice how often you do something for yourself.

6. Do you wait for others to fulfill your needs? Even worse, do you expect them to fulfill your needs?

7. Do you ignore your own needs all together?

Once we have put these things on our radar, we will begin to see patterns in our interactions and reactions to others, especially when they do not fulfill some kind of conditions we have placed upon them.

The only way to counteract not being able to receive from others is to do loving things for ourselves. Lately my mantra has been "do unto ourselves what we would have others do unto us." When we begin to take small steps for our own transformation, our good health, our creativity, our income, our peace of mind, and our general happiness, we begin to learn what it means to receive.

Do we deny ourselves things to relieve guilt or to make ourselves pay in some way? Discovering the reasons we are not able to give to ourselves is a mystery to be solved. If it were easy, we would be taking steps toward our sanity and overcoming resistance all the time.

Sometimes it takes getting sick to realize just how much we do for others at our own expense.

Sometimes it takes getting sick to be able to receive love from others! Many of us unconsciously become victims of a fate in order to be helped. Another positive action to take is to be more transparent with others about our actions. We can honestly tell someone we are relieving our guilt by giving to them. They will have a thousand times more respect for us and we will have more respect for ourselves.

It's all a work in progress for me, and I am sure for some of us this has brought up the opposite idea of entitlement and getting something for nothing. More on that later.

CREATIVE FLOW

There are many kinds of creative flow.

After committing myself to writing for nearly a year now, I have learned something about creativity. Writing requires a different sort of creativity than performing music. When I play music, I am spontaneous. I interpret music based on historical and theoretical knowledge, and combine that with feelings the music evokes, all in the moment.

What is the difference between creating your own material and performing already existing material? Since I am a performer and not drawn to composing music, I have begun to experience a different aspect of creativity in writing; a process that requires tuning into my intuition, my imagination, and my life experience.

My normal job as a classical pianist provides me with centuries of music to study, master and perform. I can never run out of material! It has provided a lifetime of discipline, creativity and satisfaction. My creativity is activated by my presence with the music as I am performing it. I have to find a way to get out of the way.

Writing makes me tap into something that is also authentically me, a creation spun from my process, my vision, and my perspective. I am the source of the material.

I wonder what percentage of writers, painters, composers, choreographers, filmmakers doubt or question themselves? There is an element of risk to truly express oneself! What does that take?

I have known world class musicians, public speakers and even those who manage groups whose perspective was askew because of their perfectionism. They could give an outstanding performance and think that it wasn't very good. They focused on a few flaws, and it was stunning to see the contrast between how they felt about it compared to what an audience experienced.

Last summer, I visited the Dali museum, learning the history of a mostly self-taught genius who had no qualms about his self expression. In fact, he walked out of his final review in art school after the two years of study, knowing that he knew more than the panel of artists questioning him.

Viewing Salvador Dali's work leaves me with the impression that he used art for his own psychological process whether that was conscious or not. One can see into his whole Being. Maybe his works have been so analysed these days that the observer sees his psychological process but Dali himself was simply expressing his soul through images, mathematics, geometry and color in the moment. His uncensored creative flow contributed to his greatness. He definitely did not care what anyone thought, and I can assure you they thought he was crazy.

I have attended concerts in which a transmission took place, and both listener and performer engaged in something bigger than themselves. I have looked at great paintings and felt the painter's feeling. I have read literature in which I felt like I was inside the book. I was directly affected by the Art, moved in some inexplicable way.

When we get in the way of ourselves, it stops that creative flow. We get self conscious and we ruminate about what others will think. This is the best way to kill that special transmission that moves an audience or stirs a crowd to its feet.

So if you are out there creating like me, it feels great to remember that it doesn't matter what anyone else thinks. We each have our unique gifts to give that are original, personal, and valuable.

Take a deep look at your experiences with creative flow. What stops it for you? How do you overcome it? What keeps you inspired?

Dare to take the risk today!

MENTORING AND LEARNING: REFLECTIONS OF A LIFELONG STUDENT

One thing I have learned about mentoring is that it can be life changing, whether I am on the teaching or the learning side. I am an eternal student, not only wanting to improve my knowledge and skills, but also yearning to have that unique relationship. If true learning is to take place, the relationship is symbiotic.

Sincere learning means to drop one's ego in order to be taught. This is the storyline behind so many Spiritual Masters, Martial Arts Sensei, modern day Yodas, and their mentees. In order to be taught, one must discover the ultimate humility in oneself, and as weird as it sounds these days, submit to the teaching.

Besides my three Spiritual Mentors, with whom I had a very strong teacher/student bond, some of my greatest teachers have been sports coaches and piano professors.

It is common for spiritual seekers to carry an idealized notion of "equality." While we are all equal as children of God, it is also true that each of us has distinct gifts, needs, and roles to play. By forcing all to be "equal," we lose the opportunity to learn from someone with more experience. That idea just isn't democratic. The ego driven desire to be someone who knows more can get in the way of collaboration and learning.

To aspire to this democratic ideal of equals is desirable and I think the time is here in which collaboration of experts is necessary. Disaster strikes when it is the blind leading the blind or in the other extreme, a clash of leader egos.

Perhaps we are leaving an era in which the Teacher/Student relationship is relevant or revered. The New Age brings with it the chance for a wheel of individuals to share their wisdom and learn from each other. There are so many cracks in the glass ceiling now that it is easier for individuals to access Truth on their own.

I will always be a great proponent of seeking out a mentor for learning more, especially a seasoned expert with a good track record. The ancient Eastern traditions with Zen Masters, Mentors, and Apprenticeships offer a unique one on one relationship that still holds water in my book.

This leads me to ask the question: what does a good teacher/leader provide?

Direction of Purpose
With a mentor comes direction of purpose and organization. Any teacher/ coach/mentor needs to supply orientation, curriculum, and skill building. This gives cohesion for a student, a class, a group or a team and prevents the experience from being a free for all. Different degrees of problems, issues and experiences will come from the students or the entire group, enhancing the learning experience for both the teacher and the student.

Perspective
Our work is truly not our own until we ourselves struggle to find solutions with the help of Grace. Self-initiated transformation is the most effective for it is truly our own path. However, someone from the outside can provide perspective. We are all blind to ourselves until we can see from our own objective observation. This is when the Work is real for us. Having someone else tell us what is wrong steals our own discovery. A good mentor will lead their student to self discovery.

An outside perspective can put us in check when our efforts are not bringing the results we wish for. We may not even be aware of our non progress, and a teacher can point that out.

Accountability

Mentors help us with accountability in ways that we cannot provide for ourselves. If they are good teachers, they show us how to become accountable to our own Sacred Will. This kind of learning requires strong doses of reality and outside perspective. A good teacher will know when to be stern about our efforts and will certainly have no fear in telling us how they see things. Sometimes it means big whacks. Ultimately, they will teach you the discipline of good practice whether that be meditation, eating habits, shooting baskets, piano playing or sales skills.

Inspiration

Mentors supply inspiration. They can be an oasis in the desert of our despair. They lift us up in times of need, encourage us when we are doubting and become our greatest cheerleader. This can make us realize what we did not get when growing up and thus what we did not learn how to do for ourselves. They grow our self esteem and break down ego. They can become a bridge to our inner transformation.

Devotion

The saying goes when the student is ready, the teacher appears. We conjure up images of Karate Kid or Luke Skywalker, countless Buddhist tales and the Diamond Sutra. No matter what field, the teacher will become devoted to a student when the student commits to doing effort as well. This really does mean a submission on the student's part in order to allow a transmission to occur.

I have known countless people who have been in spiritual groups who considered the teacher their teacher, but there was really no teacher/student relationship whatsoever. They were totally unaware of this and remained on the outside of the path, unwilling to open to being taught.

Teachers will often treat us with indifference until they see our commitment to learning from them. When that relationship forms, it is like magic and our progress fuels both the learning and the teaching. Something happens in the way trust is experienced and through that bond the real transformation happens. It is as if the relationship itself provides possibility for both parties.

As far as individuals, groups, communities or teams are concerned, it is up to the individuals themselves to discriminate when things have gone awry, when they have outgrown the teacher, or when there are elements of control and abuse.

The only way I have come to be a mentor for my piano students and my meditation students is to have been a sincere seeker myself for all of my life. I committed to learning from individuals who have brought me through the fire, stood by me in the time of trial, and who have been unafraid that I might surpass them. In fact, I have been taught that a good mentor aspires for a mentee to surpass their own skills. I have learned to trust on an intimate level which has enabled me to love better, and be fearless in my pursuit of happiness. Knowing that those skills are transferable, I can serve in a very big way.

There is a great deal of stigma around community with dynamic leaders because of the phenomenon of a teacher/preacher/guru/leader being identified with their role. This is a situation where the leader is seeking control over the will of others. The progress of the group is held back without its knowledge. There is a cultivation of dependence upon the mentor without the students noticing.

If members develop into leaders themselves, sometimes an air of competition shows up, even if it appears that the leader has been encouraging others to be leaders. Within the group, this can be very difficult to detect until one comes face to face with the leader.

I have been in a situation where I wanted to contribute to making teaching materials for an entrepreneurial group and was told no. When I asked why, the leader told me, "because I am the leader." I knew it was time to leave.

RETREATS

As summer approaches, I have been reflecting on the many retreats I have participated in over my lifetime. The modalities include cleanses, yoga, Gurdjieff movements, music, meditation, dance, relaxation, self development, motivation and combinations of the above. I realize that many of us have preconceived notions about meditation retreats, their purpose, the commitment they take and the investment required.

Meditation does not mean "escape from the world." In this day and age, there are many retreats to choose from in the rest and relaxation category, because of our fast paced, overworked lifestyle. More and more people feel the need to take time out to rejuvenate and unplug. But what if a retreat could offer a means of learning how to live in balance in your everyday life?

The kind of retreat I am writing about is not exactly in the rest and relaxation category. It is an immersion in what regular life could look like when we make right effort. It is a retreat in which one learns how to live in presence. Stress reduction will be a by-product most certainly, but the slowing of the mind and the development of greater attention is necessary to bring about permanent change in our lives.

Taking everyday tasks, for example, gardening, building, or other kinds of practical work, in a group setting, and infusing it with presence of mind exercises creates conditions for extraordinary transformation. Movements and yoga help us embody our spirituality and ground the framework to create a container for permanent change. Chanting, zikr and vocalizing calibrate the frequency of our bodies and cleanse the rust from our hearts.

The idea of a meditation retreat may bring up pictures of imposed silence and lots of sitting. Good results can be experienced from these kinds of retreats, where we have no choice about talking or sitting. But in many ways that is easier than the kind of retreat to which I am referring. When and if silence develops organically from our own impetus, it becomes our own. The choice to listen to that silence has come from an affirming active energy. The power of an active choice over passive obedience helps us to do it in our everyday lives more easily. The retreats I am talking about provide opportunity for this choice.

I am an eternal student, always wanting to improve my skills and understand more. I am like a bee gathering nectar. I feel that if I stop learning, I stagnate. I am not referring to taking in more and more information. I am referring to acquiring knowledge and understanding of my place in the world in order to be of service. This means seeking to truly Understand my Inner Process. If I am to successfully do this, the information I take in must be applied. It is not enough to hear ideas and intellectually contemplate them. I must put them to the test.

If I can be in an environment that requires me to do that, then I acquire real skills and actually experience the effect of the practice. I am taught ideas and must find a way to implement them through will power, discipline and motivation.

What if these methods taught the strengthening of those very attributes? In this way, I can implement what I learn. Active learning has always been my policy for effective results. If I have a piano student, I make sure he can master the skill before he goes home to practice it. The reinforcement of what he has already learned viscerally will make it permanent. I do not tell him how it is done and expect him to figure it out on his own at home. I make sure he has got it.

I can choose any activity as a vehicle for my spiritual transformation, but if I am to actually learn and change, my ego must be put in check. If I am identified with who I think I should be, how I want the world to see me, what kind of parent I ought to be, what kind of religion I choose, whether I am a good person or not, I block reception to the teaching. If I am filled with my own knowing and rightness, I cannot receive the gift from someone else.

Without humility, I suffer from ulterior motives of which I may be totally unconscious. In this way, I go along with the motions of the retreat and remain unaffected, unable to fully participate and thus stay outside of the Dharma Transmission. Part of the struggle to maintain attention will help me see my own identification. A retreat which offers conditions to see these kinds of things can be very disheartening to those who were expecting the "Hawaiian Relaxation Retreat."

I want to come as a blank sheet, a sponge, a child with innocent curiosity. Blessed are the children for theirs is the kingdom of heaven. If I am to absorb real teaching, I must arrive with no agenda except to learn, to try and to ask. I must make an effort toward that end, but at the same time, I must be willing to receive. Having an open mind and heart to new experience is key.

The wish and aim to learn will bring me closer to the kingdom of heaven, and my quality of effort will allow me to experience it here on earth.

GROUNDING

This past Fall I focused on what grounding means for me and for others. It is a broad subject which deserves much exploration.

For the spiritual seeker, grounding is of the utmost importance. If we think of a tree, the strength and power of the trunk and limbs comes directly from the root system. The deeper and more widespread the roots; the higher the tree can grow. Just the same with our spiritual and energetic transformation, we will only be able to reach as "high" as we are grounded below.

What does that mean in terms of the Work in everyday life?

When we consider energies and the effect they have on our lives, the more refined the energy, the more perceptive and psychic we become. As these refined energies begin to work in us, we are able to discriminate in the moment and choose right action. We can, however, acquire access to higher energies without being sufficiently grounded, and the result is a blown fuse. I have known colleagues and teachers who have become unduly ill with chronic disease due to lack of grounding. I myself was a victim of this phenomenon for many years.

One can be extremely psychokinetic, with tendencies toward a more open Being even from birth. If people like this are not totally shut down by parents and society, they may be able to maintain a tiny degree of freedom to access their true Will. These are the people who suffer most when not grounded. They are highly sensitive individuals and often turn to self medicating in one form or another. They are people who have a keen psychic sense, strong intuition, and a propensity toward the Sacred.

They have an insatiable verve for life and the gift of connectedness. These people by nature are often naturally less grounded in some ways. In fact, there are a lot of people floating around out there with huge potential to manifest their light into the world but cannot for lack of grounding.

So what does this mean and how does one stay grounded?

In spiritual work, one of the greatest tools for grounding is sensation. As one progresses down the road of transformation, sensation of the body becomes deeper and more defined, more felt, more accentuated. It is how we experience Presence. Presence actualizes our consciousness on this planet in human form. Otherwise, we swim around in our heads and imagination, not connected to the physical aspect of our existence. In fact, the more grounded we are, the more physical is our experience. This translates to a greater connection with each other and the planet through presence.

Sensation is not something that can be thought and so those who are more oriented to thinking have a harder time with this. Unfortunately, we have been taught to mainly live in our heads. Pure physical sensation has been described as heat, movement, and density among many things. When one becomes truly rooted in sensation, the awareness goes beyond just the physical realm. One can become totally aware of openings throughout the chakra system, but only with an intense physical awareness first. This is an advanced stage.

I always suggest to my students that they learn sensation as their first and foremost spiritual tool. If full body sensation is a goal, then one must start with one body part and use it as a constant reminder of the present moment. Becoming aware of sensation in a charged moment can bring us out of our thinking and into the present. The body is always in the present moment. With practice, the use of sensation becomes a great aid to our transformation.

In higher realms of freedom, sensation evolves into an enormous pool of substance that naturally includes the body. One can become aware of the physicality of the Astral Body and a Higher Being Body through resources gained in relation to higher frequencies of existence. One has access to these higher frequencies without burning up the physical body via extreme sensation.

This is experienced as a very broad and expanded physicality. In fact, it is as if the body has expanded to larger dimensions and one can physically feel that. This also becomes a radar for reading and understanding the energy patterns of other people's Being Force, whether they be alive on this planet or living eternally through their own Higher Being Body.

Often if we find ourselves unable to complete tasks, unable to have intimate relationships, unable to flow with life on earth in a satisfied and joyful manner, it is most likely due in part to lack of grounding. All of our spiritual progress as individuals and as a species depends on this foundation, so it really is one of the most basic and fundamental necessities of a fulfilling life.

Try the exercise of sensing a body part and simply notice if it is possible to:
    a.   hold that attention while doing something else
    b.   use it as a tool to bring yourself back
    c.   remind yourself to do so going into a charged situation
    d.   take a random minute to do so throughout your day

Approach your experiment with curiosity and an open mind.

CREATING GREAT WORKS
OF ART

I recently completed my second CD entitled "French" this fall and wanted to explain a little about the process just in case you wanted to get clarity on finishing your own project.

Sometimes our artistic creations must take a back seat even when we are professional artists. We have to make money and our day to day activities, consisting of earning through means of service or teaching, take precedence. No one is going to pay us for practicing, filming, writing, painting or sculpting, at least not initially. However, our daily consistent and unpaid efforts can amount to a great deal including money. It takes a leap of faith, trust in our artistry, and great conviction of purpose. We must strike a balance as artists if we want to live a quality life, earn money and produce great works of art.

With each CD, I have gotten a vision or a theme usually about two years ahead of the completion of the project. I reflect on the repertoire and its relative cohesion, and sometimes I choose pieces because I love them or have a personal relationship with them.

For French, I chose pieces that had an impact on my life while living in France for eight years. Les Barricades Mysterieuses is a piece I often heard on the steps of Sacre Coeur played by a street clown. I visited this church often after I had made the difficult choice to carry a surprise pregnancy to term.

L'Entretien des Muses represents the importance of Muses in my life and how often I am met with inspiration and innovation on a regular basis. My muses began to visit me as a young pianist living a dream life in Paris.

Ravel's Sonatine is the set of pieces I played for my young tiny French son to keep him smiling. Debussy's Suite Pour Le Piano was chosen for the gorgeous Sarabande and the way it allows me to transcend this world. It ultimately served as a gateway to a more refined technique and higher realms of interpretation.

As I undergo the process of learning the music or bringing it back, I find things developing in stages. There is the first round of getting notes, fingering, dynamics and really the basics of the music. I play for a mentor three times a year where I basically get raked over the coals and that keeps me in check.

Then there is a point where I hit a wall where I feel I can't get deeper with my interpretation or my relationship with the music. There is no end to the fixing of details. It can always get better, but I am talking about a kind of fatigue. It almost feels like the "dry period" spiritual teachers speak of before the dark night of the soul and then the big breakthrough.

My process with the music can only undergo metamorphosis if I let go to a higher force. This is a force which transcends any one of my single faculties like my brain or memory, my physicality and its relationship to the execution of the music, or the feelings that are moved in me when I hear it. I often must drill and drill to master a small two bar phrase technically. I take months and months to have the memorization just so. I am often so moved by the music, lost in feeling and emotion that it can lead to crash and burn of the notes. There is a perfect balance to executing music of this caliber.

Achieving this place of divine oneness with the music, the composer, my own Being and my audience requires solid practice on a daily basis - yet much more. I must come to understand the harmony, the form, and the patterns which come together to create the masterpiece. If I am to interpret the music well, I must look deeply phrase by phrase or chord by chord and understand why the composer wrote it the way he did. Bringing out this detail and that detail will allow cohesion for the listener. I must see the gestalt of the composition and I can only do this through living with it and experiencing a progression of insights.

I have to let go of the striving, the perfection, the performance...

It's like knowing a lover well enough to recognize the idiosyncrasies and long enough to lose each other in oneness.

I must be close to reaching a point of divine union with the music itself before I decide to go into the studio, but sometimes deadlines get in the way. You can't really push this perfect storm of execution, inspiration, and musical freedom.

I also must release myself from the painful reminder that recording adds an element of permanence and is very different than performing. That inspired performance happens when it happens and one must be prepared enough to hope that it happens in that studio. The only way to be sure is to practice your ass off even if you aren't getting paid... . yet!

The more I refine and perfect, the more I become one with the music, understanding the details while at the same time feeling something move deep inside of me. To the innocent bystanders like my daughter, my husband and my neighbors who hear the music over and over for months, it probably gets annoying. For me, it frees my soul, fulfills my purpose on this planet and provides a conduit to higher realms for those who want to listen.

THE WAY OUT
IS IN

As we open toward realms of Higher Consciousness, there is a necessity to shed the blocks that occur in the emotional and psychological realm. We are shedding the old Archetypal patterns and accepting our broadened Intellectual Understanding of the New Way. The balance of the masculine and feminine forces is also coming into play. Our access to many dimensions is actualizing.

This will look like chaos from the outside.

We must remember that at one time in history we had a highly expanded awareness of other dimensions. A cataclysm not according to law occurred and affected the way our Will operated. The subsequent sublimation of the Will to the ego has caused problems for all of us.

Part of becoming free entails shedding the old paradigm we have found ourselves in for centuries.

What does this old paradigm look like?

Our fears govern our actions. Under these circumstances, false evidence appears real. We are too paralyzed to choose and our Being is unable to be accessed. Without this access, we cannot connect to one another. We roam the earth in our sequestered world of inner considering, constantly wanting more, unable to have empathy with others, drowning in stress, anxiety and depression. These pervading negative emotions engulf our lives and make it impossible to enter the Unity of All Things. War and Dominion over others pervades.

What is the solution?

In practicing the Work, we must move toward a place of stillness in order for our Greater Awareness to be activated. Through practices that increase our attention and enable keener awareness of how we use our different centers, we grow more grounded. We begin to perceive a larger reality that encompasses somatic awareness and access to true feeling instead of negative emotion.

We must realize how we predominantly live in our thoughts.

By developing an internal observer, we will see and hear from a deeper place, a place centered in the Heart Mind. This represents a Higher Dimension, the Higher Emotional Center. It is a gateway to a profound feeling life. We enter these higher realms with the ability to experience Remorse of Conscience. This can only happen when we begin to objectively see who we really are and let go of the hold our ego has on us.

This kind of Self-observation comes about in a moment of Presence in which we see the reality of the situation and our own part in it.

This is how we take responsibility for our actions.

So often we try to solve things with our minds and our thinking. We try to develop spiritually through the thinking which never works. It cannot come from our divided capacities, namely our bodies, feelings or thinking separately, but from all three synchronized.

The manifestation resulting from the synthesis of our body, feeling and thinking develops a Watchman. Each time this Self-Remembering occurs, it is a step toward the reassembly of our Greater Selves. As we assimilate the broken structure of our psyche and emotions, we become more whole and create a Soul body, named by Gurdjieff as the Kesdjan Body. This is the vehicle through which we can experience the Higher Worlds, the World of Being and the World of Will.

The portal through which we enter these Higher Dimensions is through Being. From there, our ability to truly Understand a much larger Universe can occur.

This ability includes communication through extraordinary means, psychic connection, energetic healing, and intradimensional synthesis.

Once we are able to surrender, there is one essential element needed to be in place for these higher dimensions to be permanent states. Our Kesdjan body, a "soul body," must be developed enough to be the vessel for permanent change. The permanence requires a perfect storm in which we have developed awareness combined with surrender. We are strong enough to see and experience our Heart.

We can be opened up by many forces from the outside, from gurus to rituals, but if we have not established this spiritual body, we close right back up again. These openings can be highly detrimental to those who have no groundwork to handle the ensuing release of emotion.

In this time of Attunement, we are meant to return to the way in which our ancestors lived. Their broadened awareness and communication spanned Super Intelligences that influenced our world, the Earth, and its part in the Great Universe. There was a keen love and respect for one another, a deep reverence for the gifts of the Earth. They were part of a much larger scale of interaction between humans, nature, and the expanded worlds of synthesis and communication.

Take time for self-reflection and embrace the dark places within. I encourage us to open to a higher vibration, a calling, and the will to integrate. Let's find ways in which we can bring about stillness. Go on a solo one or two day retreat this year. Attending retreats that resonate with us and doing an Inner Work that takes no instruction will take us far.

Our transformation requires the persistence and patience to listen inside objectively, without judgement and accept as things are. We don't have to change anything, just see it. That is the first step in coming to understand our part in this great Universe and the change that is happening.

LIFE PURPOSE

In looking back, I accomplished so much last year, a book, a CD, a new global clientele and the enormous growth of my meditation groups. This is not a brag, but a hope that you will be inspired.

Someone asked me the last day of the year, "Have you always been able to manifest what you set out to do so easily?" and the answer is no. Through all of this expanded awareness practice, mindfulness and meditation, I have learned to implement what I set out to do.

I have learned about aim.

I don't question, hesitate or flounder once I have made a decision to do something. It no longer takes me a long time to make those decisions and once done, I set a specific date with specific goals and begin to take daily action. If my action is not producing results, I steer the boat in another direction, but I don't quit. I have learned discipline and how to struggle in the yes and no.

It wasn't always like that.

I was plagued with indecisiveness for fear of making a mistake or not being good enough or wondering what people might think. I was plagued with procrastination, and when the day was done, I beat myself up for it. Making myself feel inadequate was the running inner dialogue and it fulfilled the role that adults had presented to me as a child.

I somehow let anything get in the way of my desired goal. I thought procrastination was my modus operandi, but really it provided the chance for me to keep this "story" of not being good enough alive. When we are given that message as a child, whether directly or indirectly, we all find ways to perpetuate the limiting belief into adulthood.

What changed at a clear turning point was a freedom from that kind of inner turmoil. It came as a result of truly understanding with all of my Being, the crazy things my ego made me believe. It came as a result of letting go of who I perceived myself to be.

My inner work, my daily awareness and my meditation allowed me to see just how crazily things work inside of me and really in all of us, but that came after effort of a different sort.

It was daily work of first noticing that subconscious story at play, actually experiencing myself hearing the voice, then at a more advanced stage, noticing actual feelings occurring at the same time. I learned to watch my habitual, mechanical, reactional unawake self and that was the first step toward consciousness of Self.

It's not some past life stuff to learn about. It is not solely a psychological process of understanding and analysing where it all came from. Knowing what happened to you in the past does not help you notice it in the present moment. Often it can feed the story more.

The change happens in a present moment of Self-observation. That is why there is so much hubbub about learning meditation, having awareness and attention. We are developing this "muscle" of attention which eventually leads to our own freedom!

It is our mission here on earth in this lifetime to rediscover who we already are underneath the crust of our wacky ego and its shenanigans. That is our purpose and every great teacher and prophet of all religions has come here to show us that.

My hope for us all is to discover for ourselves who we truly are and why we are here, so we can manifest that into the world. We are meant to be creative, thriving, abundant, joyful and loving toward ourselves and each other.

Let's prioritize, implement, and work hard while taking time to enjoy life like there is no tomorrow. Let's get wild with passion in whatever we do, seize the day and Carpe the heck out of our diem.

INTUITIVE
JOURNALING

Upon returning from our retreat last weekend, I have been reflecting on the ways we reach our intuitive voice and truly open to Source. In essence, it means utilizing ways in which we can learn to receive those messages without the filter of logical thinking, analysis, and structure.

It is pure reception.

One element that hinders reception is control. How and why do we seek to control everything?

It feels safe, less chaotic, productive, and action oriented. We have been trained to believe that the more we do, the more action we take, the harder we push, the more method we apply, the more structure we have, the better the result.

We have become very unaccustomed to allowing.

Part of the practice during the retreat was intuitive journaling; something that does not require expertise in writing. It is free flow and the epitome of allowing. It begins to stream once we have broken past a barrier that has been keeping us feeling rather familiar and safe. It is a voice that emerges that is not under our control. We can start with a question and begin to answer that question but we must let it continue even if we are writing things like "I am not sure what else to say" or "I am not sure how to answer this question." The point is to keep writing until something starts to flow. It may seem very unrelated to the question. It will be things that really need to come out and be said.

The more we can relinquish control over the answer or its relatedness to the question, the better.

Part of the secret to intuitive journaling is to let in all impressions and write them down as we notice them. These come from our five senses including body sensations, feelings, and random thoughts. We will also receive real intuitive wisdom coming from a place of Essence. All of this input is valid and has a place in the message.

We can also do an intuitive writing exercise that involves simply recording all impressions so that we get used to noticing the many many modes of input that we usually take for granted.

Part of the reason I teach practical awareness is to learn to take in more impressions. We are usually blocked from doing that because only one of our centers, like our thinking, for example, is predominant in any given moment. We don't realize that we might be feeling from our thinking. I know that sounds strange or almost impossible but the more advanced we become at noticing what is actually going on, the more we see that we are feeling from a center other than the feeling center.

Experiencing the present moment requires the presence of all three centers whether we realize that or not. The more Presence we experience, the more we understand from an experiential viewpoint what it is to have all three faculties working and synchronized.

Many of our impressions are tainted by habitual belief and assumptions that happen so fast we can't even see it. Patterns of seeing and reacting that have been ingrained in our body since childhood which then trigger a certain feeling which then trigger a certain thought happen so instantaneously that we are unaware. Our actual taking in of information may occur well after two or three of those feedback loops have already occurred. Before we know it, we are reacting to something that truly does not even exist.

The journaling can help decipher some of this if you are open and "out of control." There is no right or wrong, but you will know when this voice from Source is speaking. There is no doubt about that. You experience something outside of your ordinary way of thinking, speaking and being.

The beauty of doing this at the retreat was that we were combining it with many modalities of being present. We were directly connecting with nature. We were unlocking code in our body through the Movements. We were acquiring greater and much more refined attention by stopping on the hour and noticing the contrast. We were spontaneously entering moments of silence that were not imposed. Finally, the group effort intensified the individual results.

I hope you will try this type of journaling on your own and see what comes up for you concerning everyday questions as well as big life dilemmas.

OPEN HEART SURGERY

My article is supposed to be finished today, but on this National Heart Day, I am sitting in the Cardiac Surgery waiting room. I have flown across the country, with about 3 hours of sleep to be able to see my father before he goes into triple bypass surgery at age 80.

When I heard the news from my sister yesterday, so many things flashed before my eyes. His life has been ultra full, his health is top notch and he can outride any of those 40-something-year-old women in the spin class. He is a disciplined athlete, esteemed cardiologist, father of six and grandfather to 10. He has lived a life of devotion to God. He's a little awkward in the affection department though his demeanor is as sweet as they come. He has made some big mistakes along the way.

He has traveled the world giving medical assistance to many in need. He has started health clinics, cardiac rehabilitation units and delivered antibiotics to remote areas. He has devoted his life to service.

Overall, looking back at his dysfunctional roots, I would say he has triumphed over some of life's biggest tests and even high jumped some seemingly impossible hurdles. He has evolved as a human here on this planet. There may be some who would not agree with me.

I did not begin to worry or panic that I might lose him. In fact, a calm came over me that was peaceful and accepting. It was not how I thought I would be upon hearing that my dad might kick the bucket in the next few days as a result of mandatory surgery. I was willing to accept that this was the end, but I didn't really believe that it was for one second. Is that called plain ole' denial, faith, a protective measure... or shock?

None of the above. The realization for me was that I am not afraid of death, my own or anyone else's. I have come to accept its inevitability and I can rest in the knowledge that life goes on after death. We have bodies for fleeting moments compared to our soul's journey.

Whether we believe in reincarnation or heaven, our eternal life is something to be realized through work and evolution on this planet. It is not some place to enjoy later. There is a mission for each one us to strive to become free in order to love. That ultimate accomplishment is called heaven on earth.

Divine Love. Sacred Love. Devotional Love.

All of these are the Beloved coming through us and if we are to experience the nature of Spirit, our mission is to learn to get out of the way and love one another, truly love one another.

We spend lifetimes trying to get this right.

So for my Dad, he has done the one thing a human is supposed to do. Amidst the misunderstandings, the broken promises, the awkward moments, the anger, the imperfection, the abandonnement, and the lack of communication, he has asked for forgiveness. Even though his actions don't always show it, he has expressed love by saying it. and... I know he loves me.

He has made a soul connection of love with me that will remain evergreen.

So what flashed before my mind in those few seconds was: mission accomplished, he has learned to love.

P.S. He made it through the surgery with flying colors!!!

VIRTUALLY TAKING IT
TO THE STREETS

Bringing my meditation school online is one of the most fulfilling things I have done in a long time. It takes work, creativity, persistence and open mindedness. I don't think I could have seen this coming 5 years ago or even a year ago.

In the first twenty years or so of developing myself and my career, I developed high level skills, both in classical music performance as well as meditation and mindful living. However, from my perspective, quotidian life has a completely different look and feel than expertise. I experience small victories and big failures, and have learned to take each in stride.

It has required a wrestle with my ego. That is the daily grind and it has become a most interesting and valued aspect of the whole picture. In fact, it is the journey that gives me staying power. How detached and "non identified" can I be with my success or my failure? If I can accept it all as it happens then I know my path is still evolving and growing.

I say this because I am on a mission.

If I don't take risks, then I cannot experience the creative edge, the place where life feels oh so real, the possibility that this teaching can catch fire and be a part of the wave of evolution on this planet. This is the place where I wake up and ask myself, "how can I serve" as if it is an adventure, a question, a soft round attention opening toward that subtle space of knowing and not knowing. The more risk I take, the more I learn about what holds me back, what doesn't work, and what not to do.

I realize that I don't like sales at all. I don't like getting myself out there and pushing my wares but guess what?

I do like being of service to people and showing them what has effectively and utterly changed my life as well as the lives of others. I can duck down under the waves of thought and the turbulence of negative emotion and glide through the water of life. That is news worth spreading. When I share the mechanics of how to do this, people are changed too. They are grateful. They are intrigued by methods that have been passed down through a thread of transmission like a secret code.

I could take it to the streets but many will not actually notice or hear unless they are looking for it, and those are the people this teaching serves. If I am to find that select tribe, then the code must pass in front of many, many eyes. The subtlety of it all rippling out from the original stone's throw goes unnoticed. Those ripples do not diminish over time but become larger and I feel it is important that the details and the absolute crux of transformation do not get watered down. The popularization could dilute the returns.

So, the original idea of bringing a spiritual teaching online can be risky and... salesy but there are millions of people out there and it is time in our own human evolution to practice mindfulness in ways that have never been "mainstream."

I recently launched my 14 day meditation challenge to 137 people in many countries around the world. It has been a huge success and a huge learning curve. Am I casting pearls before swine?

I cannot expect these methods to be wildly popular because they require a sincere effort, radical inquiry, and a burning desire for transformative change. However, there seems to be a refreshing desire for this on a wider basis. There is most certainly a need, but as I see it, the ways to effectively satisfy that need are few. The flurry of sign ups in the first day was encouraging.

To my surprise, this online meditation challenge has shown me that people are genuinely seeking ways to relieve the pain of life as we know it now. They are drowning in stress, anxiety and negativity. The increase in pain will automatically increase the desire to take the risk to relieve it.

We may not even realize we are suffering, believing that this is the way life is and always will be.

There is a certain tipping point that creates the serious seeker. All that is needed is a taste to realize just how asleep one is and then experience how sweet the nectar of peace can be.

That taste is like succulent drops of pure water after traversing the most arid desert. It brings hope and fortitude so that we can carry on knowing there is relief.

It is the sip of expanded awareness; something that has been educated out of us from all directions. I am reminded of Neo from The Matrix, taking the red pill and realizing he has been wading in a sea of hypnotized zombies plugged into a matrix. We can only know it by waking up!

I want to be of service in this lifetime and I have something of absolute value to offer, so I must reconcile and create ways to offer a profound teaching in a world that hardly tolerates keeping attention for more than 3 seconds.

Maybe that is why online marketing is the way to shout it on the mountaintops at this point.

NO STATIC
AT ALL

Last night in conversation a woman asked me whether I knew my real voice, my voice of intuition. She was asking because her intuition had recently guided her to make a decision that turned out to be bad. Now she was totally questioning whether she could trust her judgement.

I have made many big mistakes in my life because as a child I learned not to trust my intuition. In fact, what I learned to do was listen to the conditioned voice that needed to please others, be accepted by others, do what I thought others thought I should do or what I thought I should do or what my mother thought I should do. No wonder I couldn't hear my own voice!!

I can remember doubting some very big life decisions and chalking my hesitations up to fear. I ignored the quiet voice inside that whispered "something doesn't feel right about this." I experienced countless disappointments in my life as a result of not following my intuition.

With each mistake, however, I learned. I learned that (in hindsight) my authentic voice was warning me about something.

I clearly graduated from the accelerated school of hard knocks.

How do you distinguish between your conditioned responses and your authentic voice?

How can you be sure you recognize one or the other?

If you are like me, the ability to recognize your authentic voice was "educated out of you" during childhood. Repeated statements from your parents like "Oh, you are fine" when in fact you were not fine wreaked havoc on your internal radar. You learned, falsely, that you cannot trust your feelings.

Maybe as a child you intuitively picked up messages of distress from people around you who told you everything was fine. You then had to put your expert intuitive system into question. You started learning that what you saw and understood was not true.

What if you are a natural born empath and can't recognize what is yours and what is someone else's? That gift comes with its own special learning curve.

You learned to ignore your inner voice of truth. Whether it was from lack of other's honesty and integrity, from not being accepted, from being punished, shamed, bullied or simply being misunderstood, you learned that what you felt was not "appropriate."

You also learned that your honesty could get you into deep trouble.

So by trial and error as a young adult and onward, you must learn to distinguish what is real and what is not real. You cannot realize this until you make the mistakes necessary to see that what you thought was right was wrong and vice versa.

These grand mistakes are called shocks. Some of us need bigger ones than others and they are necessary in life.

Trusting your intuition and knowing your authentic voice requires wading through a lot of crusted on personality that you formed to protect yourself. Avoiding repeated disappointment is what created that false voice.

Until you start to study how you see yourself, what things influence your decisions and how identified you are with being accepted, you will continue to override your authentic voice.

You have to build a container of personal energy through Presence that allows you to be free from filtered perception. You will then no longer make decisions based on what others think. You don't have to please people anymore or seek love for the wrong reasons. You can become free, connected to Source, and know that what you once saw as a child can come alive in you again.

Experiencing your genuine self allows connection to your Being with no interference and no filter.

You become vulnerable without fear.

There is flow with no resistance.

When you next come up to a decision you are having trouble with, ask yourself:

Am I bowing to someone else's agenda?

Am I doing what society thinks is the right thing?

Am I falling prey to "comparisonitis"?

Am I afraid of what people may think?

Listening deeply to your intuition can be so foreign that at first you may not recognize it. It may be the tiny voice that has been pushed back to the far reaches of your mind. It may not make sense, but there is one thing for sure:

If you can get out of the way, there is no static at all.

I LOVE PEOPLE

Yesterday as I walked out of the Sip and Ship shop, I became strangely engulfed in a sense of total fulfillment in blossom. An observation expanded and filled me to the brim. I was experiencing a particularly keen sense of satisfaction and disproportionate joy merely from... running errands.

What had struck me in such a way that I was one with the Universe?

It was a feeling that reassured me that life is so precious. I was touched by seemingly mundane events and encounters. It made the song on the radio reach my heart. I saw the sun shining on all the cherry blossoms with new love. I felt more alive.

I came to the profound realization that I love people.

It was understanding on a different plane as if gases and air had come together to make a new hologram. It was more than 3 dimensional and it was boundless.

Reflecting on the errands, I realized that every encounter I had had from grocery clerk, barista to mail clerk involved a most gratifying Being connection.

I talk to strangers as if they are family...

However, it wasn't the first time I had seen any one of these people. They are the ones that move in constellations around my primary existence as familiar faces who participate in my everyday orbit with mutual acknowledgement that we kind of know each other but not really.

Yesterday, we had conversations. We laughed. We talked about new haircuts, being old, being young, Chris Isaak, song makeovers, teenagers and their silly ways, trust, breakups, dog issues, and of course, the weather... all in the span of one half hour.

Through that vehicle of exchange came a feeling of camaraderie; a sense that everyone is my brother or sister, that we are all parts of a whole and made of the same stuff, that we all need connection and meaning and love. It's the exchange of a certain Being substance that makes it meaningful and it doesn't feel like small talk.

I love how we all have our quirky ways, our dilemmas and our passions. Some of us meet in secret universes of knowing, mutually recognizing each other. Some of us reach out of our way to connect and through small gestures make a huge difference. Some of us meet eye to eye.

Yesterday I was grateful that I had people all around me sharing some kind of existential process that can be either enhanced or diminished according to our level of Presence. The interaction sparkles my world. Gravity expands. A magnetic connection ignites because I can choose to feel someone, reach someone, and love someone even if I don't know them.

I love people.

The rewards are infinite.

YOU ARE YOUR ATTENTION

Self-observation has been the most important yet the most difficult aspect of The Work to teach. It is the end goal, the gateway to freedom and the vehicle for having choice in our lives. The first step is developed attention.

There are three types of attention: associative, directed and a special third type that I call expanded awareness. These are wonderfully explained in Russell Schreiber's book Gurdjieff's *Transformational Psychology*.

We are very familiar with the first two types: associative attention can be observed when we watch our thinking flit from one subject to another, then it might be reminded of something by a smell, or a sound. Our thoughts change as often as the wind blows.

Any one of the senses can be stimulated and then trigger more thoughts or memories associated with it. Emotions can also be activated and those feelings can kick off another set of thoughts or memories. This is called associative thinking, and our attention takes a piggyback ride on it.

The second type of attention is directed attention; something that was "educated" into us through our caregivers and teachers. We were told to pay attention when our minds were wandering out the window in a daydream. We learned to focus when reading and paid attention to the content. We limited our field of awareness to one particular thing through a kind of effort.

Many who could not develop that kind of attention have been labeled ADD. Unfortunately, all of the constant distraction with cell phones, iPads, TV and texting has deteriorated our ability to focus and added to that statistic.

We are only able to keep our focus for a matter of seconds before it is pulled in another direction. We cannot resist the instant gratification of the next text or Facebook post.

The most recent generations have grown up with excess stimulation, constant interruptions and no time to let the mind settle on one thing to contemplate or observe it. Children under the age of three who are developing permanent lifetime neural pathways are being put in front of games and TV screens with images that change every 2 seconds.

Any of us who repeat patterns of behavior strengthen certain neural pathways which then reinforce that behavior.

This may not seem so grave until we look at what constitutes being in the present moment and why that is important.

We must evaluate the importance of Presence regarding our functioning, our happiness, our self-knowledge and our ability to thrive. To know thyself is to be free, so we must develop the third kind of attention in order to observe ourselves objectively.

This third kind of attention is the key to our spiritual development. It is the key that opens the door to Self-observation.

You see, we are our attention. Developing expanded awareness is the way we can tend to our Soul.

What constitutes expanded awareness is a kind of attention that is not directed but is focused on a broader spectrum of experiences. It entails experiencing several aspects of oneself simultaneously. It is subtle and gentle, yet it allows an entirely new impression to surface, one that can awaken insight into extreme self-honesty.

We must become aware of our associative attention and how it plays out in our subjective involvement of pattern and that requires this expanded awareness.

We have to see our "unmindfulness" in order to become mindful.

The important step here is to develop expanded awareness through simple everyday challenges involving attention. I have been teaching these techniques many many years in order to enable people to take in more impressions. In this way, they can begin to observe functioning from reaction, fueled by automatic and associative attention and manifested as negative emotion.

Expanded awareness can head this phenomenon off at the pass.

"These ideas about attention are not new... religions and virtually all schools of mindfulness training hold fast to the belief that nothing can begin to transform within us until our attention has moved from passive to active. The Buddha referred to single pointed focus, Christ, the energy of prayer, for Hindus, Raja and Bhakti yoga, and for the Zen Buddhists, the training of attention is the spiritual practice."

−C. Bourgeault

In a classic zen story, retold by Phillip Kapleau, a man approached Ikkyu, a zen master, and asked for the highest wisdom:

"Ikkyu immediately took the brush and wrote the word 'attention.' "Is that all?" asked the man, "Will you add nothing more?" Ikkyu then wrote twice running, "Attention. Attention." "Well," remarked the man rather irritably, "I really don't see much depth or subtlety to what you have written." Then Ikkyu wrote the same word three times running, "Attention. Attention. Attention."

−Philip Kapleau

Noticing the nature of our attention is life changing. There are many tools to help us develop expanded awareness and I will cover that in the next article of this three part series on Self-observation.

For now, noticing what type of attention is being used at any given moment will give you a lot of clues to how we are conducting your life.

THE SECRET WEAPON
OF PRESENCE: SENSATION

The other day someone asked me if I were to name one potent practice above all others for increasing Presence within, what would it be?

I truly had to reflect on this question for there are so many tools when working with being present out in the world. In my twelve week course, we spend weeks experimenting with different ways to notice how we are not here... and not aware of our awareness. When we wake up and realize we are here, there are actions to take to reveal more of what is going on inside of us. We can set up cues to remind us to wake up.

Meditation is also important, creating strength in single minded focus, accessing stillness and increasing the ability to watch and observe our inner landscape. Doing meditation will create the play of more refined energy with which to work, but there is something else that I would deem even more helpful out in the world.

Even after 8 years of working in a zen dojo, meditating every morning and night, plus daily yoga sessions, I still noticed that I had a lot of emotional reaction and stories playing out in my head as I went about my day.

It was not until I met my second great teacher, John MacPherson, a student of John Bennett and The Fourth Way Work, that I was shown how to use this secret weapon in ways that would change my world from black and white to color. My expanded awareness increased because I was using that subtle rounded attention to be aware of two things at once. I was not toggling between two things or multi tasking... I was understanding the use of more than one of my centers at the same time.

What am I actually talking about?

The secret weapon is sensation and it is something we can begin to use right away to understand what it means to be in our body, to be grounded and to access information from the perspective of felt sense.

The body is always in the present moment.

Asking someone to get in their body is easier said than done. We do all kinds of things to get in our body like exercise, yoga, meditation, walking, and massage. However, being in our body while doing something other than those things can prove rather difficult. One of the reasons is because the intellectual emotional complex steals the energy in the form of habitual association and analysis.

Another reason is that we have neuro pathways grooved into our mode of behavior. Our flow of ordinary associations is so habitual that it takes more attention than usual to break. We are generally not in our bodies as this is happening.

If there were any tool to help us create space outside of the energy of the psycho-emotional drama, it is sensation. Becoming aware of the physical sensation of my hands, for example, in the midst of another activity can bring breadth and perspective on what is happening within me.

One of the easiest ways to work with sensation is to maintain an awareness of a body part while doing mundane repetitive activities like folding the laundry, chopping vegetables, or gardening. This is one of the reasons we do these kinds of activities regularly during our retreats, giving the student a chance to develop skills in intentional conditions higher in energies but mimicking daily life. Once this practice is strengthened, there is a chance of developing an observer who can catch emotional wind up before it begins to happen. This takes practice, so we start with the subtle awareness of our hands and maintain that while doing something less charged like chopping wood.

The other important result of using sensation is that we are grounded and able to accumulate higher energies and transform our attention into food for the soul.

Grounding is more than contact with the earth, although this is very very important. When we incorporate literally, we have a new impression of the energy of not only the body, but also the energy of emotion, thought, like and dislike, our environment and nature. We are able to take in a new mode of information in terms of felt sense of these energies. We are open to a new way of seeing called Self-observation.

We are meant to be in these bodies of ours, incarnating to the degree that we have new understanding and actual transformation. Working with this kind of expanded awareness generates sensitive energy which is conducive to connecting us with the here and now. The more that happens, the more we experience objective awareness which leads to a higher order of experience.

PRISONERS OF AN UNSEEN WAR

We create our own reality inside and out.

For me, understanding this has been my life purpose.

If we are to find our way to love - loving ourselves as well as others - we have to learn to see how we walk the earth oblivious to our own prison. We can feel the consequences of our sleep well enough, but we do not know how to escape.

I believe the best tactic is Self-observation. Please don't take my word for it. I ask that we find out from our own experience. The more free we become, the more we realize just how unable we were able to live in peace and harmony. When we practice true Self-observation, we see that we are rarely all here utilizing our freedom of choice.

The good news is once something has been observed, it changes.

Our aim is to strive for three centered awareness; an awareness that is expanded beyond any one center of perception, that is, the thinking, the emotions or the body. We can only arrive at this unified state by trying to incorporate the body into the habitual psycho-emotional drama in which we are trapped.

We must acquire information about the habitual state of consciousness in which we live, if we are to escape our solitary confinement.

The greatest illusion is that we think we are conscious of ourselves when we can articulate our feelings and what is seemingly going on inside.

These are usually wanderings of the mind based on analysis and a mentally constructed sense of self. Our analysis is tainted by our conditioning so we really have no objective sense of who we are and why we do the things we do.

I know this sounds disconcerting and no one really likes to hear that they don't realize what is going on inside of them. In fact, we don't want to believe that. If it is true, almost everything we know ourselves to be, is false.

Can we suspend our disbelief for a brief time? What if we were to question it all? What if that were to lead us to a greater truth and freedom?

If we decide that we are already winning the battle, we lose the chance of discovering the territory to be gained.

To become truly self-conscious leads to self-remembering. The importance of this lies in our evolution. If we do not question the reason we repeat patterns over lifetimes, we remain eternally locked in the cycle of death and rebirth. The only answer is to see and know thyself objectively.

When I say self-consciousness, I am not talking about a state of nervousness where we think everyone is looking at us. I am talking about being aware of our awareness as we go about life. The recognition of our own Presence is developed through the practice of Self-observation. That is when we enter the Present Moment aware of ourselves in a new and fresh way that can see the pattern or feel the emotion or sense the archaic automatic bodily response. Once we become skilled at recognizing that we are bombarded with automatic associations and judgement, regardless of how much conscious will we ascribe to our thoughts, feelings or actions, we get closer to the truth of ourselves.

There are several requirements for experiencing Self-observation which the author Red Hawk so eloquently points out in his book *Self-observation*.
   1) We must remain impartial with no judgement of what we see.
   2) We must not try to change what we see.
   3) True Self-observation cannot be achieved without sensation.
   4) This requires brutal self-honesty.

With these parameters in place, we can see the challenge put before us.

It takes a real struggle to notice something and not judge it. Our ego is constantly weighing whether something is good or bad. It is the seat of like and dislike and it runs the campaign. If our work is to drive the ego back, then we must resist the inclination to judge whether something is good or bad. Equally when we justify our actions or blame them on anything and everything, we remain the prisoner of judgement and take no responsibility for our acts. The minute we do this, it no longer remains self-observation.

Likewise, we have to consciously struggle not to change what we see, for when we do, it too has become the property of our associative, analysing, categorizing process of good or bad. When we want to change it, it implies that what we have seen is "no good." This takes enormous discipline to overcome a lifetime of letting our head lead the offensive.

The body, always in the present moment, will never do this. It takes in information so quickly with no filter that we would do well to start to listen to how it experiences the energy of thoughts, feelings, likes and dislikes. If we can incorporate the use of sensation on a regular basis, this will lead to knowing thyself on a broader spectrum. We may begin to experience our lives on a new level and understand our patterns from a new perspective.

We can try to visualize things of a positive nature or say affirmations until we are blue in the face but they will never acquire the energy necessary to overturn the pattern if they come from thought. To penetrate our self-sabotage and understand what holds us back, we have to see it in a way that reveals the locked in automatic conditioning.

When we are aiming for brutal self honesty, we must ride the energy of yes and no. We aren't going to like what we see. We will try to hide from the perceived enemy. That has been our motivation since we were children looking for cover.

With efforts to gain clarity on what is really going on, we become stronger. We get better at the practice. We learn acceptance. We will see how horribly we treat ourselves and recognize the warzone that we uphold. If we do that, imagine how we could treat others.

Let's end the war.

SOUL FOOD

What we feed grows.

There are many kinds of food that we put into our organism. Attention to nutritional whole food is the way to stay healthy. We take care of our body by feeding it the right balance of vitamins and minerals through unprocessed foods free of pesticides, herbicides and hormones.

There are two other foods that are essential to our health as human beings and without which we could not live.

The second food is air. We cannot last more than a few minutes without it circulating through our system and into our brain. However, there is something more we share in the air that we breath that feeds our soul. These are finer particles of which we partake consciously and intentionally.

When we take a conscious breath, aware that we are aware and aware of the air we breathe, aware of the sensation of that breath, something more feeds us. We take in a finer substance that has been there for eternity. This substance feeds our consciousness. We experience presence through conscious breath. This practice becomes our gateway between the inner and the outer.

The third kind of food is impressions and we would most certainly die without them. Solitary confinement, for example, can bring about hallucinations and mental illness. Our sensory perception feeds all of the many parts of us, and most importantly, feeds our attention. When we work to notice what is really going on around us and inside of us, we develop a new kind of attention which becomes food for our transformation.

This is how Self-observation becomes the key for feeding ourselves a higher and more refined level of impressions. If our impressions are constantly filtered by automatically processed responses and habitual reaction, we are giving our soul nothing but Cheetos and Coke.

Our brain is like a binary computer and meant to function as a survival mechanism. Through analysis, comparison and memory, our experiences are filed away as good or bad, safe or unsafe according to its survival benefit. This is what created "I like this and I don't like that" and is based on what created "safe" regardless of if it was harmful, cruel or crazy.

Through our education and our society, we have primarily developed the thinking, this binary computer as the primary intake system. The formatory apparatus, as it has been described by Gurdjieff, has taken control!!

If we don't learn how to take in pure organic and objective impressions of what is happening, then we get our stock answer, "the processed food." The filing system takes over, performs search and retrieval to pull out the memory file which says that thing has been labeled bad, we react and we can no longer objectively see what is in front of us.

Let's give an example that will help us see how this center, the intellectual center, works.

We may have had a parent who had high demands or was extremely critical. As we did things not to their liking, we learned that our actions were bad even if they were authentic and soulful to us. Formatory apparatus filed away certain behaviors that pleased them (good behavior) and ones that didn't (bad behavior). However, those certain "good" behaviors may have been denying ourselves something in order to please. We continue that habit through various forms like eating disorders, overworking, lack of self care and the whole myriad of self sabotage because that is our habitual "safe," "being in control," and "being loved." We don't realize we are under the influence, drinking the same old libation that got us "love" a long time ago.

The emotional center takes in impressions, but we may not realize that it too has its set of automatic habitual responses that have been neurologically grooved into our system. It works in conjunction with the thinking center and provides a reactional feedback loop almost impossible to escape unless we learn to observe it.

The emotions are energy moving through our bodies: vibration on many levels and they play a big part in our survival. We feel emotion as love, empathy, or sorrow and we experience all kinds of negative emotion like anxiety, fear, self-pity, confusion, overwhelm, worry, depression, elation and happiness as real. However, many of us think emotion instead of feeling it, analysing good or bad which means judgement and then adjusting the emotion accordingly. For example, we may react to something someone says because it has kicked off an automatic association that is no longer valid. We cannot hear objectively what that person is saying because the stock emotional response has already been retrieved by the thinking. Thus emotions get all caught up in a habitual thinking-emotional complex.

The third means of taking in the food of impressions is the body. We can sense our body and it can also take in information about thought, emotion, environment, nature and beyond. When we are angry, we can sense our chest tighten or our jaw clench, and adrenaline rush. Our body may become hot, tense, detect distress or relax. We may sense these aspects of emotion instead of feeling the emotion. Our body can also sense the energy of thought in the way it races or sense the way it acts on our body and our concentration.

We cannot think sensation and so when we use intellectual center to find sensation, it can make us believe we are observing something in our body that is really relegated to our thinking only. Most of us are totally unaware that we are doing this because we can articulate what is going on inside of us. It is most often from the perspective of the thinking.

So... we can see that there is much work to be done to see if we actually sense our body, feel our emotions or think our thoughts. We are inclined to feed ourselves predominantly from one center if we haven't oriented ourselves to developing attention and integrating all three centers. Our spiritual work is to notice how we take in information as impressions through each of these modes.

To take in things objectively is like eating a beautiful array of organic colored vegetables. It feeds expanded awareness which then grows.

When we are present, there is a synthesis of impressions from all of these different parts and we begin to see what is deep inside of us from a new perspective: one that is free of our conditioned responses.

TYRANNY OF
THE EGO

Tyranny is the cruel, unjust, and arbitrary use of power and control. In ancient Greece, a tyrant was a ruler who seized power and usurped legitimate sovereignty. His subjects were victims of his passions and unjust desires, which he substituted for laws.

We have a tyrant inside. We are victims of it's negative emotions, likes and dislikes, fears, and doubts. We fall prey to its reactive nature and believe the demons that haunt us are very very real.

How can we recognize this inner tyrant?

It is most certainly the cause of our frustration and unhappiness. It hinders us from feeling in harmony with God and others. This illegitimate ruler sits on a throne constructed of mirrors, a projection system that makes us feel threatened when we are not. We believe it's negative emotions are real.

The tyrant's right hand man is "identification" Through identification it perpetuates fear, anger and other negative emotion. We then "feel" these emotions and become hopelessly lost in a web of illusion.

These seemingly real situations then create obstacles for us in our work, our relationships and our lives. They create self-fulfilling prophesies.

Identification comes in many forms, including self-sabotage, self-deprecation, depression, and the like.

Some self-help methods stress the importance of expressing negative emotions so they don't fester or create stagnant energy. While this might be better than repression, expressing a negative emotion will not cure the root cause of its existence. This root cause is like the little black seed found deep within a wart. The tiny black seed must be removed for the wart to go away.

So it is with our negative emotions. We must see how our ego plays the role of taskmaster. The ego is not meant to take the place of our Divine Will. Our Will follows the path of least resistance toward God and ego doesn't. The ego was meant to serve as a fight or flight system to protect us.

Through a revolution of Self-observation, we can break down this tyranny.

Self-observation is the first tool for catching the tyrant in action. Little by little, we become aware of how little choice we exercise in our life. We keep falling in the same hole and wonder how we didn't see it coming. The more we develop expanded awareness to take in more impressions, the more we can dig underneath these illusory negative emotions and walk around the hole!! This is how self-observation works.

When negative emotions like jealousy, anger, sadness and resentment are in full force in our bodies, the adrenalin and physical symptoms are in full swing. Those physical responses trigger more emotions in us which then trigger thoughts that move around and around in circles.

If we can notice any part of this whole automatic feedback apparatus, we may gain insight into something that is happening often inside of us that we didn't see before.

Noticing this sequence can unravel the whole package.

The first step is to simply notice it *without changing anything*. We will begin to notice that as we experience a negative emotion, another voice is saying "I shouldn't be feeling this" or " oh, this is because of such and such." We may know that what we are feeling is irrational, but we can't stop it. We are in a constant state of identifying with those many parts of us and what they think we should do. Our only recourse is to watch and accept, not label and analyse.

As we practice watching, we begin to notice more and more about the feedback loop in action. It is subtle and difficult to see because we are so used to doing it.

For example, we recently came back from a retreat where one participant noticed that his reaction regarding a particular intuition exercise we did with a random partner, brought an overall feeling he had not noticed before. He began worrying he had offended the other person by not confirming what they had intuited. His logical mind knew this was ridiculous and that she really didn't care at all. However, a whole web of thoughts around what the other person might be feeling concerning him ensued.

The value here is that he noticed more about an overall feeling and the accompanying rampant thoughts. It was even more than just the feelings; it was everything lined up in a moment of Self-observation. A new picture emerged that connected the dots in a way he could not see before because he stayed with it. In the following weeks, he was able to recognize that this phenomenon happened often inside of himself concerning his boss and his peers also.

This experience at the retreat brought new understanding of how a state of identification with certain thoughts takes control and puts him into pattern. Through staying with the feelings and thought, he gained insight into how he identifies with his own insecurity.

We have a way to vanquish this dictator, but it is not by overthrowing him. This tyranny must be observed and accepted for what it is for us to be free of it.

LETTING GO

Letting go of something is hard. Whether it is a habit, a method, an organization, a job, or a person, the process of letting go is like the process of grieving. The resistance prior to the release can be intense and scary.

What is it, in letting go, that seems so risky?

In my past experience, it is often the fear of feeling like a failure after having tried so hard. Sometimes it is my desire for security, albeit a false one, that I just can't imagine living without.

To enable growth, change is required. The more we grasp and hold on tight when we know something is not expanding and evolving, the harder the hit when we know it is time to release it. It seems that the more we push toward a goal or a certain outcome when clearly something is not working, the more we know it is time to find another way, no matter how painful that may be.

If it isn't working, feels abusive or negative, lacks inspiration, feels like a burden, why would that be so difficult to let go?

Part of us is so invested that it becomes a huge hit to our ego to think that we have been doing something the wrong way. We are told never to give up and to persist toward our dreams, goals and desires. We try to let go of sub-optimal choices sometimes as a matter of survival, but we often run into resistance and stubborn attachment.

Often, it is not the dream or target we need to let go of, but the method in which we approach achieving the goal, especially if there is no evident success toward that goal with the current approach. The mixed message of allowing things to occur and never giving up can get us stuck in the mud. There is a balance of doing and allowing that holds the key to success, so let's address what happens when we try to make things happen and they don't.

Have you ever seen things come easily to one person, and yet someone else does the same "method" or system and gets absolutely nowhere? What is the difference? What factor is present for things to manifest in the way we would like them to go?

One of the problems buried in this question has to do with the way we "think things should go" or should be. We drive and push toward our version of the way it should look, but along the way we find out that the "should" gets in the way. When progress toward an end is not happening, that is our signal to let go of the pushing, the driving, and the "making it happen."

Have you ever made huge efforts to produce or understand something, without success, and the minute you let go it all starts rushing in? We can only try our best toward an end, but recognize when to give way and allow.

I have found that letting go in itself is a process of metamorphosis. It takes courage to risk, to accept "failure," and to trust that another way will emerge. The first step however is the recognition that things really are not working, and unfortunately we have an uncanny knack for denial. We will justify all kinds of unwanted occurrences and turn a blind eye to what is actually occurring because we so badly "need and "want" it to work.

There has to be an acceptance of the fact that the old way did not work - and this does not mean giving up. It means letting the energetic process unfold without our control. When things aren't working, we often bargain with ourselves to make it seem like everything is OK. We make excuses and justify our behavior. Seeing objectively is so difficult when we are totally invested.

So how do we get uninvested?

We must believe in our goals and dreams but accept that it might not happen the way we envisioned. It does not mean sacrificing our conviction or lowering our sights. Knowing and accepting that there is a direction, a way, or a flow, and then reading the signs becomes part of this process. A failure can be just another part of the learning curve that leads us to our ultimate goal.

In the heat of the moment, the crisis, and the meltdown, we lose sight that this too is a necessary part of the process. Without the contrast, we cannot learn. Without the "failure," we cannot find more efficient and effective ways. Without the discomfort and challenge, we cannot know ease.

The final stage of letting go is acceptance. When we accept and let go, space becomes available, and there is room for growth. How many times have you resisted that dreaded action only to find that once you did, a whole new world opened up? In hindsight, you find that the only means to the end was to let go.

I dare you... You won't be sorry.

A ZEN STORY

I could have been very content in a monastery locked away from the world up on a mountain top, but my love of being out in the hustle and bustle, needing the messy interaction of people, and relishing the glitz and glam trumped that card.

I chose the monastery of life, whichalso included the formal study of meditation from personal mentors in several esoteric schools. I did that for 21 years and my dedication to personal transformation will forever remain alive.

The mystical, magical side of things has always fascinated me. My life has been full of synchronicities, perfect timing and help from above. I don't construct "signs from the Universe" or take warning if the stars are not aligned. However, I am keyed in and notice how things are connected.

I do look for the Sacred in all that I do. Even my Rocket espresso machine is a vessel for gratitude each morning.

Early on I started spontaneously "meditating" on my own, contacting my Guides, Ascended Masters, and Angels. I needed all the help I could get, but from the looks of my life, that wasn't really working.

When I found my first spiritual school, living in Paris as a daring twenty something, I wandered into it somewhat haphazardly. I was looking for a yoga class that had been recommended to me by my ex boyfriend's girlfriend whose father was a Buddhist monk in Le Havre. We had been at a wild party when she spoke of a Zen Dojo aka Integral Yoga Institute, hidden in the heart of the 9th arrondissement.

I needed relief from the anxiety and stress of being an esteemed student of classical music at the Conservatoire. I needed to try something wholesome in contrast to the drinking and drugging that was pulling me further and further down with no relief from the pressure, the competition, or the fear of failure.

I decided to attend said yoga class which unbeknownst to me was followed by a Zen meditation that would change my life forever.

First of all, the teacher, Raymond Kotai Lambert, was cross eyed and practically blind from being tortured by the Nazis. He was sought out and captured because of a letter he had written to his father, dissing the Germans and their maneuvers in France. He was not a Jew, a gypsy or a threat.

I would come to find out that thereafter, he had studied Hatha Yoga extensively in India for years, Irano-Egyptian Yoga in the Middle East and was a chosen student of the Zen lineage of Taisen Deshimaru Roshi of which I also would be chosen and initiated. He had been a circus acrobat in his early years in France and his sense of humor was truly profound.

That evening I did my first formal meditation where there was a "holder of the energy," a real Zen Master or Roshi, and I must admit I was extremely curious.

I had no idea about the meditation part until some of the members changed to black robes after the yoga class and lined up outside of the room. I was herded into place sans black robe, nervous and barely understanding the new French vocabulary whispered back and forth about what to do.

Lined up, we entered in a walking meditation (kinhin), something I would come to use as a powerful tool of transformation. Each step required a conscious inhale and exhale. We took our places seated in a "square circle" facing the wall, but not before there were bows, followed by seated cantilever swaying from larger to smaller arcs then various other machinations of which I had no idea what, how or why. Of course, I simply copied the best I could, all the while thinking that this was a bunch of ritualistic hootenanny of which I wanted no part.

What the hell had I gotten myself into now?

The ritual started with utter silence, painful, squirmy, silence that resounded so loudly in my ears, I almost jumped up, screamed and ran out of the door to the nearest chic Parisian bar. The thoughts were rushing in at a speed with which I could barely keep up. Why do people do this? What was I doing here? How could I have trapped myself as a prisoner like this? I am nowhere near the door! All this ritual just reminded me of the hypocrisy of church. Maybe I should have never come here. I am a fish out of water. I can't breath. I am starting to panic. I can't do this... .

Just when I could stand it no longer, the bells and chanting began. Thank God! Something so beautiful... I thought I had died and gone to heaven. At this point, I could have considered a moaning sick cow music to my ears. It broke the horrible suffering of the unbearable "silence" and gave me something to wonder about, something on which to focus.

Over the next 6 years, this would become my time of deepest reverent prayer.

Oh no... .more silence and this time the agitation was so great within me that I started counting specks on the wall from the new fangled paint job. My legs were throbbing, I longed to move but I didn't for fear of what someone might think. Everyone else appeared perfectly still, peaceful and unified with an unknown force of which I was not a part. Any movement would not go unnoticed.

How long could this last?

Suddenly, I heard the whack of a paddle. What the hell? I slowly turned my head to glance down the line and saw the teacher with a long paddle (*kaisaku) graciously doling out the torture after each student bowed in submission, with hands together. They then leaned their head right, whack, head left, whack ,and bowed again in gratitude.

This was the last straw. I would not be the victim of some sadistic cult leader. I began to get very hot, my heart was pounding in fear, and that buzzing started to roar in my ears. Surely I was going to faint. My mind began to scheme how to get out of there before he got to me and then I figured out that if I didn't bow down and ask for it, he would pass me by.

My heart was pounding so hard that I was sure he could see it when he arrived, looming large behind me. When I didn't do anything, he himself leaned my head right, thwack, then leaned my head left, bigger thwack, and gently pushed my head into a bow that greeted my hands which had somehow miraculously come together without my knowing. His hand remained on my head, I felt, in some kind of reassurance.

It was ritual I could not understand.

It was ritual against which I wanted to rebel.

It was so foreign to my experience that I judged it up and down as abuse, unnecessary submission, and ridiculous beyond measure.

But in that moment, tears began to stream down my face. These were not tears of pain from a paddle which actually didn't hurt at all. They were tears of release, tears of letting go, tears of relief from the incessant disturbance in which I had been drowning not only seconds before, but a whole lifetime.

All went quiet for a fleeting moment in which every worry, judgement and criticism melted in a pool before me.

I knew that I was on my way home.

NEGATIVE EMOTIONS

Negative emotions are the first and fastest place we go when we encounter friction or suffering. It is the nature of sleep to immediately shield ourselves against the forces that can awaken us.

Negative emotions are a reaction, not a perception. In this sense, they are not really emotions. They are defense mechanisms. They actually prevent the possibility of full emotion.

With negative emotions, we turn away from what is really happening. We dig a hole and bury our awareness in it.

Negative emotions have us see the world in relation to ourselves instead of ourselves in relation to a much much larger world and the laws governing it. We don't actually see the world. We respond to it and see that.

Negative emotions are harmful not so much for what they are, but because they steal our ability to control our state of consciousness. recapturing this ability is what transformation is all about.

–Peter Ingle, The Little Book of Transforming Negative Emotions

I have some challenges for you this week.

In my group classes, we are digging deep into Self-Study that will allow us to see into our negative emotions.

The goal: to discover how not-real they are.

The not-goal: to explain, correct, or eliminate them.

If we want to be objective, we have to look at things like a scientist, without analysis, assumption and, most importantly, without trying to change anything.

We can't understand anything if we keep trying to "fix" it. And if we analyze or explain something, it comes from the perspective of our intellect, and is not a true observation.

Did you ever notice that knowing "your story" never actually stops all the negative emotion from happening? Analysing the reasons why we do what we do does not turn the faucet off.

Have you felt relief from beating a pillow or expressing all this anger and found that it went away forever? No amount of expressing something that is not real will get rid of it.

The whole point is to UNDERSTAND, with all the many parts of you, that it isn't real.

So when everyone in class was talking about trying to stop it or make it better, they demostrated that they judge themselves or others for having these "emotions" in the first place. Of course, it isn't a comfortable place to be in so we naturally want to get out of that "very icky feeling."

It was cleverly pointed out in class,"Hey, if you don't like the station, change the channel."

This is exactly what I am proposing we do NOT do.

Staying on that channel, tuning into that frequency from all aspects, our body, our mind and our thinking, yes, that horrible inner talk that feeds the whole habitual reactive system will be more beneficial than changing the station.

We need to watch it, feel it, listen to that little voice. We must Do it as if we were watching someone else.

We can't change the channel.

If we can do that, another kind of energy starts to work.

The observer gets stronger.

As the observer gets stronger, the multiple parts of us that like this, don't want that, feel they deserve this, aren't good enough for that, overwhelmed by this, incensed by someone's actions, agitated by incompetence, flippin off the driver, kissing the bosses ass, and neglecting their health, will get weaker.

We don't have to attach a story to it as an excuse for what we do.

We don't have to beat pillows in order to relieve something that is not us.

When we can watch it, we practice Self-Acceptance on a grand scale.

Here's a challenge for this week:

Try not to express your complaining, bitching, and moaning. I am not asking you to suppress these emotions. I am asking you to "cook" in them, a term I learned from Russell Schreiber.

If something you perceive as bad happens, refrain from talking about it. If you experience misfortune, don't voice it.

If you see someone being unthoughtful or mean, don't fight back and don't criticize.

If the day has not gone as planned, fuck it and don't complain.

If you feel you must show how you know more, don't.

If you feel compelled to justify your actions, don't.

Do not outwardly express your negativity, but notice it from the inside.

See how this effort feels to you.

Notice how it affects the negative emotion itself.

Notice how long you remain in your negative state.

What feeds it or chokes it?

THE OLD BEGGAR

"If you don't know fear, you will never know fearlessness."

–Pema Chodron

Lately I have been having small waves of fear about my upcoming speaking engagements. I am slightly inexperienced at this and the thought of organizing all of these thoughts and topics seems daunting. Part of me easily holds this fear at bay and part of me struggles to not become a slave to it.

I know I will do the talks to the best of my ability. I will work toward making my ideas presentable and clear, but until I start writing things down and organizing, I remain in a paralytic limbo. It is almost as if the fear keeps me from getting started, and yet I know taking action will solve the problem.

I know I am getting closer to what I am meant to be doing because these feelings are aroused in me. Every time I have reached into the unknown, said yes whether I knew I could do it or not, accepted a mission with blind trust, or booked a concert of very difficult music, this feeling slightly held me under but didn't drown me.

I know it as a part of me that really cares and it has helped create another part of me that is fearless. If I avoid the fear, then I never learn what it is to overcome it. I never know what it feels like to realize that much of the anxiety was over a non existent built up pie in the sky nightmare scene generally rooted in what other people think of me. Once through the other side, I see its irrelevance and am more able to ignore the shenanigans of the bogey monsters and things that go bump in the night.

My accumulated experience allows me to remember that it is just my imagination. I lock down in the future which holds me prisoner. I now know from overcoming previous fear that it is part of the game, and not to be taken seriously.

If not, I cannot move forward. I would become paralyzed worrying about what might or might not happen. This would then feed the inertia that kept me from taking any risk.

In hindsight, I only wish that I had had more courage or perhaps foolishness as a twenty-something-year-old. The risk takers feel fear but they do it anyway.

What is this quality in me that goes forward despite fear?

What is it that pushes me through the fire?

There must be a drive stronger than the fear and an awareness that my trepidation is unfounded. The only way I have gotten stronger is by experiencing this over and over so I have the power to detach and not identify with the insecure part.

Of course with age comes the ability to care less about what others think and a desperation to get it done.

When I look back at my life - playing prominent concerts in Europe, reaching out to top world renowned musicians with whom to collaborate, booking gigs and not knowing how in the world I was going to get it done in time - I realize I am a risk taker. Every result of taking those risks, whether it was success or failure, has made me understand the illusory nature of fear.

It is something that still creeps up like a nagging old beggar knocking at my door.

But now, I greet the beggar, "Hey I know you. I remember you, come sit at my table and have a good meal so you don't have to linger like a needy dog. Let me see you and hear your concerns and know that you are the visitor that comes around when I am on the threshold of a new dawn and a breakthrough. I welcome you. Every time you visit, I know I am on the precipice of my own growth."

And so, fear has become an old friend that doesn't have the power to consume me like he used to. He is still by my side and with a wink and a nod, I simply step around and go on my merry way.

How do you experience fear?

What keeps you going in the face of fear?

Do you get paralyzed and feel like you can't go forward because of fear?

THE GRADUATE

The lump in my throat is pretty big... bigger than usual.

I am ditching my plans for another spiritual article because what I have encountered this week ranks among the most touching events of my entire life.

It is quintessentially spiritual.

Perhaps in writing this piece more will be revealed to you and me about why it feels so poignant and deep.

If you have children, you will understand the lengths we go to to make sure life is good for them. We sacrifice our time, contribute resources and hope for the best. If we are conscious at all, we will learn to stay out of the way and let them learn their own life lessons. We can only protect, advise and guide so much.

For me, the greatest lesson as a parent has been to learn to trust.

I still struggle with it.

We never know where someone will end up, and we can point in this or that direction, but ultimately they choose. In fact, their life truly becomes their own when they don't need us anymore.

That is the time to celebrate and grieve. At least, that is what it is feeling like to me.

Today I am a proud parent of a college graduate. I am proud for what he has accomplished despite some of the struggle and strife in his life. If I am proud it may seem I am taking some of the credit, but I am not. I just feel proud.

And sad.

And nostalgic.

There is a bittersweet sense of the passage of time from my perspective. It is a feeling I am slightly unfamiliar with, but it feels like one of the more important ones. In fact, it makes me know my life is rich.

These are the kinds of feelings that make me know the deep meaning of having a family, of raising children, and of close lifetime relationships.

It was no ordinary graduation. I didn't watch my son walk across a stage with hundreds of other students. I watched him bare his artistic soul in a once in a lifetime concert in which he was featured. He chose the repertoire, the musicians, and wrote the program notes.

Instead of doing the concert at the Conservatory Recital Hall, he chose the Red Poppy Art House in the Mission District of San Francisco, which had personal meaning to him as well as many artists that he served by volunteering there.

It was highly personal for family members who flew in from everywhere to witness, to listen, and to cook, clean and decorate.

It was well attended by his professors, fellow students and colleagues.

This was no ordinary graduation indeed.

Perhaps the poignancy for me lies in the fact that I too remember my senior recital and how important it was. I too struggled through the conservatory life to become a professional classical musician. I understood the devotion, the will to serve through music, and the desire to be successful in a highly competitive world.

I witnessed my son breaking a certain stereotypical mold by adding original jazz music to the standard classical repertoire. Everything had his personal out of the box creative stamp on it.

I could only feel that this is the way musicians should be: close to the creative pulse of original music. It wasn't stodgy, typical or boring. He demonstrated musical prowess, strong technique and intense passion.

Last but not least is the backstory that makes it a trifecta win, a hit it out of the ballpark kind of graduation.

He is intelligent beyond measure, so as a child, hard work was foreign to him. However, when he was expelled from an elite prep school after 10th grade, he decided to devote his life to music instead of drugs. The goal of being a music major in that short amount of time was almost unfathomable.

It would take more than hard work by anyone's standards.

He entered the San Francisco Conservatory with a scholarship four years ago and never looked back.

Today I, with my family, stand before a top rate professional Classical/ Jazz musician who chose to pursue his passion and follow his dream.

May he be met with all the success life can offer.

THE MANY "I"S

There are so many parts of us that compete for space.

There is the I that wants to be noticed and loved, the I that takes and the I that gives.

When I experience that push and pull within myself, I observe the battle that ensues. When I fight against my own self-pity and say you are better than that or bigger than that, I know the struggle.

I know that it is the battle of a divided self.

It was P.D. Ouspensky who likened this phenomenon to a person being like a house in which only one room is lit up at a time. We compartmentalize everything and are blind to what we were saying or doing minutes before.

All of us contradict ourselves on a regular basis. I urge you to do your own survey of how often that is happening within a day or even an hour.

We want to be good spiritual seekers attending to our practice, but when it is time to use some self-control or conscious effort in everyday life, it slips out the window.

How many times have we gone on a diet or quit smoking/drinking and experienced that evil person in us that takes over and says "ahh one slice of cake/one cig/one drink won't hurt." It is another part of us that takes over.

We chalk it up to no will power, but that is not the half of what is going on.

One part of us cannot see or know another part of us. The lights are on in the room that most suits the moment. In addition, who is deciding what suits most?

We have a secondary issue in which our higher nature battles the lower nature.

Have you ever listened to the crazy person on the bus who talks out loud?

We can see this character and that character having a conversation, berating the other one, providing running commentary, or cursing nonstop. We can watch that person having conversation with the multiple personalities within themselves.

We think how sad this is and how cut off from reality this person is, but we don't realize that that is what is going on inside our own head constantly without externally verbalizing it. We think we are so much more put together, whereas we have simply learned to ignore it.

The voices in our heads are so habitual that we don't hear them anymore.

I have always thought it would be an amazing invention to have a device hooked to our body that printed out our thoughts and feelings at warp speed so that we could actually see the incredible whirlwind of contradiction, anxiety and self-judgement that happens in nanoseconds.

The whole point of a spiritual practice and being mindful is to be able to notice this stuff. That is not a new idea.

John Bennett, author and student of Gurdjieff, called this the divided self. It is a state of being that sucks the higher energies of transformation away from us.

He explains that we are hypnotized by our reactions, our preferences, our beliefs and our habit of thought and this inhibits the awakening of consciousness.

We have a full repertoire of roles we play as actors on a stage and those roles are generated from a deep desire to be accepted, loved, and recognized.

All of these different roles give our lives a certain shape and it is up to us to begin the work of recognizing how they stop us from progressing. That takes consciousness.

Simply noticing without becoming too involved in the battle is a way to gain some perspective. When that battle begins within myself, my ability to simply notice and become aware that I am aware of the situation creates a place for something new to enter.

This is how the real battle is won.

A great exercise is to act like we are visitors within our own body, something Russell Schreiber puts forth in his book *Gurdjieff's Transformational Psychology*. We will develop the Inner Observer this way. We can do this for a finite period of time, for example, while we are driving to work, doing the dishes or walking to the store. We then notice what our body does and how it does it without analysis. We can observe as if we are unfamiliar with the activity and watch our body, our feelings, and our mind do this activity.

We are "participating" as an outsider with the intent to learn more about our automatic behavior.

As we improve with this technique, we may notice that our attention is now in a new place and not lost in thought. We can develop a way to be more objective. In so doing, we have a chance to see what makes the divided self exist in the first place. We may start to understand where our reactions come from. We may notice what enables us to persevere in the face of this inner battle.

These are all things that contribute to our freedom. We must find and see it for ourselves in order to permanently change it.

We are so ready for a fix from the outside that we are reluctant to do this work ourselves. We live in a society that is habituated to quick fixes from pills to "clearings." Let me ask, has something that someone else has cleared stayed away for good?

We may find temporary relief, but until we understand the phenomena that occur within us, the phenomena that cause our suffering spiritually, emotionally, psychically and physically, we cannot be free of them. Someone else doing the fixing will not give us the kind of insight we need from ourselves.

I have found the only permanent change that occurred for me was when I was making an effort to see into myself objectively while simultaneously opening to healing from God.

I encourage you to keep striving to see in ways that are not obvious. It takes a certain intentional curiosity to look within and actually see. This is not the knowledge of "your story," but the true understanding of how you are identified with it. This has to occur in the moment: in a moment of presence that can see the whole. That is the only way to "drop" the story!

Practicing participation can bring you to that place of presence and integration. Integration will bring the many "I"s together. You will catch yourself as an outsider observing things that you thought was actually you.

You will see the ways of a fragmented self.

Only this perspective can bring about cohesion.

MESMERIZED

Yesterday I wandered around my old college campus putting up posters for our upcoming retreat. Each time I go back, something in my visceral memory is activated. I can remember certain feelings and attitudes vividly.

They are both positive and negative and give me perspective on how far I have come from those days of confusion, ambition and insecurity.

I was so lost in the memories and feelings that I reached in my purse for a non-existent cigarette as I left Kane Hall.

Wow, that was a wake up call.

I was hopelessly lost and lost in hope back then.

For this article, my point is that there has always been a feeling at the University that elicits of hope and promise for all who have been there to learn. It is an institution where people make their careers come alive. Being a student made me feel like a renegade. I don't exactly know what I mean by that statement except that I remembered the feeling of considering doing something I had never done before. I remembered the feeling of possibility.

If you haven't walked around your college campus for 10 or 20 years, I highly recommend it.

I was there for about an hour and a half, walking amongst the gorgeous cherry tree orchard, the elegant gothic style libraries and small hallways of the philosophy and comparative religion departments.

Many of those particular hallways were unfamiliar to me as I spent most of my time in a 12 by 12 cubicle with a piano and a pack of cigarettes.

There were not as many students liting up compared to back then, but I did notice something very disturbing, so disturbing that I left feeling a little hopeless.

I began to wonder if anyone would see the beautiful colored posters I had made for our meditation retreat. They were eye catching with powerful copy and a good student price.

I began to wonder if anyone these days really notices anything around them anymore.

As I wandered through the halls, I looked at people's appearance, how close or far they sat from each other. I looked for young lovers kissing or groups of activists talking in heightened tones, or people sitting around laughing and playing hacky sack. I looked for readers laying under the trees and women clumped together in those tight knit circles of "important conversation."

In the student union, I looked for groups eating together, joking and gregarious.

I walked through the square where people used to sit on the benches, people watching.

As I passed people on the pathways, I tried to make eye contact... that kind of eye contact that shows mutual recognition. It wasn't flirting or weird eye contact, just a silent greeting that so often used to happen.

I sat in the library and closed my eyes remembering the exquisite silence that used to engulf me.

Today, I could only hear a symphony of click clicks of the computers.

When a young man opened the door before me and held it as I went out, I looked back to say thank you, but he was buried in his phone.

In fact, everywhere I looked people were mesmerized by their phones. No one looked up as I passed and looked at them. No one was having conversations with each other; all were too busy having virtual conversation with someone under their craned neck.

There was no laughter or clumps of people, no arguments, no lovers... just a ghost town with shells of human beings plugged in.

No one made eye contact in passing. No one talked to each other. No one looked up when someone coughed.

I realized I was walking through a sea of zombies oblivious to their world around them. It was a brave new world in which the majority were so absorbed in that little box that nothing else could possibly matter.

The woman of their dreams could walk right by unnoticed.

The recognition of mutual Being presence through simple eye contact is a relic gone by.

In that hour and a half, I made eye contact with 2 out of some odd 202.

I tried not to become completely sad and I still hold that back even as I write, thinking this is how old people feel in a changing world.

But I am not old...

I am not pining for the past either. I am pining for the radiant exuberant life force in all of us to wake up and connect.

Now I am worried that people locked to the screen cannot cross the street safely.

Let's forget noticing an energetic in the room, or enhancing our intuitive nature by taking in more and more subtle nuance. Only the crude and sensational can now get our attention at this point... or a good instagram post.

My walk through that campus brought to my attention that we are living virtually, under the demands of an ever pinging device vying for our attention... calling for our love.

We are addicted to this instant gratification that has so cleverly drawn us in.

Only we can choose to be here now.

Maybe someone will notice the flyer.

SACRED MOMENTUM

When I think back to some of the most profound moments in my spiritual journey, they have occurred at retreats. I can remember those moments of opening and clarity as if they were now. Time became infinite and still and that is why I can still feel it.

These are not just any kind of meditation retreats, but an environment set up with conditions for higher learning. They have a unique flavor because of the work we do together in so many forms of meditation.

Even brushing our teeth can become an exercise in presence, so put people together working at being present through practical methods and we get breakthrough to understanding.

Why is this environment so conducive to promoting presence?

To some who arrive and begin the daily activities, it may seem like not much is going on if they don't begin to apply their efforts toward being here now. It is a golden opportunity to understand being present but it has to come from their own initiative.

The only way I can describe these retreats is that we delve into a deeper experience that is not apparent from the outside. There are certain activities like meditation or the movements that bring us into focus and are more obviously geared toward presence and stillness. There are other activities like practical work in which we must initiate our own "being here."

When we start to understand that there is more going on than meets the eye, we have entered into the inner sanctum, so to speak. We become aware of the inner and the outer simultaneously. We become a part of a profound connection amongst the participants in times when it is not obvious to do so. These could be times when we are transitioning from one activity to another, or cooking with one another or eating together at the table.

These are the times when most let their efforts to be present go out the window.

One of the most effective parts of the day is what we call "practical work." We gather in groups and perform mundane chores, or work on a project to improve the retreat property. This is the time of day when the retreat most resembles everyday life, and it is easy for us to forget why we are doing what we are doing.

I can remember having great resistance to the practical work. I would go out there kicking and screaming, wondering why we do this. Over the years, the practical work has included grooming a ski slope, building terraced gardens, roofing, dry walling, weeding, erecting a shelter, designing and building a portable dance floor, and digging a ditch. I don't like to do these things, but here are some amazing facts I have learned about practical work at our retreats:

- Participants see more when they don't like something.
- An opportunity to make a new kind of effort can bring us closer to our suffering.
- We forget more easily doing an everyday life kind of thing, so when we do remember ourselves in this setting, it stays with us.

I have had my greatest flashes of insight, heart openings and deeper awareness of the unity of myself with others during the practical work.

Because it is harder to remember ourselves during the hammering or shoveling, when we do, it is much more effective and we own it. Often we do not have the skillset and are learning how to use a nail gun, to shovel without hurting our back, to line up roof tiles so they don't mess up the whole pattern and the like. A kind of presence has to come forward and we all help each other by making our own individual effort. Those that do know how to hold their attention affect those that don't. In that way, my presence becomes a service to someone brand new.

If this sounds unappealing, I wholeheartedly understand. Who wants to spend good money to come work like that? We can decide "that just isn't for me" because we don't like work or we can take a chance to see what it is all about.

Our curiosity and our aim to be free will get us there. It is eye and heart opening.

When we combine the mundane with the more esoteric endeavors, we get a perfect cocktail for transformation. The perfume of freedom wafts through the air. The atmosphere becomes loaded in a way that is tangible. We succumb to the Presence of something higher that is available like never before.

When we decide to let down our guard and surrender to it, the magic happens. Once it starts to happen, everyone starts to feel it and then the doorway opens for us all to step through.

Sacred Momentum.

LIMITING BELIEFS

Can we recognize our own limiting beliefs?

We all have a story we tell ourselves; a kind of picture we have of our potential and capabilities. However, most of us do not realize that it is just a story. We have been telling ourselves this story for so long that it has become our truth.

Our identification with this story inhibits our freedom to choose, Sometimes we make crazy decisions or sabotage our own progress, or we choose partners that do not have our best interests in mind. We listen to our story, make these "choices," and afterward, we wonder why.

Where does this story come from?

It is a result of the conditioning we receive at an early age from our parents, our environment, society, and circumstances. It comes from the pain of being a free but vulnerable human being in a world of unfree and wounded people. In this environment, we do not grow up in freedom, but instead we experience pain, feel threatened, and learn to protect ourselves. If we are not encouraged to be free through development of our Will, we don't accept ourselves for who we are. Instead we create stories around who we are and what we believe.

If we did not learn proper boundaries, or were violated in some way, then part of our story is the idea that we have no control.

If we were not given the freedom to make mistakes, then our story says we have to be perfect.

If we had real desires and dreams that were discouraged or crushed, we developed stories around why we could not do what we really wanted to do.

Believing these stories about ourselves perpetuates our conditioning, and manifests these thought/feeling forms into reality. We stop objectively seeing the way things are because our stories have overridden our perception. Belief in our stories is truly limiting, and the opposite of consciousness.

The first step in working with limiting beliefs is to observe ourselves operating from these stories. When we do this, we can recognize our identification with a role or scenario.

One need only look at one's life circumstances to see where stories are at play. For example, if we are depressed, having financial woes, in a bad relationship, feeling isolated, have no inertia or drive, keep getting into trouble, have no success from our efforts, etc, then we can bet that our identification with "the story" is behind it (note: it is tempting to say we are just victims of fate or bad luck, but that in itself is identification with being a victim of something that has been done to us from the outside.)

Questioning our own beliefs is a good start. What is our story? Do we believe we are worthy of the greatest things in life, a fulfilling job, a loving relationship, spiritual freedom, abundance in all aspects of life, things coming easily to us, deep satisfaction and inner peace? Are we able to do more than just think those good thoughts by feeling them on a vibrational level so that the Universe will meet us with a resounding yes?

The Universe will meet and mirror the degree to which we are free from "our story."

First step, notice what we are saying to ourselves on a daily basis.

The only way to notice is to develop a keener sense of awareness around these stories.

Nothing is coming in very objectively so we must catch ourselves doing things habitually If we can get ahead of that stock response and listen for other things coming in from an objective perspective, we can start to notice how the limiting beliefs have their power.

The goal is to take in objective information about the way we see things. We will start to get a picture of how we weave the limiting beliefs into our system of impressions. and perhaps be able to separate that from what we actually experience.

Learning how to observe ourselves is a skill and a practice. It entails several factors that will be discussed in another article.

These practices will lead you to understand how your limiting beliefs kick in well before you realize it.

CHILDREN: OUR GREATEST TEACHERS

One of the greatest rewards of parenthood, besides the joy of seeing our children grow into amazing people, is that we learn so much about ourselves. The times when I am most frustrated are usually related to what I need to see within myself.

We can certainly apply this to our partners or even the relationship with ourselves, but there is something more charged about our relationship with our own children. We are more identified with the outcome.

If we are to get our children to develop discipline and a sense of responsibility within themselves, we must understand this in our own experience. So often we chastise kids for not doing this or not doing that after we have asked many many times. There are all kinds of things coming up in this situation:

1) control issues
2) the inherent inability in us as humans to adhere to an aim
3) perpetual insecurity
4) lack of empathy

Let's address each one to better understand why we end up in a cycle of punishment and rewards instead of instilling better values by which to live.

1) Control

When we ask children to do something, we expect them to do it because we have asked. We are the parents, their guides and provide the structure. Many construe this as being "in control."

However, when we ask someone to do something, there is free will involved. If we demand by dangling our conditional love over their heads they learn to do things out of desire to be loved. If we threaten with consequences, they are motivated by fear.

There are endless ways to exert control over our children because they are vulnerable and dependent.

This is how we destroy their trust and their ability to act from will. When we ourselves act out of insecurity that we are not good parents and "can't control" our children, we often resort to draconian measures because we ourselves have not learned to act from will. We often parent out of fear that we ourselves will not be loved and thus develop this in our children. We do this by being too lenient or by trying to take control and withholding our love if they do not obey.

2) Multiplicity of "I"s

One of the problems with getting kids to do something is that we as humans operate from a multiplicity of "I"s so to achieve an aim is very difficult. One part of us wants to daydream and ponder, another play, another talk with friends, another live in a clean room and another wants to be a good daughter. All of these different parts of us compete for space and we can imagine which one wins out as children. This is the ordinary state of affairs for all of us. If we are unaware of this condition in ourselves, we have a hard time understanding why a kid hasn't cleaned their room yet.

Of course, there are those children who have been threatened with consequences or withdrawal of love (this comes in the form of shaming, parental withdrawal and parental anger). Most of us have grown up this way and so, it is natural that we perpetuate that pattern. Unless we have gained some cohesion with our multiple "I"s, we will continue to use these tactics. It is seemingly the only way to get them to do anything unfortunately.

Ideally we want our children to want to do their chores because they understand their part in the family. They understand the consequences of their own actions without someone implementing external ones.

If they can experience why it is important to have a clean room for themselves and not because we have asked, demanded or threatened, then they have coalesced some of their "I"s. They have an understanding that they can find things easier because they couldn't when it was messy. Their room smells better so kids don't think they are gross. They have a heightened sense of self-esteem when things are in order.

They have to learn this for themselves by experiencing the negative consequences of having a messy room.

We all learn this way. As adults, we have formulated ways of replicating our parents' fear tactics and unreasonable conditions within ourselves because we were not given a chance to learn responsibility and consequences of our own actions. We have been robbed of free will. Our spiritual development is learning that we inherently have it.

3)   Insecurity

At a very early age, we were taught that certain action or non action was displeasing to someone else. We developed an identification with being the pleaser in order to get love or we developed an identification with being a rebel in order to preserve some sense of independence from outside forces. Both are survival tactics. This is how our egos develop so strongly. We were not meant to live by survival tactics and so as adults, we get in trouble in both our personal and professional relationships.

We act out of insecurity because that has been developed in us. We then perpetuate it in our children by fearing that they won't love us if we don't give in (i.e. they learn they can get away with not cleaning their room). We may fear that we aren't good parents if they don't obey and are out of control. We have no idea that our self-image is wrapped up in our parenting.

We have learned to live with the fear of not being loved so what makes us think we can do differently when it comes to parenting?

When we take ultra control with threats, it might be because we never had control as children using our free will. Now we must exert it on someone else or on situations in order to make ourselves feel safe. It has nothing to do with discipline.

4) Empathy

Finally, when we begin to work on ourselves, we begin to have insight into what is happening with our children. We begin to understand full well why they couldn't get something done. We understand why we ourselves are so bad at gentle reminders of follow through. We realize that if we can't do it with ourselves, how the hell could we expect ourselves to do it with our children.

If we can act out of empathy, we eliminate our identification with being a good parent or needing to get what we deserve. We stop acting out of conditional love or what other people think of our parenting.

We act out of understanding that these children need to learn to gather many "I"s toward a common aim in order to get things done. They are learning and they need to make lots of mistakes in order to take their life in their own hands and act out of integrity and self-will instead of someone else's agenda.

They will wander, we understand, we remind and we love them because they are learning.

In my experience, they always clean their room when they have lost something or people don't want to hang out with them in their room or... they want to live differently. Not because I told them over and over in a constant battle of wills, shame and threats.

Watching my parenting can become a barometer for how I manage my inner life. Do I have an inner tyrant? Do I sway and bend with the wind and not get anything done? Do I always aim to please?

If I watch the interaction between me and my children, I have a very good idea about the interaction of me with me.

ENERGETIC SAVINGS
AND LOAN

My life is drastically different than when I first started using these methods of transformation. I have a sense of obligation to pay forward what was taught to me, not only because it works but because it is the way toward us living harmoniously together.

I have had amazing spiritual teachers: people who devoted their lives to passing on their wisdom about how to be free and live a life of abundance and peace.

I too had to be devoted as a student in order for anything to really happen. I had to make a commitment to do the work, attend retreats, show up at meetings even when I didn't want to. I had to keep trying when I couldn't find my way out of self-pity for days and days.

Last night a member of our meditation group offered her clear observation of carrying one tiny statement her husband made into the future with her. She remained in that moment in the past, feeling more and more sorry for herself, angry at how insensitive someone could be to her needs, wondering if anyone really cared and it went on and on. She caught herself some hours later and had enough consciousness to see that she wasn't in the present. She was very much living in that past moment and it was tainting her attitude, her mood, and her interaction with everyone around her. She put into question her marriage, her life and her happiness.

She however had enough "energy" from doing this kind of work to see that she was generating the negative emotion and realized he might have meant no ill will towards her. She released the hold her ego had on her by choosing in a moment of inner struggle, to let go and surrender the fight.

She could see in a new way how she was still living in that past moment over and over for the last 6 hours.

She understood in a new light what was causing her suffering.

This may seem obvious to you reading this story, but try it when you are all "caught up" in anger or depression.

If this was easy, we would be easily extricating ourselves from these types of situations when we are in deep angst. There would be no such thing as blame, self-pity, self-importance, self-justification and guilt.

When we find ourselves lost in this complicated web we weave, there has been a lot of energy spent on weaving it. In fact, the higher frequency of energetic vibration that can help us see, gets spent when we do this. If we don't have enough refined energy saved in our account, we are constantly depleting any possibility of getting around these emotions which feel so real to us and cause us so much suffering.

My spiritual work helped me realize that freedom is the ability to choose not to go there.

If my energetic account is filled with higher energies, I have enough force to enable me to see and to choose.

If I am constantly giving way to feeling resentment, anger or justification for feeling that said negative emotion, then I leak any chance of getting out of it. In other words I spend the good energy.

What a catch 22!

So how does one keep the "energy account" full?

Meditation will most certainly add to the savings. Even if we are struggling to stay present and think it is the worst meditation we have ever had, the struggle itself creates higher energies. This is conscious labor.

Every time we go to the cushion when we don't want to, it is conscious labor and intentional suffering.

Every time we resist complaining (this does not mean not expressing your needs), resist flying off the handle, stay instead of storming off, listen when we want to hang up, speak when we want to scream, breath when our body is panicking or internally take note when our heart is pounding into our throat, we create higher energies.

Our tiny struggle is the essence of staying simultaneously in the yes and no and the only chance for something greater from the outside to come in.

This is a Sacred Law.

When we bear the unpleasant manifestations of others, we resist flying down the rabbit hole of being justified... justified in our anger, our self-pity, our rightness and our blame.

When we are able to stop and consider where somebody may be coming from, we can rest assured our savings are intact and we draw upon our resources. This enables us to not take something personally.

Here's the great thing about this bank account:

The more we "intentionally suffer" in the ways I have just described, the bigger the energetic savings gets and the easier it is to do the intentional suffering.

There comes a tipping point when a new kind of savings gets created, a proper investment account of higher energies which helps us to become more conscious. Not only do we see, we transform.

The great thing about this new conscious energetic account is that its tipping point leads to freedom, permanent freedom if the soup is just right. Being in the yes and no of this account allows God to enter into your heart in such a way that you step into a new dimension of living.

In this dimension, we laugh off statements of others. We take very little personally. We understand and see into someone else's state so that it never has to be about us and our bruised ego.

We have empathy... And choice.

If something bothers us, it lasts for seconds or a minute not hours or days.

If we are conscious of the impending doom, we can head it off at the pass. In fact, it can be that things don't bother us at all and life is wonderful despite all the pesky human contact that used to entangle our lives with expectation and frustration.

We can have community without competition or feeling threatened.

We can be inspired instead of scared, have understanding instead of being offended, be helpful instead of blaming.

We can be free... if only we try again and again to struggle in those tiny moments.

OUTSIDE OF TIME: A PERSPECTIVE ON RETREATS

Standing outside of time where different points of awareness sync up was an aspect of last week's Awareness School retreat. It was as if we entered a sacred and eternal constant. This is the place that fills me with a substance I can't describe. It is visceral and palpable and... beyond explanation.

This can be for all of us. It is where we are all connected.

To bring this forward into everyday life is why we do the retreats. Our aim is to understand an awareness of both inner and outer self in the diversity of life. We as individuals walk amongst each other, share ideas, projects and meals. We each bring to the table a certain flavor. Life can be seen from as many perspectives as there are people. Rather than getting sucked into the fray, we maintain our presence of self while participating in life.

We can learn to track our individual state and at the same time gain heightened awareness of those around us. In retreat, we are moving as a unit of people from activity to activity, like being in spiritual camp. We try to notice not only an energetic play between us, but one that we create together specific to the mix of individuals attending. For this reason, each retreat is different and can never be reproduced.

That unique mix this year created a most profound event. We all described entering moments of presence, recognizing subtle shifts of consciousness. As the week progressed, we became much more still; the moments of silence bringing us closer together in a common container. We had a chance to notice much much more.

Each of us came with individual aims, and realized it takes consistent practice and a build up of higher energies to make choices in any given moment toward that aim. These minute efforts coalesced the many parts of us that normally would unconsciously pull us in all directions from second to second. Once we got this, we were struck by the level at which we could do what we set out to do. We understood Sacred Momentum. We learned what right effort felt like on a micro and macro level to produce real results.

It is how we overcome resistance.

It is how we get out of the way.

It is how we see the barriers that separate us from each other.

Many efforts became an experience of the simultaneous push and pull. It meant experiencing the difficult and painful things we saw or couldn't do and accepted them in that moment. This is the only way we could recognize what is us and what is not us.

The Movements classes were effective for this very thing. They served the purpose of learning how to be "all there." If our emotions were flailing about, the part that is supposed to keep track of various gestures could not do its job. If there was fatigue or lack of energy, we learned it was impossible to implement the combinations. Through present action and impartially taking the gestures, we could alter the intricate web of deception and see what was previously inaccessible. In the moment, we could step into a brighter future. We learned to laugh in the face of such challenge.

Those who were there will never look at themselves or each other the same way. We can be guided from a new template, available whenever we enter that place outside of time/space that connects us forever. We will be reminded at random times of such moments and sink deeper into self-remembrance. We came to learn that very thing and were blessed with a multitude of reference points.

I sit today steeped in a wealth of gratitude for this Work, the dedication of the participants and the possibility for the future. The music, the various individual insights, the collective progress keeps coming back to me in waves and I know those of us there must all feel this.

There was something there in the format, the methods and the present moment that enabled us to expand and grow.

BAD HABITS

I talk about choice a lot in my writings, on my website and with my students. Sometimes when we think we are making a choice, we are just acting out of habit. Habits perpetuate suffering. Our ability to actually choose could change all that.

We get into tailspins that are inextricably painful. Do you have episodes of anxiety and fear about your present situation or future scenarios that are really extremely difficult to quell?

Do you often get subterranean tension with a partner that never gets flushed out and dealt with?

Do you persist in feelings of resentment about something that is in the past?

Do you have a pervading sadness that you cannot shake?

Are you seething with anger that is misplaced, unfounded, or uncontrollably stuffed to the far reaches of your consciousness?

There are so many red flags that can help you see the habit. Yes, you must first notice that it is habit, automatic, mechanical and illusion. If that can occur, you have a way in.

If you have experienced any of the above scenarios, you know how hard it is to extricate yourself from these negative feelings no matter how hard you try. In fact, some of your efforts to fix begin to be part of the habitual chain reaction that makes things worse.

Some of your efforts to "feel better" come from the part of you that can't stand that you are fallible, vulnerable and in pain. It will justify all attempts to skirt the real issues, actually promote behavior to keep it all going and discourage the ability to choose something different.
Choosing something different begins to erode "its" power.

As I work with people privately, I notice more and more how we all take for granted that what we are experiencing is real. It certainly feels real. Further along, there is a realization that it isn't real, but still no luck in escaping the sticky web we weave.

What most have in common is that these constructs are a result of thinking and are not based in objectivity. Our identification with our ideas about ourselves has us believing they are real. When we catch ourselves, we want to change it... we don't accept it

No energy to experience and accept the pattern.

Survival mode run amok...

This is why I do what I do. I teach people how to become more objective through the skill of observation. Presence consists of developing a concentration that enables us to see. It is the synchronization of centers. Sometimes this isn't so pleasant nor is it easy, but the benefits of learning this skill will change lives forever. It is a gift that keeps on giving, developing and evolving the more free we become.

Mostly these days I find people are attracted to things that will make them "feel good" in response to the amount of suffering and negativity they are experiencing. Once the feel good session is over, the negativity comes rolling back in with a vengeance because it has not been dealt with and so... we seek the feel good again. The feel good methods range from the spiritual to the detrimental and everything in between including the myriad of distractions we have created to keep our suffering a moving target.

Money, fame, power, martyrdom even... Spirituality.

Learning self-observation requires that we simultaneously experience our thinking, feeling and bodily sensation. We then and only then are enlightened to the fact that we are highly compartmentalized, especially in our thinking with no means of escape.

It is frustrating and scary to see ourselves feel and act the way we do with no "control" over that anxiety, that anger, or the actions that keep us separate from one another. This makes us go running to the temporary "feel good" and we may not realize that our temporary "feel good" is a habitual system that promotes feeling bad because it doesn't fix it.

No choice.

Starts to feel like prison.

There is a way out but it won't be easy or pleasant and you will have to accept some disturbing things about yourself. There is a price and you have to really want to pay it. You have to be fed up with the way things are in your life. You can head these "negative experiences" off at the pass with choice, but you have to make one clear choice before that, which often comes in a moment of inexplicable grace.

You have to decide you really want the freedom, like an inextinguishable fire that burns within and... you are willing to do what it takes.

MAY THE FORCE BE WITH YOU

Do you find you go through surges and waves of productivity?

What stops us from getting things done?

Sometimes we figure out that some of our most productive days are ones where we let go of pushing toward a goal and relentlessly trying to make it happen. If there is too much resistance and everything is going all wrong, we know the timing is not right.

We must also push against our tendency to get distracted or procrastinate in order to fulfil an aim that we had for the day.

We can understand that divine timing means the presence of... The Third Force, and may have nothing to do with timing at all but our awareness of the interaction of three important forces.

Being blind to the Third Force can create a lot of havoc in our lives.

We can try all we want to make something happen, but if there is no recognition that a Second Force is necessary in the form of resistance, we will not get the results we want.

For any endeavor to have a result, an outcome, a new direction or level, there must be three forces present, the affirming, the denying and the reconciling. We can't get the reconciling force unless the first two are there.

The First Force is known as positive, masculine, yang, active or affirming, The Second Force can include negative, feminine, yin, passive, receptive or denying.

We never hear much about the Third Force known as the reconciling or neutralizing factor. All three forces must be present for actualization of a process. We usually don't notice the third force so keying into this can change everything for you.

If we look at an Enneagram, the symbol of process and transformation, the triangle represents the Sacred Law of Three. These are points 0(9), 3 and 6. This law works in conjunction with the Law of Seven, represented by the hexagram superimposed on top. The hexagram represents the process, and the triangle represents points of reception of forces outside the process.

Of course, many people have come to know the Enneagram from the personality enneagram, and in Wikipedia, unfortunately that is the only definition. This has nothing to do with the Enneagram brought to the West by G. I. Gurdjieff. It was an ancient symbol used by Wisdom Schools and Central Asian Brotherhoods for the very purpose of studying process and Sacred Alchemy of Transformation.

The Law of Three works everywhere in our lives. Have you ever noticed when you push and push to make something happen and get nowhere, but the minute you give up, let go, and accept, it somehow miraculously comes together? That is the Third Force in action.

We can't remember a word or name and it comes to us the minute we quit trying.

Writer's block, that gives way to a flood of ideas by writing anyway.

A relationship that begins to flourish after much misunderstanding and fighting.

Money that appears where before there was none.

Dissipation of reaction, anxiety and worry.

The Third Force comes in if both the Holy Affirming and Holy Denying Forces are present. If we can become familiar with these first two forces and use them properly, the Third Force is activated.

We can learn to be present with the yes and the no, seeing both the positive and negative sides of our nature pushing against each other in the same moment.

One of the most important things we can discover is that Self-observation can be the Second Force pushing against our "comfort zone." That comfort zone may be defined as how we constantly judge ourselves and others. It may be how we work ourselves to death in order to feel a sense of accomplishment. It may be procrastinating to the point that guilt overwhelms us.

That sounds more like misery than comfort, but that is where we are caught if we don't observe it. Our constant habit of evaluating our actions as good or bad is one way we live mechanically, unless we push against it with the effort to observe these shenanigans.

Learning how to observe, through conscious effort, creates an intentional Second Force. It is the quintessential definition of mindfulness.

That buzz word, mindfulness, is omnipresent right now, but is there an understanding of how to do it, what it is, and how it works???

We believe it is to relieve symptoms of suffering like worry, insomnia, anxiety, but we don't really know how to be present and make that happen.

It isn't about keeping our focus either.

Mindfulness is an expanded awareness and the ability to objectively observe without trying to change anything. This way we stay in the feeling we think is "bad"; the feeling we think we shouldn't have, or that we must change. If we go to the place of needing to change it, we have stepped out of the realm of Observation and remain with the First Force only.

When we stay with "negative emotion," it is "uncomfortable," and that very discomfort, that suffering, creates the exact cocktail for freedom from it.

It is the thing that will enable us to manifest. It is the thing that will put us in the right vibratory dimension to attract abundance.

This is how to co-create our life.

This is the presence of... The Third Force.

This is why Luke Skywalker had to learn to understand his anger in order to let go to a higher order for the Force to become effective.

Our Self-Acceptance is created by an effort to accept what we see in a present moment without trying to change it. When that is achieved, the Third Force moves in and one experiences freedom from the fight.

Pick an aim each day that may be a little difficult for you. Start to notice and identify what you think are the subtle denying forces that come into play. It may be your procrastination or distractions. Notice how the Third Force comes into effect and what you did or didn't do to allow it.

May The Force Be With You.

HOW MUCH CAN
YOU BEAR

Bearing the unpleasant manifestations of others is a core practice of our work. It is an integral aspect of understanding acceptance, and is the definition of effective karma yoga. Day to day living inevitably offers me many opportunities to practice with family members, friends and colleagues.

I have found that bearing the unpleasant manifestations of others releases me of their energy.

I don't dwell in the negative.

I learn non-reaction.

I gain empathy.

When I make a big deal about someone's ill behavior, I reinforce the vibration of the wave they started. I immerse myself in the habit of being right and criticizing. By pointing out the wrongdoing of others, part of me justifies to the world that I am not like that person.

Which part of me needs to prove that?

The struggle to not express negative emotions brings about transformation by creating friction.

When I bear the unpleasantness of others I resist the expression of my own negative emotions. I struggle to not argue, to not have to be right or to not have to point out the faults of said person to others.

This means pushing against strong habits to create inner energetic movement.

When I purposefully create struggle within myself, I create friction which then combusts into a new fire of consciousness. I unify the many parts of me that want to be seen and heard in certain ways.

I believe when people act in strange reactive ways, it means they are triggered and very much hooked into their identity with things like being a victim, or needing to be in control, or a collective anger. This list is endless.

When I react to that person's identification, it is usually because I have no empathy, no insight, no understanding of that person's irrational negative behavior. More often than not, if I am not on my toes, I will take their actions personally and begin to react according to my own identifications..

It is very difficult to step back and have compassion, understanding and maintain distance. When I take the first steps of resisting a reaction, I will create an intentional friction within myself.

This friction will enable me to begin to see my own identification with being justified about my behavior.

In essence, if I don't create that friction within myself, I am participating in the same story as the person I am complaining about, fighting with, or reacting to. I assist their "matrix."

The only way for me to learn to be compassionate and empathetic is to resist the expression of my negative emotion concerning someone else's behavior. I will then have to deal with an inner dilemma and observe what it is in me that needs to express such things.

It will stop arguments dead in their tracks.

It curbs gossip.

It puts projection into check.

I will begin to see what makes the other person tick.

I will begin to see what makes me tick.

Most importantly, it enables me to learn through intentional action to become the master of the many parts of me that want to carry on in reaction, in sorrow, in anger, and in persecution.

When I pick up the gauntlet of talking about someone else's faults, I am most assuredly building up my own beliefs about myself. I am blind to the fact that I am complaining just as much as that other person had been doing.

I stoop to their level, match their vibration, and create a symbiotic feeding frenzy.

This week let's rise above the urge to:
- talk poorly about someone
- react to a negative comment someone has made
- argue back even if you "know" they are wrong
- justify your indignation

What effect does it have within yourself and with the other person?

THAT OLE TIME RELIGION

Each year I take time out for myself to regroup, to rejuvenate and to question. As you read this I could be in the woods on solo retreat.

Daily, I am driven to get small goals done. I strive to make self-imposed deadlines and push myself to new heights in both of my businesses. In addition to that, I hold learning in high regard, so I read everyday.

My daily sitting meditation is my spiritual sustenance, my devotional connection to Source, my dip into the Sacred Well of Peace.

I also take care of my body, my temple, by getting exercise, drinking clean water, eating organic food and avoiding processed food of any kind.

These things are the rules by which I live, but I am not obsessed with them. There is that part of me that can get very identified with "living the right life."

Even spirituality can take on the self-righteous aspects of "look how devout I am." This is when spiritual practices become a slippery slope.

I am referring to practices and beliefs which exist to relieve guilt or to puff up our self-image, drive our ambition, or get us noticed for "doing the right thing."

Sometimes our identification with our spirituality creeps up on us unrecognized. We are doing it for the right reasons. We know that it puts us in balance with positive effects rippling throughout our lives.

However, we can be so identified with our spirituality that it becomes spiritual pride. St. John of the Cross writes volumes on this subject and so does Buddha.

When we are able to choose right action in daily life, then we know our spiritual principles have infused into our lives. Otherwise, we are not living in integrity. Choosing right action from our authentic selves is difficult and even trying creates growth. When we are awake, we are better able to manifest values from the unseen world.

It is the only way we can put theory into practice.

I got disillusioned with religion long ago, feeling that it has turned our world upside down. The teachings of the Great Masters has become distorted. This distortion is the result of our individual and collective identification to serve our ego. Our ego believes in it's own self-righteousness, and sees it's shadow in others. The more we bury things in the shadows, the more fundamental and extreme our religion becomes. We are intolerant of others and isolate ourselves further from "those that can't see" or "those that can't do"... We make a distinction between us and the "sinners" even if we aren't outwardly condemning them.

We see ourselves separate from God as well.

The very thing we seek to heal and amend becomes the cause of our separation from each other. We hide behind our religion. We practice it so fervently that the shadows burst out at the seams, leaking sideways anger, binge eating or behaving self-destructively.

Unfortunately, we can make eating organic food or exercise our religion.

We can make being rich and successful our religion.

Even environmental causes and charity work can become religion.

Does your religion represent your attachment to self image, ambition, security, perfection, being "good" or being accepted?

I ask you today, could you walk away from your religion if you had to?

Does it hold for you your entire identity? Could you let go of your rigid beliefs, and evergreen self-improvement schedule, your agendas and your glorified purpose and imagine who you would be without it?

This week, let go, even if it is for a short period of time and imagine.

Take a step back to question if you have made your spiritual practices or ambitions your religion.

Take a personal day to do nothing, absolutely nothing.

Throw a wrench in your ever productive schedule.

Take two hours to sit in contemplation on who you would be without your attachment. Walk away from the pressing needs of your desk and get outside.

Ask yourself what is really important. Ask yourself if you indeed are identified with doing well, being spiritual, being the best, attaining enlightenment, helping others, or being a good person etc.

When you are identified with something you think is good, it can get turned upside down. It boosts the ego not the soul.

When it separates you from others, something has run quite amok.

I hope it will get you questioning!

BEINGS OF LIGHT

We are Beings of Light.

Each and every one of us.

It is our responsibility to fulfill a certain purpose on this planet and we have been given all the equipment to do so, but most of us don't realize the power we have.

We know we only use a small portion of our brain for example.

We know it is easier to cave in to fear than act out of love.

We know that sometimes it is really hard to be here at this time. There is negativity all around and it's being fed to us on a constant basis. We are being trained to live in fear. Many are turning to hurting themselves, surely a reflection of the collective and individual inner state. Many have learned to distrust their bodies. Many have put their intuition on pause.

We don't need to look very far to see that this is real and true.

We can keep our blinders on for convenience, but that won't work for long. Things will only get more difficult if we don't face the facts before us.

I urge you in this time of great upheaval to take the road less traveled.

It is time for us to wake up now if we are to accomplish what we came here for.

Our purpose in a nutshell is to learn to love. That comes down to every small choice we make in daily life all the way up to forgiving ourselves and others in a big way.

The big stuff is harder of course, but we have to start trying. When we live blaming others for our sorrow, we are not taking responsibility for our own behavior and our own reactions.

We are not taking responsibility for our own life.

Staying angry and resentful is the biggest love energy leak I know. If we can step into love, we get amazing fringe benefits.

Everything comes into place. Life is no longer difficult no matter what comes our way.

We see the pertinence of everything that happens and are more able to accept what is. That is way easier than all this suffering.

If we do this together now, we accomplish something that has been waiting to happen since... forever. Jesus, Mary, Buddha, Mohammed, Zarathustra, Padmasambhava, Confucius, and Kuan Yin among others came to show us in ancient times that it can be done.

The modern day saints and enlightened leaders are too long to list. Some of my favorites are Mother Teresa, Martin Luther King, Krishnamurti, Gurdjieff, Jeanne de Salzmann, Pema Chodron, Maya Angelou, Eckhart Tolle, Thomas Merton, Marianne Williamson and The Dalai Lama.

Please add your favorites to the list.

We are meant to cocreate as stewards of God. When Love is bursting forth in us, the Source of all things is operating through us.

We can end war.

We can stop suffering.

We can sustain human existence on the planet.

We can begin to recognize the purpose that has been before us all along.

What is it going to take for us to realize what is needed?

Let's all do our part and make it happen.

I'm all in... are you?

THE FIFTH
DIMENSION

I am listening to a lot of "spiritual teachers" online these days, trying to discern what is being said out there on the interwebs. I notice waves of topics in common.

There is a lot of talk about the 5th dimension, something I have been talking about with my groups for years. For the purpose of clarity, and to ride the wave with my other colleagues online, I want to say that the 5th dimension is now becoming the next "it" topic. Perhaps because so many are now beginning to understand what "it" is and where the planet is headed.

Peace will guide the planet.

We are in the midst of "A Love Revolution" that in hindsight will appear monumental compared to the 60's.

Even movies like Interstellar and Arrival, for instance, are beginning to more concretely present the notion of consciousness outside of the time space continuum. People who have experienced certain levels of freedom, Nirvikalpa Samadhi, the opening of Higher Centers, and enlightenment, can confirm right away their experience of living in the 5th dimension and beyond.

We easily understand 3 dimensions from a spatial and physical point of view, but it also refers to our level of consciousness. If our efforts are based in the 3 dimensional world, they remain on a functional level having to do with our thinking/conceptual life, our emotions and the body intelligence.

We must work in this realm to fortify the groundwork for connecting to our Higher Centers and the 5th dimensional consciousness.

The fourth dimension is seated in time and our perception of it. It is also the world of relative Being in which archetypes, non physical Beings, and overarching collective consciousness is coalesced.

The 5th dimension is the world of Being, the understanding of the Unity and Diversity of all things, outside of time and space. Love enters our heart on a deep level in this dimension so we enter a consciousness in which we have empathy. We experience the reality that we are each other. I am you and you are me. We are made of the same stuff that exists outside of time and space.

The Moon in the 7th House

This is the Heart Mind to which every religion and spiritual path directs us. This is what will manifest en masse in the Age of Aquarius, but it has to happen through our awakening, through our attention, through expanded awareness.

Jupiter is aligned with Mars and you know what that means...

We are at critical mass.

It is time to constantly question whether we actually are awake or not. When we assume we are, we close the door to expansion.

It is better to question and verify, because the majority of us are walking around in conscious sleep thinking we are awake.

The best tactic is to assume we are not awake until we can verify for ourselves when we wake up that indeed we were not. Ha!

Perhaps because of all the work people have already done, it will be easier for everyone to access this expanded consciousness. Afterall monks, nuns and general meditators have been contributing to this higher collective consciousness for centuries. We have been graced with Enlightened Beings to show us that we are capable as humans of having God Consciousness.

They lived by example to show us what is possible... and necessary.

I feel compelled to talk more openly about all of this at this time because I think most are much more open to the idea that through spiritual endeavors, our life becomes easier and we change the planet at the same time, a win win.

Love will steer the stars.

We are ready to embrace a lifestyle that will promote refinement of energies.

Energy does not go away, it transmutes, and that is what is happening to us when we experience 5th dimension consciousness. The higher our energetic substance transmutes the more we experience the cosmic traits of harmony and understanding. At the same time, we raise the lowest common denominator of the collective.

Minds of Liberation

We do this through mindfulness, awareness, and attention plus opening to the divine.

Mystic Crystal Revelations

That phenomenon will have an effect on the collective consciousness and my theory is that because of this, we will access 5th dimensional consciousness much more easily.

Golden Living Dreams of Visions

Higher consciousness constitutes understanding what life is like under the influence of fewer laws, instead of causality, accident, and no choice. We are less determined by our own conditioning and more in line with direct God contact.

So let the sun shine in...

TIL DEATH
DO US PART

How could 18 years of marriage feel like the blink of an eye? Three six year periods seems like nothing. We all know how fast six years can pass and yet for a teenager that is high school and the majority of middle school.

In those terms, it's an eternity.

These 18 years of marriage, however, are measured in Sunday morning pancakes, piano sonatas, birthday parties, graduations of every kind including kindergarten rainbow bridge ceremonies and memorable "when are we gonna get there" family trips.

They include moments of understanding where two souls have met in indescribable places in which poignant eternity and vulnerable connection intersect.

They encompass births that happened right upstairs and more deaths, both literal and figurative than we care to speak of.

Time has slipped through our fingers while standing still for us to become who we are meant to be.

We have cried buckets of tears and laughed our heads off.

We have been there in sickness and in health, for richer and for poorer, through unfounded fears, for better and for way worse than I could have ever expected.

It has even come down to dumping piles of unraked leaves on the kitchen floor, hanging up on each other from time to time, and plenty of walking out in self-righteous huffs.

It took ten years of being together to not be together and to admit, with backs to the wall, our own silly part in the deal: that we are not here to fix anyone else or wait for them to rise to their potential. We aren't together to hope that the other will change or eventually "get it."

We aren't together to blame each other for our own lack of boundaries, our gashed expectations or our lingering self-pity.

With each year, we realize better ways to communicate our own needs without fear of losing the magic. We realize the importance of our own independent struggle and respect that.

We have learned to own our part in the matter (for the most part) and we don't take every little thing seriously or God forbid, personally.

We know that through our individual transformation, we affect each other in the most positive ways. We stand as unique pillars of strength that bear the weight of our collective burden.

We are mirrors for each other in ways we can hardly stand or even don't, but we know in our heart of hearts, it is true.

We have realized the importance of expressing our gratitude and acknowledging in little everyday ways each other's hopes and joys.

We have come to recognize what it takes to support and to sacrifice without throwing the baby out with the bathwater and resenting it til the cows come home.

We have learned to forgive and to accept and so.... we have learned to love, not just pretend love... real love.

What a treasure to share... what a miracle to behold!

EVERY BREATH
YOU TAKE

Every breath I take has the potential for higher consciousness. I can use breath as a practice, just like I use meditation, only a lot more often. There is a substance in the air, finer than the molecules of oxygen, nitrogen, and hydrogen that we breathe. This finer substance is available to us as food for our soul. I can only draw from this pool of finer substance if I am here, present, and remembering.

In the beginning of my practice with breath, I would forget all the time. It was only in a time of frustration or crisis that I would use the breath to center and "calm down." As my pool of consciousness grew, so too did a new practice of Self-Remembrance.

I remember that there is nothing to change and everything to accept. In these small seconds, I fill my bucket of consciousness. With that consciousness, I have learned to see more and more of who I am, and what is behind all of my suffering.

When I first started realizing what was really up with me, I became lost and full of despair. I realized my life was built on false pretenses and negative beliefs. It was almost as if my ego got a whiff of being caught and poured on the heat.

This is the point where I fell into wanting to improve myself.

My own journey became obsessed with fixing myself. I was looking for a way out of my madness. I wanted to be free of my self-sabotage. I only had to look at my life to see nothing was in sync with truth and sincerity. I did not realize there is nothing to fix.

Every breath I take is my most powerful tool.

It is that simple. It is that pure, and it's easy to forget until it isn't.

With each conscious breath, I accept what is.

THE GIFT
OF DEATH

You don't know what you've got til it's gone.

This seems to be the beauty of death and loss. It provides contrast for us to deeply appreciate what we do have.

Recently, I lost an old family friend though I had not had contact with him for many years. It was a tragic death and he was a bright light extinguished way too soon. He had sparkling charisma and a highly magnetic creative force that I see living on in his children.

He suffered greatly this go around.

If this was painful for me, I cannot imagine the pain it was for his family. I know right now they must wander through life only half here, lost in memory and shock. The only thing I know to compare it to is lovesickness where pervading pain seeps into every crack and we fake our way through everyday life.

Perhaps it is the tragic nature of his death and the painful life he was living in the end that makes it all that much more difficult, but who can really quantify this kind of grief.

For those left behind, this loss inspires us to live life more to the fullest. It reminds us how temporary and fleeting things can be. Though death is more extreme, it applies to losing a home, a job, a lover or a friend.

The ensuing adjustment can add value to our future if we allow it.

I see myself dropping what I thought was important these last weeks to spend time with my son who is visiting for the funeral. I can put the ever important deadlines aside and take a weekend with my husband. It has put things into perspective about what actually is important. It brings me closer to appreciating what I do have.

That appreciation would not be as heartfelt if it weren't for the loss.

I have watched how this death has affected my children and realize its relevance as a necessary component. We can learn that death brings us closer to life, that people do suffer in deep ways, that no matter how much help we offer someone, they are ultimately responsible for their experience here.

Every gesture of kindness and connection now has more depth... until we forget again. The relationship we have with family members gets stronger.

The permanent nature, that feeling of never being able to see that person again makes our relationship with others that much more meaningful.

On a lesser scale, when we get the new home or job, we embrace it differently because of the hardship. The contrast makes things better and much more appreciated.

In this present situation, I can look around and see that everyone who knew our friend Park is just a little bit closer to who is left here in the circles of family and friends. We do not go untouched and though we may not feel the pang as much as his immediate family, we know something has changed in us that will not go back to the way it was before.

When we lose someone we love, we go forever changed for the better though it comes in the form of suffering.

We feel compelled to reach out to people we don't communicate with enough. We remember how important it is to connect and to make the effort to stay connected. We also stay comforted in the fact that we all have an eternal spirit that lives on outside of our body, an eternal light body that we can always stay in contact with.

We come to know this keenly only through death of loved ones.

Our memory of the energy and spirit of those who have left us lives on through eternity. We cherish the times we did have and realize in a new way the importance of now.

The gift of death makes things more precious: the songs he sung, the enthusiasm he brought to a room, the unfailing sense of humor and those red shoes.

We will miss you Park.

Your immeasurable gift reminds us to fight, to laugh, and to love.

A THIEF IN THE NIGHT

Resentment goes around like a thief in the night. He slips through the back door just when you look the other way. He creeps up slowly and goes, "BOO."

This week I have been looking at resentment in us and how it comes about.

The definition of resentment is bitter indignation of having been treated unfairly.

I start by noticing that it has to do with how we perceive other people's actions toward us. Something gets interpreted as unfair or thoughtless. Inconsiderate is most assuredly included in the basket. We then get disgruntled and feel bad about certain behaviors.

We become justified in our resentment.

The more I looked at different scenarios, the more I noticed that resentment really has nothing to do with what someone else has done. It has more to do with how we are feeling about what someone else has done.

We have certain expectations about how we think people should act or how we would like them to act, but more often than not, they don't. What are we to do with these gashed hopes of how we want things to be?

As I explored more about where resentment comes from, I realized the thief has a very solid accomplice most of the time, and knows how to become practically invisible. This accomplice makes it convenient for the thief to enter and in fact invites him as a partner in crime.

When we feel resentment, we need look no further than our own self and the way we make boundaries.

Let me give you an example that may elucidate the picture better.

If I have a mentee who misses their session and doesn't call, they owe me money anyway. I am not obligated to make up the session. Perhaps the student has a really good excuse or not but asks for another session anyway. I have plenty of things to consider.

Do I have time outside of my usual working schedule that I am willing to sacrifice? This could mean my rare personal time, family time, writing time etc. Perhaps something in me is unable to say "no, your loss" because I want to appear a nice person, or I want to please others even at my own expense. Maybe it just isn't that big a deal to disrupt my time for an hour. I have to decide if I am OK with giving something away because of someone else's forgetfulness/disregard/disorganization.

In fact, if I decide to make up this session, I am not really doing those people any favors. I send the message that it's OK to miss a session with no notice because I'll bend... I'm flex... I'm kind..etc.

If I keep my boundary clear, I won't make it up because that is my policy, especially if the excuse is... we forgot. They will learn that it is not OK to not show and that I don't do make ups for that.

However, if my boundaries are screwed up, I say yes let's make it up
    a.   because I am identified with being a nice person
    b.   have a hard time saying no
    c.   am a people pleaser at my own expense
    d.   don't want to seem mean or not understanding

Each of these reasons have to do with what other people think or how I think others will perceive me. They are not founded in following my own conscience, much less the policies I made explicit to my students when they signed on.

As the make up session rolls around, I find myself wishing I had never said yes. It is now infringing on something that I hardly have time for... and all just to be a nice person??

I begin to wish I had never said yes and wonder how they could even ask for the makeup? Why don't they have enough sense or insight to know that they are infringing? Or that they have no right? Or that they are not following policy? Or that they don't have the sense to not ask? How could they be so insensitive, and so on.

All kinds of mental scenarios could build up that make them the culprits, but it is my own lack of boundary that has brought this situation on.

I did not say "no make up session" and would have been completely justified in doing so.

For any of the above reasons and beyond, I did say yes not really wanting to, but did it anyway and then stewed in resentment.

I ask you to find times when you are resenting someone for something and let me know if the accomplice, lack of boundary, isn't behind the scenes.

Do you have any example of being justified in your resentment?

Do people have that much power over you and your inner state?

Check Your Boundaries!

THE SPECIAL SAUCE

I am lucky to have had several long term "Yodas" in my life.

The methods I learned were well established from the Zen Buddhist tradition and the methods of the Fourth Way. These teachings carry high transmission and require one part process, one part free will, and one part willingness to receive. Without that balance, nothing is guaranteed.

I was given a certain plan of action through specific meditations, practices or a combination of both, but that didn't mean it was going to work.

There was an inner teaching within the teaching that I was to access.

The secret to my transformation was my willingness to act and be acted upon in perfect balance, so that something greater could come in. When there was this willingness to accept the gift of the inner teaching, something very subtle began to happen, and it required human to human.

I may not have felt I even needed that kind of intermediary because I already had a relationship with the Divine. However, the symbiotic human exchange provided a shortcut to understanding profound human connection. I learned how to receive, how to respect and how to love.

That can spice up anyone's life.

When we believe we don't need anyone else's help, it's true. We have direct access to Source and we can discover our own path to God Consciousness. However, when we let in Love from Higher Realms through the transmission of someone else, we gain trust in the human ingredients.

Letting love burst into our hearts is delectable. If it happens, we are then equipped to contribute to the planet, making it easier for everyone else to get there: another crack in the glass ceiling, so to speak.

When we burst forth as stewards of a Higher Source, completely embodied and co-creating with God, it is so we can relate in oneness to everyone and everything else.

That is how a harmonious planet earth will evolve.

I speak from my experience of intense one on one study with mentors seated in very high stations, who made it easier for me to access the Higher.

It was mystical and magical. The taste will forever remain with me.

Receiving the true living dharma from another person is the special sauce in the spiritual recipe.

I have learned so much from great books. I have experienced expansion through prayer and meditation. However, the most meaningful part of my spiritual path has been my relationship with my teachers, who understood my quest and could give me answers. Each was right for different reasons, and at different stages of my development.

I encourage all of us to seek a relationship with someone who can teach the ways of meditation and the present moment. A teacher holds us accountable (not always comfortable) and we gain humility when allowing someone to come in and help. We learn respect.

We often justify not seeking this help by requiring perfection and superhuman qualities in a teacher. Conveniently, we will never find that person.

Our ego will always find a way to wiggle out...

I have found that letting someone teach me, no matter what the realm, be it spiritual, business or artistic endeavors has been one of the greatest gifts of learning. Even now as a professional musician, I consult my mentor who knocks me into line.

I will forever be grateful for all of my teachers' insights, their persistence and their faith in me. I appreciate being called on my own bullshit and being held accountable. Most importantly, I appreciate the special attendance from someone which allowed me to feel love and gain self-respect so that I could go forth and do the same.

If you have never had a real one on one relationship with a teacher, it's worth seeking and it is never too late to learn.

Questions:

What are your experiences with teachers?

How has outside help propelled you forward in your career and personal transformation?

Are you willing to let someone in?

LISTEN

When I listen closely with all parts of me from an integration I cannot explain, I experience a deep sense of trust.

I realize the more I feel this trust, the more I see what was missing from so much of my life. When I felt scared, anxious, and so willing to please without any regard to what I really wanted, it was from lack of trust. There was no solid foundation from which to say no.

The more I listen in stillness within myself, the more I experience a consciousness that connects me to an eternal force. It represents strength within me and becomes that upon which I lean. In fact, it is the very thing that allows me to take greater and greater risks. Those risks come in the form of creativity and love with little regard to what anyone might think.

This integration is a result of years of inner work and observation of my thinking, my feelings, and my body, even after I acquired an expanded perspective from beyond the three. In this subtle, yet deep awareness, I see God within myself, that which is perfection, that which can love. This is very foreign to the way I have been taught to regard myself.

For most of us, feeling love for ourselves seems arrogant and full of pride, but I have discovered that trying to keep that arrogance in check has stopped me from realizing my greatness.

I have cut myself off from my power because of the false fear of being self-centered. There was no room for my greatness.

As I listen inside, watching with eagle eye, I begin to see that spark that I could not recognize before, that I would not let myself embrace.

As I hear the celestial sounds of my own Being, thought completely subsided, I melt in gratitude for the fantastical journey that started with unflinching faith and conviction, now bolstered by trust in a process well beyond just my effort.

The more I am able to trust, the more I am able to let go and take the next leap.

How can I describe to you what I hear as trust?

It is no longer shrouded in self-doubt and yet there is a questioning vigilance toward what is really happening within me. I have strength to look. I take the risk to feel.

Absence of fear.

Desire to create.

Solidity, security, and relief.

I can look back and realize how much my life depended on me protecting me from me.

Ironically, I listen and realize that I Am... a merge with eternal consciousness that I thought at one time was not me. The gates were closed because I had locked them up and thrown away the key, vowing to fight the good fight in the name of survival.

As I listen, there is a sweet longing for all of us to let go more, to try harder, to not give up, to question, to be brave and to allow. I hear all of us really wanting that, each in our own individual way. I hear our fear and our pain.

As I listen, the earth too sings its song of longing as the aspen leaves rustle and the waves come crashing into me. Her power is something to behold, as a force that will vanquish the foe, as a lesson to be learned and a connection to be had.

Then there is the music of the spheres; the almighty vibration of higher frequency that can only come to me in a synchronistic flow of understanding of something more precious and holy than words can describe. Everything fits and everything is miraculously infinite in fractal cohesion. The Laws of the Universe abide and I am distinctly part of that system.

I listen and know that I am enough. In fact, I am not only enough, I am powerful beyond any stretch of the imagination. I can embrace the power that once scared me, that got shut down, that doesn't belong in a world of fear.

Listen... can you hear it?

INTENTIONAL
INNER FRICTION

I notice resistance revealing itself in small ways throughout my day in the form of distraction, procrastination, and fear.

I am listening to discussions in a new way, oriented toward how people deal with resistance. I start to hear how many excuses we make for ourselves.

My depth of perception concerning resistance and how we use it is expanding.

Because of Newton's Third Law of Motion, we know nothing goes forward without resistance. For every action, there is an equal and opposing reaction. It's the law, and if we accept that it's true, we find ourselves better able to understand what is happening to us when we meet with resistance coming at us.

My basic premise is that resistance is an inside job, whether we attract situations that match our vibration or take things in our own hands and use resistance to deal with our lower nature.

We must first recognize in life that everything we do will be met with resistance, whether it is from the outside or from our own intentional application of it.

There is a huge difference between these two aspects.

Let's take the example of steering a boat. If we are in control of the rudder, we can make small course corrections as the wind or the current push us out of line.

There are two forces, the wind and the rudder and those together propel us forward in the direction we want to go. If we didn't apply any resistance, the wind or current would blow us in any which way until something else out of our control blows us the other way. We become victims of fate.

This is how life is for many people who do not understand how to use resistance or inner friction to produce the Third Force. For them, life is a series of tragedies, dramas and setbacks to be used as excuses for not living the life they want.

Do you know anyone who is constantly living in the drama of life? Do you notice that some people attract major strife, tragedy and difficulty?

For all of us, shit happens. The wind will blow our boat off course, just because we have gotten in the boat in the first place. We have to take the responsibility to steer it.

Part of the magic of using resistance against our own lower nature is that we are intentionally choosing to create inner friction. When we choose the road less traveled, choose to confront our pain, take the scary risk, we have the chance to experience the two forces inside of ourselves that we usually avoid. This is the only way we can invite Third Force.

It cannot exist without the two forces being present simultaneously.

When we rest in our comfort zone, there is only one force present. We avoid the "pain," the "fear," and unfortunately, the "gain." On the other hand, many of us are attached to suffering so let's not get the masochists and workaholics all excited.

This is not about suffering as a way to move forward. It is about choosing to put oneself through the fire to ignite the magic.

Sometimes that can come in the form of letting go, if we are the type to drive ourselves to the point of exhaustion, determined to not let anything get in our way. Remember, that kind of push will be met with equal and opposing force.

Conversely, we can avoid the work of our own transformation and have other people "clear it," but sooner or later the resistance of our own unhappiness, dissatisfaction, and return of the problem we were originally trying to fix will require us to do something for ourselves.

If we can intentionally bring about the inner friction, either letting go or taking action, we take responsibility and a finer energy is produced. This is how we raise our vibration in a permanent way. This means we no longer attract shocks of massive proportions in the form of hurricanes and giant squalls to get the message across.

Life gets easier. We start manifesting what we want. We learn to steer the boat away from the storm.

How does this look for us in terms of daily life?

First we must understand that our fear is the result of identification with certain thoughts or false beliefs, so it kicks up a survival mode response. If uncertain outcome is involved, and any risk or creative endeavor we take falls under that category, then our lower nature will grab on and automatically react in fear.

Things that are not life or death situations morph into eminent threat. We are given the instruction at central command to avoid at all costs, and so we learn to procrastinate through distraction, perfectionism, overwhelm and attracting "disastrous situations" to use as excuses.

When we find ourselves procrastinating, taking one small step means taking the rudder in your hand. If you are a writer with writer's block, sitting down to write at the same time everyday, even if it comes out nonsense is taking that step.

If you are riddled with anxiety, finding ways to be still on the inside provides intentional resistance and will reveal the pain that causes it in the first place. Recognizing the things we do to avoid that pain is subtle, so taking one small step toward peering in will reap great rewards.

Sitting in the anxiety and trying to observe it from a neutral perspective without trying to change it or judge is the missing force, the rudder against the current.

Instead of pushing it away or masking symptoms, we discover the source. This is the Third force streaming in to allow us to see deeper parts of ourselves.

Learning how to apply the missing force through intentional inner friction is the most profound and fruitful spiritual work.

Please let me know your experience with resistance. Try working with it and let me know how it goes. What are situations in your life that have required you to apply resistance that brought about a revelation of sorts? Can you recognize energy leaks in the form of negative emotion, and anxiety and simply watch them?

Work with ways to apply your own "resistance" against your comfort zones.

May The Force Be With You.

VALUING IMPERFECTION

Valuing imperfection seems practically impossible for us.

Part of us cannot stand being flawed: so let's discover how this became so highly developed in us.

Why is self-acceptance so damn difficult?

Were we treated so poorly by our parents, teachers and friends that we carry on the pattern internally? Even most of us who seemingly came from a loving household carry traces of this perfectionism.

It is in our DNA. It appears as self-preservation to mask the contradiction within us. When we believe in our self-importance, but our experience reveals otherwise, we begin the self-bashing for not being better than what we expected. It's like a tennis game that's going on without our knowledge.

We only need turn the lights on in the ball court to begin to struggle with self-loathing.

Inherently, there is a wisdom so vast within us that knows, that accepts, that loves unconditionally but we have lost our way.

Why does another part of us pick up the self bashing so vehemently? One would think there was within us a failsafe system to access the good wisdom of truth about ourselves no matter what happens. But the truth about us is contradictory to that with which we are identified, it isn't what we like, it isn't what our ego deems as good. We have built up stories and beliefs our whole life to cover up the truth about ourselves.

The truth will reveal what we hide with our self importance and our self-loathing.

To let go of the self-loathing would be to accept our imperfection, but what may be hard wired is:
1) I won't be loved
2) I have failed
3) I'm not good enough
4) I'll be alone

Even spirituality and trying to become free can get morphed into trying to become perfect.

The more suffering we experienced in early life, the more we unknowingly perpetuate the self-loathing. That early abuse becomes a gift if it spurs us on to discover that we ourselves are now carrying the pattern forward.

We have all suffered because of the way the world is and our conditioning leads us to this ugly place of self-deprecation, non acceptance and self loathing. We live distorted lives without learning methods to help us see within and accept. Unfortunately, most every self-help method gives us the message that we need to change.

The real spiritual practice that will unravel all the self-sabotage is the practice of objective Self-observation. We must start with the smaller things and it must always involve a sensate knowledge of our feelings and our experience.

Of course, our parents did not expect us to be perfect! We built that into the mix, and our distorted self-perception created an intolerable monster.

We can study this monster when we see it as the secondary phase of Self-observation.

It is the danger zone.

It comes after we observe our disconnection, our fallibility, and our identification with things that give us false meaning in life. It is noticing ourselves all caught up and then judging. We try to change it.

We push it deeper into the shadows. We project it onto others. We take action to punish ourselves in a perpetual and inescapable downward spiral.

This is the place where we must choose to do something different. As we see the contradiction of our situation, we have a chance to let the oxygen starved Light Being that is really us take part. If we struggle to accept the condition we now see within, we strengthen that Light Being, our Essence.

We are all afraid to feel this sorry state of affairs within ourselves because then we must admit our own imperfection and our loss of control. We experience the self-divided. It is just too vulnerable and we have spent our whole life building walls to protect ourselves from this vulnerability.

The proud overcoat that has taken on gargantuan proportions must be removed.

Brick by brick, we must uncover our imperfect self in all its glory.

We must lose control... ..

Our pursuit of happiness has been too long the search for love and acceptance from the outside because we haven't discovered how to do it from the inside. This is the root of the chase for money in and of itself, fame, and power.

This is the root of our twisted sense of self and the unconscious sabotage we create to maintain the bashing. As long as we cannot accept our contradictions and love who we are, we will create ways to punish ourselves.

too fat, too lazy, too poor, too lonely, too unsuccessful, too persecuted, too you- name- it

and we actually manifest it so we can say, "see I told you so"

It takes courage to accept what is.

It's hard to catch it because it is an ingrained habit. We know something isn't right by the way our life is manifesting. We can blame it on everything under the sun, but nothing will change until we embrace who we are and what we keep doing to ourselves.

We don't have to change a thing about our imperfect selves.

We only need to accept what we see.

INNER CONSIDERING

Inner considering is a fourth way term referring to the phenomenon of putting importance on what others think.

We create scenarios which are false in order to reiterate and uphold the patterns learned so long ago about what "should be." When this happens, the best thing to do is to notice the inner considering for what it is, nothing based in truth. By trying to do that, we begin to develop an Observer who can then separate from the story and the identification just by seeing it in the moment.

Inner Considering is a condition we all live with until we learn to detach ourselves from those thoughts. Our negative emotion and inner considering when boiled down to the root of the matter is caused by identification. When we are identified with certain ideas about ourselves, it causes us to put importance on what others think!

We can carry a stressful or difficult situation with us for a long time before we are really able to let go of it. We wallow in what we think we could have done better or how we should have acted. All of these ruminating thoughts are the result of putting importance on what others think.

When we consider internally, it is all about us and how people see us. There is never any consideration to what the other person is actually feeling. Our thoughts revolve around how we are seen, what others think of us, the impressions we have made, whether we are accepted or loved, and what we should have done better.

If we could externally consider, we would take into consideration others' feelings and circumstances. We would have empathy for their situation or mood. We may not agree with them but we would understand why or how they could think the way they do. We may not feel the same way, but we don't resent them for their choices.

Inner considering is so common within us that we hardly notice to what extent we do it. With more presence by integrating our thoughts, feeling and body simultaneously, we start to notice more about this within us. If we are working with the power of presence to learn and observe more about ourselves, we will notice how often we are affected by inner considering.

Inner considering is a huge energy leak. It diminishes all the good meditation and presence work we have done. Struggling with our inner considering is one of the strongest practices I know. When we are present, inner considering cannot exist. We work by staying collected and bringing ourselves back to the present even when we are plagued by these thoughts.

When you find yourself lost in wondering why you said this or how could you have done that, bring sensation to a part of your body immediately. Begin to watch these thoughts. Notice the nature of these thoughts and how they are based in some kind of fear of what someone else thinks. Do not try to label anything or change anything. Simply try to watch it and accept the state that you are in. This inner struggle alone will shift the energy.

ENERGY LEAKS

In my groups and individual mentoring, I often see themes emerging.

One such theme is "containers."

The inner efforts we make to stay present create a "container." As this container becomes stronger, it makes it easier for us to be present.

As I have worked over the years, I have learned it is possible to reach a tipping point of higher energy, where one can have breakthroughs to higher understanding. At this point, my heart is able to open because of the safety of the container. Permanent freedom comes from a well developed container. This container is a developed spiritual body that can enable retention of refined energies. Gurdjieff called this body the Kesdjan Body.

Some people assume that we already have this "extra body." People speak of an astral body, or a soul, as if it is ours by right. But this is a body we must develop through our inner work.

The trick to developing a strong spiritual body is spiritual practice focused on energy leaks. If we can understand what leaks higher energies, we plug up holes in our bucket of consciousness. Even if we cannot perceive immediate results from our efforts, we gain force.

We get an A for effort in spiritual school because of the energy upgrade that it creates. We may get a sense of more cohesion rather than a frenetic dispersed "feeling." After a while, ease of decision making, stronger boundaries that were not there before, and less reaction are indicators of fewer energy leaks.

When the scale really tips, because we have been doing daily practices of intentional "effort," we have the opportunity for tremendous growth and freedom.

Balancing the affirming and receptive aspects of our effort is key at the tipping point. Like a cat at the mouse hole, we will be ready when the energy is just right.

Consistent effort is very important for plugging up the leaks.

Some of the major leaks to notice and work with are:
   1) reactive emotion
   2) distracted thought
   3) excessive drug/alcohol use
   4) dependence on distractions
   5) lack of boundary
   6) constant diet of negativity/intensity

The dispersed energy of reactive emotions occurs when we identify with certain roles and thoughts. When we find ourselves reacting, the best practice is to "cook" in it and watch it. When we do not express the emotion outwardly, for example, keep our negative thoughts to ourselves, it causes a desired inner friction and reflects proper effort. This does not mean you need to suppress the emotion - that is the ego's response to judging what we are identified with. Staying with it means you acknowledge it, observe it and feel it to find out more.

Distracted thought is easy to detect, and simply bringing ourselves back to task with no judgement is the practice. Every time we bring bodily sensation into the mix as we notice the distracted state, we are present and we have just created energy upgrade.

Obviously, it is up to us to regulate our drug and alcohol consumption, but unless we have learned to catalyse energies under the influence of permanent freedom, these substances will diminish our higher energies needed for transformation. We may be working hard to enhance attention, create inner friction through sustaining the yes and no within ourselves, meditate every day and then deplete all the good energy through excessive and consistent drug and alcohol use.

We will be living the life of Sisyphus rolling the stone up the hill every day and wondering why all our efforts are not getting us further along.

Dependence on distraction simply keeps us from facing the difficult things within. If we never have moments of stillness and feel we must fill the void with input, we do not get a chance to increase awareness of inner phenomena. Through attention, awareness is increased which will help us with the previous 3 leaks. Some examples of distraction are the phone, social media, TV, sports, and serial new relationships. Other signs of distraction are constant new projects that never get finished, procrastination in excess and lack of follow through. We may have shiny object syndrome where we are pulled from one thing to another without ever really applying the benefits we have learned or struggling to finish the work.

Lack of boundary gives rise to blame and anger, not to mention depression, anxiety and fatigue. When we do not take responsibility for our own feelings, we miss the real Work at hand. We deprive ourselves of the opportunity to shed light on our states of identification. We buffer ourselves from seeing the intricate web our ego weaves and continue to suffer and blame others. We pick up the energy of others and are unable to distinguish what is us or not us. We become a sponge for people's negative and positive energy. Big energy leaks like that can even affect our health quite dramatically.

What we feed grows so a constant diet of negativity, violence, pain and even exaggerated input to all the senses will numb us to the subtle. Sex is no longer exciting without the pain associated with it, movies are boring if there are not so many frames per second. Our attention need not be engaged because of the overstimulation and we remain asleep to the very process that will upgrade our energy system. The only result will be that we need more and more because we have not developed a way to take in a finer substance.

Walk in nature and take in the very subtle nuance of color and sound. Sit still for a day and do nothing. This develops our attention and thus raises the energy level.

As we work with conscious effort, attention and expanded awareness, it gets easier to spot the energy leaking activities and behaviors.

Have faith that no effort goes unrewarded and our bucket will soon be brimming over.

Our life will then look and feel completely different:

We will have empathy where we were once offended.

We will find ourselves choosing not to react.

We will no longer be paralyzed by fear.

We will not measure our self-worth by what others think.

Our senses will become increasingly attuned to our inner voice streaming from our true essence.

Indecision will be an issue of the past.

We will finish what we started, in fact, we will be able to do more than we ever dreamed we were capable of doing.

We will move gracefully toward self-acceptance thus learning to love others more deeply.

TIPPING POINT

Surely most blogs, social media posts and news bites will mention one subject this week. Yes, it is on all our minds and in our hearts, and we are collectively grieving the numerous attacks on innocent people around the world. Not only are we collectively grieving, we are succumbing to fear which is permeating our media and our lives.

I ask us now to understand that we are being called to collectively look within to find the real enemy. The scenarios on the planet are outward manifestations of our interior landscape. It is a macrocosm of the fear we experience on a daily basis and the war we wage against ourselves.

No amount of retaliation will heal the situation. We have learned very well that violence begets violence. Lack of empathy and understanding around the whole situation is what perpetuates it.

There comes a time when we must put down our weapons and embrace that which is within us that needs attention. Doing this will curtail the need to look outside of ourselves for happiness and approval. This exterior need has gotten us where we are today. We will kill for it and we will be killed.

I ask each of us to search deep within and experience fear and vulnerability for the purpose of our own transformation, self-acceptance and love. Only then can we embrace one another in security and trust. There will be no more dominion over others. There will be no more extreme greed. We will no longer have the need to kill each other.

This weekend I experienced utter sadness and despair for this planet and our predicament. If we do not wake up, it will be mass destruction in the form of war and an eternal chase for a moving target.

However, as I pondered and prayed, something began to shift within me. It came as a small realization at first but then swept over me like a tsunami. My deeper freedom and self-transformation is always like a moving target. I felt the need to stop chasing, searching, and aiming.

I began to understand a new point of surrender to enable reception.

It started as a reflection on my business and life; one in which I perceived my desire to constantly drive toward goals. I can do everything right. I can take every step required. I maintain discipline, consistency and develop relationships but where is the ease? Where is the art of receiving?

I believe from the vulnerable state of the collective, I was able to more easily step into my own vulnerable state. What am I actually afraid of? Where does this belief come from that I must work so hard in order to get the results I want? Am I receiving in my relationships or do I make it happen?

This started a new cascade of insights in regard to the lost art of reception, a feminine principle that has been socialized out of us. I will kill parts of me to make something happen. Somewhere along the way I sacrificed the belief that things can come to me easily just because I deserve it. I had forgotten to call in grace and ask for healing, for help, for love and to believe that I can have that too.

In my vulnerability, I began to realize my neglect of self; a neglect that robs me of receiving. Through great tears of breakthrough, I knew that I am worthy and I can forgive myself. I can be loved, I can receive abundance easily, I can have peace and understanding and in allowing this, I accept in myself that which has been so ignored.

That led to a greater knowledge and understanding of my desire to deeply connect with others. I cherished my husband like never before this weekend. I am filled with gratitude for my three beautiful children. I accept loving them, appreciating them, and supporting them. I am better equipped to accept love from them.

There is also power in coming together as groups and community. A system of competition feels almost laughable at this point. The new paradigm is collaboration.

The existence of us versus them, we are right they are wrong - is absurd. It smacks of the collective shadow that is looming over us all.

This was my small individual transformation, but it contributes to our universal transformation and tips the scale from fear to love. Do not underestimate the power of individual metamorphosis and its contribution to the planet.

This week, I implore us to take part in tipping the scale:

1)   Take time to reflect in stillness about the sadness and vulnerability within ourselves. That is the only place where we will discover the seeds of our own prison. Peace on earth is dependent on peace within each and every one of us.

2)   Stay away from the media. None of us need to listen to reports of violence over and over. Yes stay abreast of current events, but don't listen to story after story about it all. In this way, we resist falling into dire fear by re-experiencing the trauma over and over.

3)   Spend time with loved ones and friends. Take part in some kind of art form. Sing, laugh and dance in the kitchen, one of my favorite healing activities.

4)   Finally, send love to each and every human on this planet. Let's find it in our heart to forgive, for when we do this, we forgive ourselves and heal.

THE IMPORTANCE
OF CONTRAST

Without contrast, we cannot appreciate things. We cannot see how blessed we are. In fact, the greater the contrast we experience in life, the more we do not take things for granted.

What I mean by contrast is the darker more unpleasant experiences in life. Without our troubles and difficulties, we would not appreciate when we don't have them.

Take illness as an example. When we are in pain for a long period of time, we are ultra relieved when it stops, even more so than someone who has only had acute pain for a day. With a prolonged health issue, we experience overjoyed relief when it stops.

All of this came to my mind yesterday as I walked in the perfect weather yesterday. It was not just another beautiful day. This day came after months and months of cold rainy weather here in Seattle. We have been truly starved of sun this Spring so much so that things were not germinating. The soil is so saturated that things are way behind.

Spring is a difficult month for me anyway because of my expectations. I sometimes get lucky but most of the time it is a lot colder with a few sunbreaks here and there along the way. We enjoy the beauty of the flowers and the lush green, but there is a cold bite in the air.

This Spring has been unbearable for not just me but many. The most rainfall in history since it has been being recorded. The temperature hasnot risen and stayed steadily warmer for more than a day. This comes on the heels of the rainiest and coldest winter on record for the Northwest.

For a native Floridian, that is torture. I have to immerse myself in hot baths often to get my body temperature up.

So you can imagine the joy and pure bliss all of us experienced yesterday as temperatures broke into the high seventies. Everyone is out walking, gardening, or sunbathing. People are high on life, love, light and warmth. This weather was so appreciated that it struck a chord in me.

People in Florida do not experience this contrast.

Contrast provided a deeper sense of gratitude and relief.

So we must appreciate the great contrast we feel when we heal from abuse. We appreciate a non abusive situation and do not take for granted what life could be like.

People who have healed from health conditions do not take their health for granted. People who have lived with great lack do not take their meals for granted. Those who have suffered great loss appreciate much more profoundly their new founded security.

CLEANLINESS IS NEXT TO GODLINESS

Today I am sitting in my new office with a new desk, light streaming in from the southern exposure french doors next to me. There are no papers piled up, no post-its everywhere. Just clean space. I have strategically placed things of certain significance from my life as inspiration and reminders. They are to renew a fresh perspective daily.

It is arranged in a private corner of my piano studio: my sanctuary that I have christened my office. I honestly don't know why it took me so long to do this.

The table is the first piece of furniture I bought from a flea market in Paris, not just any flea market but the famous Marché aux Puces de St. Ouen in Clignancourt. It is a 1920's deco style table with curved legs, a rare find these days. St Ouen served in the court of King Clotaire whose son Dagobert I convinced Ouen (Owen) not to become a monk. He, however, went about France founding monasteries and promoting spirituality. Wow that was a tangent, but I love French history and it seems pertinent to my mission.

The picture of my children at our old beach house reminds me to keep family and leisure time a priority. There is also a small clock from Toledo resting against the picture to say take time for travel and discovery.

My Grandmother's large shell ashtray from said beach house, now filled with shells I have collected from all over the planet, keeps the wisdom of the ancestors alive. My renewed focus on the power of women coming together and supporting one another is represented here.

Pens float in a tiny Irish pitcher to spur me on to write everyday. Just like practicing the piano, writing requires the subtle discipline of daily doing, not waiting for perfect conditions or lots of time. The Irish part represents wit, humor, loving kindness and the fantastic influence Irish people have had in my life, especially my husband and my piano mentor.

On the other side of the desk are a piece of pottery from Mexico from the first trip I took with my husband, some fabric fortune cookies made by one of my best piano students and an alabaster cup and saucer, albeit chipped, from my first spiritual teacher to remember that life can be like a cup of tea, filled to the brim and to be shared with the company of others.

The marble lamp with a flower cut shade is from my mother's bedside table and stands out as a memory of something both precious and painful from my childhood.

The Moroccan dish is a gift from my middle son from a trip he took where he "heard the call." I put my earbuds there to remember to heed the call and always always listen.

The artsy postcard of a bee represents personal transformation and the preservation of our planet. It is the mascot of my spiritual school. The bee collects the pollen, inherent Sacred Truth, and miraculously converts it into honey, our alchemical personal spiritual experience. As well, I love nothing more than honey and beeswax, the smell, the taste, the feel and the cleansing satisfaction it brings.

Finally, a check from the Gratitude Bank of the Universe to remind me that money is an energetic flow that I can give and receive with ease.

I know these are all "just things" but they came together like a tapestry of items from all over the house. Nothing is new, just rearranged, and that creates the antidote for lack.

My old IKEA desk was an ancient stacking ground shoved into the corner of a multi-purpose room. It was so crammed with books, bank statements, and things I wanted to save as absolute must do's from 4 years ago that I went seeking light and view in the kitchen. I chose the most public place in the house with no regard for my own space. It was also a dumping ground for everyone else's shit.

Something came over me last weekend and in order to clean the desk, I had to clean out the closet and shelves to put some of the books away. That opened another can of worms, loads of memories and reminders of failed business attempts, newly found lost items and a lot of emotional baggage. At one point during the process, there was a 4X4 pile of CD's, books and papers on the floor to go out of the house.

Purge. Holy Purging.

I have cried more than once about my life decisions, the old self-doubt, all the extreme fruitless effort, and my relentless clinging to crippled hopes and dreams. I heard echoes of my delusional wish for something better, something more and all the evidence of my belief that I am not enough. I found old parts of me that once believed success came from the outside; that things would be better if..., that sacrificing who I am would bring about a way to support my vision.

I recycled it. I threw it away. I gave it to charity.

As I write, I feel the poignancy and sacred maneuver of what I just accomplished. I have dusted away the self-pity and nourished the undeserving waif who so needs my forgiveness.

I stand in gratitude for what I have and where I am. I forgive myself for such imperfection. I marvel at this new environment both inside and out.

With an enhanced sense of clarity and relief, I truly understand a most important edict: Cleanliness is next to Godliness.

I HONOR YOU

Today I want to honor...

Those of you who feel like crap,
Those who cannot shake a terrible feeling of disappointment,
Those who feel nobody gets you,
Those who cannot shirk an impending sense of doom,
Those who are tired of making efforts,
Those who don't know if it's going to work,
Those who keep cringing in fear but don't know why,
Those who are convinced they are not going to be successful,
Those who are afraid of themselves,
Those who wallow in guilt for what they have said or done,
Those who dread getting up,
Those whose minds are racing,
Those who keep bursting into tears and don't know why,
Those who feel like giving up,
Those who are angry at themselves for not making better choices,
Those who feel trapped,
Those who really care about what everyone thinks,
Those who can't pinpoint where these awful feelings come from,
Those who live in fear of doing something wrong,
Those who feel they are not enough just as they are,
Those who secretly suffer with no one to talk to,
Those who hide their pain,
Those who cannot accept help,
Those who blame everyone else for their unhappiness,
Those whose greatest weakness is shaming themselves,
Those who cannot find a way to escape,

Those who pretend everything is alright,
Those who disregard their own wishes in order to please,
Those who mistreat themselves,
Those who are angry about their misfortune,
Those who wish they hadn't,
Those who wish they had,
Those who find fault in everyone,
Those who want to be seen and heard,
Those who look for love in all the wrong places,
Those who cannot go on...

because you are not alone.

I have been there too.

I honor you today because you are me and I am you. We share a common human experience no matter where we are in the stages of transformation with these things.

I honor you because I know how hopeless it feels and I also want you to know there is a way out, I promise. There is a way out, but you have to trust and perhaps trust is not yet part of your repertoire.

There is Reality behind these illusions.

There is Love and you can have it.

Your process requires belief in a chance at freedom, faith that it can happen, and trust that it is yours.

Trust comes from your ultimate vulnerability and surrender.

You can take the risk because you have nothing to lose but that long list above.

I'll whisper in your ear... "let go!"

God will catch you.

IN SERVICE

I work fervently in service hoping that... it serves.

Why do I do that? Because someone did it for me in a way that brought me to an everlasting freedom. What I mean by this freedom is having an infinite energy source to enable conscious choice, knowledge of the magical ways of energy, waking in gratitude, and experiencing non reaction and fulfillment.

I want that for everyone and so I am driven by something deep in my heart. It is the knowledge that if I can have this, so can someone else. If I can rise up like a phoenix from the ashes, so can someone else. If I can heal from tremendous sexual abuse and parental alienation, then so can someone else. If I can reroute deeply grooved neural pathways of self-loathing, so can someone else.

That pain incited me to be a true seeker. At some point in my life, the self-medicating had to stop. The futile relationships that simply reenacted the past had to stop. The debilitating self-sabotage that so frustratingly disabled my efforts had to stop.

I resisted my own path to transformation. Everyone does and this makes my job even harder.

I am transmitting an esoteric teaching that is life changing but how many people are running around looking for that?

Not many...

They are all looking for ways to improve their business, their relationships, their health and their life. They want it to be easy and fast. If I bundled this up in a glitzy package that promised a six figure income, they might start come running.

The beautiful thing about what I do is that it is not for the masses. It is not for those who need pop spirituality or quick fixes; it is for the seekers. They have to get a whiff and realize this is what they have been looking for. They have to sense that it will reveal the underbelly of their greatest fears and make them struggle with the parts that get perpetually pushed into the shadows.

Some of them may be seeking in the wrong places, not realizing that the foundation of suffering is identification with false stories and wacky self-images. It takes a lot of work with attention to get free from these stories. The stories do not dissipate just from knowing where they came from or that they exist. Developing ways to recognize what identification is and how it works is unknowingly what they are after.

This can get very messy.

Real freedom comes from catching ourselves in the act, a truly humbling experience. Catching ourselves requires the uptake of certain practices that can make us uncomfortable. No more pretending to be positive and zen like.

These practices help us wake up.

If we can endure the discomfort of watching the negativity, the subsequent awakening can be very encouraging. A new octave of transformation can begin. It starts to feel like a new lease on life.

Now some people will give spiritual transformation a go, but run away the minute they touch upon a glimmer of the dark side. It is too painful and too scary. They will then seek something that will make them think they are progressing but subconsciously know it keeps them one step away from true self-discovery.

Oh the games we play with ourselves.

Suddenly, another life shock will come along that lets them know that it isn't really working. They realize they have been letting life slip by in low grade unhappiness, tolerating situations that are truly unbearable, avoiding their freedom in codependent mirages of security, and generally neglecting their own needs. They can only hide from themselves for so long before the dam breaks.

It is simply easier in the short run to stuff it into the shadows until it gets messy, very messy.

They have developed such intricate webs of self-deception that it is really difficult to find the exit door.

The specific inner work I practice and teach is a chance to experience web extrication, extreme self-acceptance which then manifests in all areas of life.

When it is right on the inside, it gets right on the outside and ironically affects all of those in the near vicinity. There is no aspect of life that will go unaffected.

Win–Win.

It isn't glitzy and it's not easy, but it works.

THE BLESSED SEASON
OF LIGHT AND DARK

I love the darkness of the winter. For me, it is a time to be quiet, spiral inward, and reflect.

I am forever perplexed by the busyness that goes with the holidays and I annually vow not to get sucked in, but I do every time, because I love to give and I love to gather with friends and loved ones. This comes in the form of music, food, dinners, gifts, and decorating.
There are a couple of weeks where I get more busy than any other time of year.

I love the much needed sparkle of lights around my very dark home in the Pacific Northwest. This has been an especially dark winter full of rain, so I can enjoy the lights of the tree and mantle with my coffee even in the morning.

I have many concerts that bring joy to so many people.

I host a Solstice lighting ceremony for the Awareness School, a Christmas Eve dinner, a Christmas brunch with immediate family and then "family Christmas" with friends on the 28th. I know it's too much, but each event brings together people that I love.

I usually collapse for a few days after that.

I make quince jelly in one weekend in November for teachers, neighbors, family and friends so I don't go out and do much shopping. I stopped that long ago.

I love to cook so these meals don't feel like a burden but more of a creative endeavor that we all get to enjoy.

I have come to realize that the most precious part is having all of my children in the house even though they steal my chargers, borrow the car and leave coffee cups all over the house. They are happy to see each other and I enjoy the back and forth banter of these creative visionaries and rebels.

It's a juggle of light and dark. It's an inner fight to remain calm against all odds. I act like it is all OK, but inside I get frustrated with the effort and then something gives way. I remember that the spirit of humanity, the hope and goodwill of our planet is based on caring and giving. Without it, we are lost.

I remember why I am running around and let go of trying to get anything done in a hurry. I accept that it took 5 hours to get errands done. I smile and strike up conversation in lines. I take advantage of traffic jams by praying. I learn to share my private spaces and hide the chargers.

I don't stress over the third grocery trip in two days for forgotten items.

I am grateful for any parking spot I can get.

When the Solstice rolls around, we as an eclectic mix of seekers gather in utter darkness in my dining room; no house lights, no outdoor lights, no cell phones to light our way. I journey deep within as I wait for the guests to fill the room while they stumble over steps, feel around for a seat, some squirming and many stomachs growling. We take in the darkness, a rare treat. We experience stillness together with no agenda except to be.

We are prepared to meet the darkness within.

The first candle lit is dramatic and the glow increases as we call in our intentions with the lighting of each candle. The star represents our personal wishes and collective prayers for humanity and burns brightly into the evening. We are witness to each other in a new way. Each year is different and each year is very sacred.

I cherish the deep reverence I have for the darkness of this special night and the community that has formed.

I wish for each of you a most blessed season of light and dark, of giving and receiving, of effort and rest.

May you find peace in your heart and joy with family and friends this season.

GO AHEAD,
PUSH MY BUTTONS

One of my mentors has a saying that goes, "if you think you are enlightened, spend some time with your family," which I recently did on a trip to Mexico for one week. I was so excited to chill out with my children and my husband in the sun, far away from work, school, stress and schedule. I wanted to call it Mexico, unplugged...

My first mistake was to expect that I was immune to this saying and that, above all, we were in need of each other's company after 4 months of not being all together. Two of my children are already in college with independent lives of their own and maneuvering their way into adulthood. We were in close quarters in a foreign country, albeit Los Cabos is more like Mexican Las Vegas where everyone speaks English and caters to the tourist. My second mistake was assuming that I would not fall prey to the issues encountered at the last family vacation rafting down the Rogue River in Oregon in even smaller quarters.

We were all excited to spend a vacation together, get some sun, swim, and enjoy each other's company. We are generally a loving family and open to each other's input... ...sort of. As the week went on, I found myself struggling not to react to certain comments and behaviors from one or more of my children. The struggle became a quest to not take things personally, to not take sides, to see into another's pain and insecurity, and to strive toward empathy. My efforts circled around understanding what was me and what was not me.

When do I ignore certain aggressive behavior and when do I call someone on it. This led to questioning whether someone else's behavior actually was aggressive and aimed toward me, or was that my delusion?

Could my husband help me verify if I was delusional or not? Does anyone else see this going on? Am I in my own world, imagining the subterranean interaction between myself and different members of the family? Passive aggression, scapegoats, black sheeps, projection... .Tumbling down the rabbit hole of questions, analysis, irritation, and inner reaction has to come to a head at some point, either processed internally or spewed out ineffectively in the wrong places. This boiling point became clear to all of us at dinner in a restaurant. Unfortunately for innocent bystanders, who only needed to observe our body language and decibel level, it was also clear.

Perhaps the mistake for all of us was the inability to communicate effectively in a way that feelings were expressed without being tainted by resentment and blame. It was all loaded statements and smoking guns. How do we get around this, because in the end we really know we love each other even if in the moment it doesn't feel like it.

Sometimes the boiling point enables us to say what we have not been able to say, only very ineffectively. It gives us a chance to see our anger and perhaps get closer to what the real feelings that we have been suppressing are. An angry intercourse can bring out resentment in both parties and for me in this case the only way to wriggle out was to remember to sense my body. Somehow that jerked my feelings into place or at least made me aware of them period.

That is a scary place and requires pride to move aside: another difficulty in said environment.

As I struggled with my own pride and stubbornness, and struggle to sense my body, I could hear for just a brief moment the plea of the other person, the need for him to be heard, the need to be understood and the requirement of me to get out of the way of my habitual associations and beliefs. My children know exactly how to push my buttons, so I am on guard and at this point the guard needed to be let down. I have usually chosen ferocity in the lion's den as a means to skirt around my feelings but that is not what it felt like this time. This new gained sense of other allowed my defensiveness and anger to dissipate and yet allowed me to express the feelings I needed to express.

Alone in my bedroom where I could truly let down my guard in the aftermath, I became a reduction of tears and remorse in which I realized the hideous webs we weave with each other. I saw the prison of pattern our parents hand down which we so unconsciously pass on. I wallowed in remorse for the way I have been raised, for the love I did not get, for the heroic attempts I have made to overcome that upbringing, for the probable overcompensation I have done and worse, the failed avoidance of perpetuating the same thing.

In the end, I must face myself and hold myself accountable for what is mine, realizing that other family members are also struggling with the same thing. If I am the victim of blame and feel it is unjustified, my buttons are pushed. If someone reminds me that I am just like the person I have worked hard not to be like, my buttons are pushed.

If I recognize that I am not that person and never could be, I begin to remove that fear. If I recognize someone's situation and have empathy for their feelings, see into their accusations, accept my part in the interaction and have enough distance to question what is not mine, there is a chance for reconciliation and healing.

Perhaps Mexico unplugged meant a chance for some key interactions to occur. Ones which may not necessarily have been pleasant, but ones that brought us closer to each other by way of expressing and understanding each other's pain. It got us closer to unraveling the great mystery of human relations, family ties, and moving through barriers with those we have chosen to be with on this Earth this go around.

It forced us to face a strong undercurrent which had been pulling us further apart. We were unplugged from the myriad of vehicles that keep us distracted from each other, ourselves and our feelings. We only had each other as checks and balances in a delicate ebb and flow of connection, self-preservation and fear. We got sun, swimming and much much more than we bargained for.

THE LAUNCH

I am in the midst of an online launch and that may not mean anything to those who are unfamiliar with the concept.

I laugh because I hear my husband, who works for a large company, talk about launches all the time. Basically, it is fundamentally a very hectic and demanding process.

For an online launch however there is a stage of letting people know about your service or upcoming course over the period of a month or so. There are posts and ads and contacting individuals about said upcoming event, all the while, behind the scenes, I am working technically to put all of the moving parts together.

Producing a course online looks easier than it is and for the technically challenged, it can sometimes feel like a nightmare. Thank goodness I have help with that. Even small changes for an image block or logo size can take time. Last night I spent an hour on what my assistant came in and did in 5 minutes. Oh well, that is why I have tech support.

I mostly focus on the content: content that reflects a lifetime of work, both my personal evolution and my work with others. It is the perfect balance of an introduction to ideas of how to work spiritually, and material that can be used over and over for long periods of time. Each module has a theme or idea that one can delve into for a week to get the feet wet or a month or more to actually discover what it really does. It is designed to be a course to do over and over in order to grow each time.

There are so many paths of transformation and what I have found about this particular method I use is that it is absolutely practical. I am teaching concrete ways to find out what mindfulness actually is, what presence actually consists of and how to go about working with it. It is the only method I have found that goes into such depth about using attention beyond thought energy and why that can take you out of your thought prison.

For most of us, we try to use the very thing that got us into trouble in the first place... thought.

When you strengthen attention and awareness, it feeds into the ability to see into our suffering from a new place. This Self-observation leads to self-acceptance. I must say over and over that it is difficult to observe oneself. There is no end to strengthening this practice, but I have never found methods that teach how until I came across Ouspensky many years ago. I subsequently found a teacher who taught me the ways of this particular kind of integrated awareness.

What is rare is to find a living teaching of transmission that uses these methods.

I have encountered practices of other sorts and delved into spiritual schools that asked me to open my heart, but there was so much in the way that I couldn't.

Having someone show me how to have enough presence to look inside and pull things out of the shadows simply by not pushing away the negative emotions was life changing. When I could do that without judging (deeming some behavior or "feeling" as bad or good), I could actually begin to see what lay behind these ridiculous traps of self-pity and self-importance, blame and guilt.

If we can learn the fundamentals of attention, expanded awareness, and presence, we build up a safe container to see. We don't have to change anything, just see it. That is real acceptance.

Having said all this, a course that will get one started on these fundamentals can change lives forever. It becomes a lifetime of work that yields results.

It is the gift that keeps on giving, but it isn't always pretty or easy. That is when we know it is an effective spiritual practice.

There is work involved and we must want it.

We must be backed up against a wall so that it speaks to us.

Perhaps we have had enough of the self-destructive behaviors we cannot stop.

Perhaps we are tired of feeling isolated and alone in our suffering.

Perhaps things are just bad enough that this peaks our curiosity.

Our usual first line of defense is to numb the symptoms through distraction, overworking, and denial. This comes in the form of addiction to food, alcohol, sex, drugs and sports to self-improvement and exercise. Wanting to be better, wanting to masque the pain, and wanting to escape will catch up with us.

Maybe we know deep inside that something really isn't working and it is time to find practices that reveal the truth of how we are living.

The beauty of it is that each week, we do a group meeting with people from all over the world and share and see that we all have so much in common. Together we can go very very far. An individual practicing the sacred wisdom of masters is powerful; a group practicing it is profound beyond all measure.

THE POWER OF A WOMEN'S GROUP

When seeking transformation, the power of a group cannot be underestimated. Let's face it, we are more effective together than competing or working on our own. We live in an ever growing atmosphere of isolation and fear. We don't go out as much to do anything and we are not connecting face to face. It is important for us to remember the beauty of coming together.

From small organizations and businesses to women's gatherings and spiritual groups, we have the chance to experience what it means to work together. When we gather toward a common goal, intent on allowing each to contribute to the whole, we gain more force than our own individual efforts can produce.

I have experienced the extraordinary phenomenon of accelerated transformation through participation in and facilitation of group retreats over the last 20 years. One of the purposes of the Awareness School retreats is to allow people to understand what happens when people gather to meditate and work mindfully together. Something more happens to all of us simply because of the group. If a magnetic center is formed in a group that has been together for a while, a distinct momentum affects everyone.

My motivation for writing this piece is to speak about the magic that happens when women gather. This can happen in something as informal as a Mom's group or a book club.

I have just finished an extraordinary long weekend with my mastermind women's group: a set of powerful women leaders coming together for support, transformation and healing.

We are diverse yet hold a common thread of spiritual women in business for themselves: each involved in sacred commerce, a term I learned from the book, Sacred Commerce.

Their definition of this term is: the party-cipation of the community in the exchange of products, information, and services that contribute to the revealing of the Divine (i.e. beauty, goodness, and truth) in all, and where spirituality — the return to the Self — is the bottom line.

Along with this common aim of sacred commerce, we understand the bottom line to our success is through mutual support. This not only refers to business, but also personal transformation. Healing the bond between women that has been fractured by the Patriarchy is also an important aspect of our time together.

When women gather, there is a magical feel to it and some women even gather for the purpose of magic itself. Our culture has long condemned this ancient ritual connected with nature and the rhythm of the moon. The practice of women gathering holds the power of healing the wounds of history when women were burned at the stake for being midwives, healers and psychics. We were taught that it was dangerous to practice ancient arts in circle. We were taught to compete. We were taught that to be successful we must do it at the expense of others. We were taught to go underground.

Mostly we were taught that it is unsafe to heed the call to gather. Something inherent in our nature. We began to sow the seeds of dysfunction between mothers and daughters.

We forgot to trust one another.

The power of women gathering at this time is to sever our connection with a dark past. Through support and love in circle, we rectify the mother wounds and the sister wounds. As one of us accepts and sees the pain of the past, we all face what is locked in our deepest selves.

What we do for the one, we do for all.

Many years ago I was in circle with women to celebrate the spiritual wheel of the year. We studied the significance of nature on our psyche and our connection to it. We made things together, sang songs, and created family gatherings that pertained to the seasons. The mere fact that we would meet monthly, listen to each other's stories of birth, death, and relationship, created a strong bond. Moreover, this little family, like my new mastermind today, was able to bring back important elements of what women have done for centuries.

We are now reclaiming our power to sit at the table equally with our brothers who are also learning a new way. The patriarchy is crumbling and our men need only hold the door in protection and love to support this in happening. We will walk through the door with ease and grace to take our place at that table.

We are all learning to hold each other up, to see the gifts of the other and to hold each other in reverence and acceptance rather than competing. This is not the rise of women into power over men. This is the emancipation of women all over the world to stand equally with men, so that together we are co-creators of a new world where war and dominion are a thing of the past.

I AM NOT YOUR TYPICAL MEDITATION TEACHER

The fact that I come from a troubled background has most likely shaped who I am and why I do what I do. I sought ways to relieve my pain and confusion, my isolation and my fear. I wondered as a kid how I got myself in such an unsatisfying situation. I remember feeling so sorry for myself when I looked around and was convinced that everyone else had it so much better. I just knew that some people had loving families and Moms that came to their rescue. I was probably seething with jealousy and I took it upon myself to be tough, to be invincible, and to not let things get to me.

I hid the pain of years of abuse that came at me from all angles, from a creepy perverted teacher who sexually abused me to absentee parents, plus a healthy dose of criticism that I took to heart.

Perhaps the most amazing revelation as a result of Fourth Way practices was actually hearing and seeing the critical monster within me for what it was.

I realized early on that music was my saving grace. I could find love there without the pesky human contact. It filled my soul the way no human possibly could. I chose to go into a career of high level performance probably so someone would notice me and my good deeds. At the same time, I did love sharing and being part of such profound beauty.

I am a classical pianist, something that takes discipline and commitment.

How commendable!

The problem was that everything looked great from the outside but nothing was right on the inside. The self-bashing, the fear of not being good enough, the love affair with perfectionism and proving myself, and the reputation to uphold became too much for me.

All the while, my other dark side fed on drugs, sex and... well not rock and roll. I could not have been a better example of a living contradiction. I am sure many of you can relate to this.

I found meditation and yoga blended in a unique combination at a dojo in Paris where I was engaged in high level studies. Even after 6 years of this, I couldn't feel the love outside of that dojo. All of that was a means to "fix myself" and yes it helped tremendously. It curbed the sharp edge of anxiety and fear, but I was still living a lie and it bothered me.

When I found the Fourth Way work, I learned how to live life and recognize the lie through practices done out in everyday life not just on a cushion in silence. I was "Zenning out" as in motorcycle maintenance and more. I was out there in the trenches living the practices and learning who I really was.

It brought me to a kind of freedom that I believe made me fearless in the wake of what previously seemed insurmountable. I could grapple with that part of me that needed to "fix me." I learned how to have a truly fulfilling relationship after so many false starts and relentless boundary benders.

I learned how to stand in the face of all the shit that came my way and not let it get to me. That was the new invincible me that really could stand aside, wave my red cape in front of the bull, balance the tightrope of promise, and dive with surrender into what is.

I could play music without the baggage of needing approval and recognition. I began to play for the sake of personal expression and giving from the heart.

So this is why the typical notion of a meditation teacher "oming it up" in zen like fashion for all to see is not really me.

I dance in the kitchen and even video it for social media to keep myself in check, to challenge the notion that I care what others think of me, to remain a free spirit against all odds.

These practices enabled me to get out of my OWN world and my own depression and begin to love life.

When I do things that show that I don't care about what other people think - it's very freeing.

I don't believe that meditation has to be all about stillness on a cushion though I absolutely do that every day.

Sitting makes room for the God part in me to be recognized and so does practicing presence out in life - it all translates to living life more fully.

None of us have to sacrifice who we are to do this work. It is about how to live life and not get bothered by it.

I AM

_____

Purely and simply.
I am a Mom.
I am a daughter.
I am a pianist.
I am a wife.
I am a teacher.
I am a mentor.
I am a friend.
I am a sister to many.

I am so many things and yet when I look within, above and beyond, I am a deeper essence, something much more. My journey is to discover and remain present with that part of me.

I get in trouble when I believe things should be a certain way or my behavior needs to reflect a certain role. What are my roles? What are my "beliefs"? Do I have a sense of being separate from those beliefs?

In order to do anything well, we as humans must be invested and identified with a role, however, that is also what gets us into trouble.

We can be identified with things like being perfect, being strong, being evolved, being spiritual, being productive and behind that identification comes the underlying chief feature of I'm not enough or I need to be loved..

We also get mired in mechanical patterns of self-destructive behavior in order to live out identification with self-hatred. We learn ways to shut down to keep ourselves from seeing the contradiction within us.

We see only the negative results of our behavior and can't figure out how we got there.

We often experience our inability to extract ourselves from negative emotion.

Negative states are the hallmark of identification and a good red flag to help us notice that we are indeed hooked.

Here's what I do: when I find myself in a state of anxiety, disgruntled and short fused, I know right away that it is a result of identification with something. I set out to discover through bringing sensation to my body just exactly what it is. I don't necessarily have to stop what I am doing. I simply bring sensation into the picture as a measure to see something outside of my habitual scope.

I also don't push that negativity away. I remain in the yes and no of it. I strive to be present enough and separated enough to watch and observe it without trying to change it. This feels like a subtle inner effort. It is the struggle to get free by going against my desire to get rid of said "bad state." Instead, I abide in the negative thoughts and feelings, watching what my body senses, listening to the thoughts that swirl, and perceiving the flavor of this state. With this effort, something melts.

The fact that I have woken up enough to even try to struggle with the negative emotion means something is changing. Otherwise, I remain locked in my self-pity or my guilt until something wakes me up, until things feel so bad that I am desperate to find a way out. If I don't find a way around the "story," I simply accept that and know that I have tried my hardest. On some level, something has changed just because I am being present with it, but I may not perceive the immediate results.

We can carry things like being offended for many days, hanging on to a moment in the past when we took something very personally. We can even live years in that situation, resenting and blaming. We rest in our comfort zone of blame instead of taking responsibility for our own feelings and states of identification.

This is not an easy process. Our first inclination is to get rid of a negative state through some kind of distraction. We want the good and fight the bad with tooth and nail as if it shouldn't belong.

The irony here is that the more we hide from it and push it away, the more it rears its ugly head and we find ourselves in a conundrum.

So be conscious of what follows your I am statements. Let it be a cue. 'I am' can precede an array of negative emotions, self-constructed stories, and hopeful aspirations. 'I am' can precede spoken affirmations that never take flight.

If our behavior contradicts that said image of self, we falter and fall into false states of negativity. We are unable to resolve the contradiction in ourselves. We rely on "buffers" like blame, guilt and self-justification to keep ourselves from having to see that contradiction. I am angry. I am frustrated. I am guilty. I am justified in my anger. The very 'I am' in which we are deeply rooted results in our illusory world of suffering and we get very very stuck. We cannot forgive. We block ourselves from ourselves and thus from everyone else.

The only way out is to acknowledge this state of identification. We must learn how to become present enough to catch ourselves identified. Observing our "I am" brings brutal self-honesty into the picture. If we have been weaving the web of deception long enough, it will seem almost impossible to do this.

All the walls that have been cleverly built will have to come down.

Begin with the simple practice of noticing when you say I am and what follows that statement. For example, I am tired may have a certain flavor of "poor me" and that is what we must catch. We catch it by noticing the small things first, then gradually uncovering the bigger underlying story.

ACCELERATED TRANSFORMATION

Group work, a practice of the Fourth Way, creates accelerated transformation.

The first line of work is work on oneself, for which we must all take responsibility.

The second line, group work, accelerates individual transformation because of the collection of energy that is formed by the efforts of the group. The efforts of many contribute to a whole, thus raising all boats in the tide.

Joining a group each week to share our work and witness each other's observations offers a chance for deep humility and brutal self-honesty. We feel accountable to each other in this setting. This accountability factor keeps us all going.

Each person's offering does not have to get extremely personal either. We simply need to bring what we observed about ourselves in concrete examples and specific situations. These are not memories or analysis of something after the fact. There are no opinions being thrown about, no suggestions, and no theoreticals.

Our aim is to be objective, seeing in real time in a present moment. The trick is to catch ourselves not in the present. The telltale signs of reaction, blame, projection and self-justification are opportunities to take action with newly developed methods of attention. What we bring to the meeting is exactly what we noticed in that present moment. It is never hindsight. We don't define or label, just present the facts.

This is not easy and it requires the practice of taking in impressions objectively.

There is something very special and poignant about witnessing other people's present moments. Not only do we learn what a present moment looks like, but we enter into that person's present moment in a way that affects us. Their present moment is our present moment. Everyone gets better and better at it as we go along, and thus we bond in ways that are unusual and extremely beneficial.

When we all contribute, we get a tenfold acceleration of results. Things start to move very quickly. One person begins to say what another person needs to hear. Another becomes a reflection for what the other needs to learn.

Working in a group can also sometimes rub someone the wrong way, precisely the perfect time to observe what is actually going on within themselves. That pesky human contact, irritation and impatience becomes grist for the mill.

Even when people come together for a short time, a matrix is formed so that one person's energy completes part of the wheel. We can move as one through a process. We find a new and fresh set of conditions from which to learn.

Finally, we learn something about service and contributing to a whole. It is not all take and no give. It is not all about our own progress. Our progress becomes a contribution unto itself.

This fits into the third line of work, Work for the Work.

THE SPIRITUAL ALCHEMY OF GIVING SOMETHING UP

Inner friction is a way to facilitate transformation. It is the spiritual alchemy of giving something up. It turns lead into gold.

This is not a new idea.

Every religion includes practices to create this environment of purposeful resistance within oneself. The aim of each is to grapple with our lower nature.

Mr. Gurdjieff called it Conscious Labor and Intentional Suffering.

The most common form of this practice is fasting. Working with any of our obvious addictions can bring us face to face with the subtleties of the subversive tactics of our ego. Our addiction to self-importance and superiority can be just as dangerous as dependance on drugs, food, or alcohol.

In fact, things that seem "moral" may be a worse addiction, promoting an illusion of self and pushing our uglier parts into the dark recesses of our psyche. The stronger our addiction to "self-improvement," to being positive, to being "good," to being enlightened, holy, pure, successful, and intact, the further we get away from our essence. This is called spiritual pride.

Initially working with something simple can be the best tactic.

Having grown up in the Episcopal church, I have maintained a tradition of giving up small things during Lent. Even though I spend all my days aiming toward intentional inner friction within myself, I get especially ramped up for the Lenten season.

Forty days of anything will yield mega results unless we have chosen something that is too easy. The nature of our choice should require inner struggle.

Giving up alcohol, sugar, morning coffee, going out to eat, netflix, internet or any other beloved habit can be extremely effective.

What about giving up complaining or doling out opinions? If we are quick to speak and not listen, how about not talking until someone asks us a question?

Adding a discipline like meditation, exercise, stopping for a brief pause on the hour is also recommended.

Adding a daily gratitude practice can be life changing.

As the struggle crops up, the importance is to recognize the struggle of opposing forces within ourselves. Becoming aware of sensation in our body while the struggle is happening will open our eyes to phenomena that may exist behind the actual addiction/discipline.

Work of this sort becomes the gateway to a flood of new impressions.

That is how we learn about ourselves and feed our consciousness. The more we begin to see, the closer we get to accepting our mechanical nature. We know much more vividly how it operates. We experience our own prison.

In a way, things can seem worse before they get better when we see "the terror of the situation," but it is the only way through. We can't do it by not seeing. We can't continue to numb ourselves into oblivion. We hide in our identification with what is good or bad, for instance, with being a nice person, or with being disciplined in a practice, or with pleasing others.

... And the same goes when we struggle with a more obvious addiction.

This is why in my courses, in my mentoring and in my groups, we work with doing things we don't like. We start with small practices and work our way up to seeing how we act so inauthentically.

Acting inauthentically is often concurrent with doing what we like and staying in a comfort zone. That comfort zone may be persistent self-loathing, self-bashing, guilt and shame.

I wish us all strength and courage in our choices for the 40 day period. Even the smallest struggle reaps great benefits and prepares us for the deep dive!

RELIEF, RELEASE AND GRATITUDE

This morning, relaxed with my coffee, I sit on the brink of tears, poised in the place of wonder and awe, relief and unfolding. It is a poignant feeling of relief, release, and GRATITUDE.

I attempt to describe the vibration in my body, the presence, a subtle joy and a quiet satisfaction, not elation, not a high, but a feeling after a big push of effort.

Though I am still creating the final modules of my ecourse and far from done, the people are here. I am running 3 groups simultaneously, plus counseling one on one. I think back to when I had 2 people in my living room many many years ago. I did not give up even though it felt hopeless.

I think back to the many times a particular group would spontaneously dissolve and I wondered if I should have quit when out of nowhere a new one would form in its place. This is the healthy nature of groups I have discovered. If they last for a long time with the same members, things involute and become very very stagnant.

I have held the space consistently for 15 years with a group ebbing and flowing, giving even those two people at one point everything I could because they wanted to be there. I have held movements classes with small attendance. I have held the faith.

After twenty years I have learned to trust my vision to build a global community of people who practice the profound ways of Presence so that their hearts can open, so that they can show up and be of service to themselves, their families and the planet.

It is a chance to experience community on a very deep level where love abounds. I cannot help but say it is the microcosm of the way things could be for all of us.

Somehow I stumbled upon a way, a teaching, a vehicle that was so far reaching beyond anything I had ever seen, that still to this day, it is still yielding results for me. I have gone on many a reconnaissance mission to keep myself up to date, informed and even on the search for new ideas. In the end, I fall back to these principles that have taken me to places I never imagined.

The retreats which I facilitate continue to provide profound experiences. The energies collect there for those present as we journey through our individual path together in consistent effort over a concentrated period of time. It is something we can aspire to in regular life, but there is nothing to describe what reaches us deep in our hearts on these retreats. We create a container that assists this heart opening.

When I think of the beauty in my life, the moments of feeling deep meaning and purpose, I recall various retreats where I tapped into something eternal. Those occurrences will always be with me, like a forever living moment, not a memory. It is what I long for others to experience. It was these moments that made me realize that life has so much more to offer than we realize.

I continue to hold the vision of a month to 3 month long retreat on a big property that I own (hopefully where it is warm) where people can learn a way of life.

I knew when my heart burst open long ago and I stepped in sync with The Beloved that my path to share "the how," as my teachers did for me, was a reality.

Today I stand in utter gratitude for my own persistence and vision and for those who have shown me the way. I realize the profound importance this Work has in the world. It is a teaching that runs through a lineage of those who sense the baraka. I am thanking those who are showing up at this time and in the future, to receive the transmission, and then pass it on.

My husband and I realized last night that there are 3 groups running simultaneously and I bow my head, hands together, in hopes that I may be an effective vehicle for this information.

I look back at the long road from whence I have come and I feel relief, release and gratitude. Big Gratitude.

PAST, PRESENT, AND FUTURE

Why are we so compelled to know about our future or our past?

Truly the majority of us have no access to what has happened or will happen, and so we pay big bucks for everything future and everything past, looking for answers to our big questions about us in the present.

It's true that no one is really asking about now, and I have my theories about that.

We believe we already know about now. We believe we know who we are and how we operate.

This is the big elephant in the room. It isn't easy to convince anyone they don't know what's really behind their behavior. No one wants to know because we think we already know. In fact, when we do want to know it's usually when things really aren't going well.

No wiggle room and backed into a corner... there is a need.

The irony here is that most of the time the things that get us truly upset are a result of the illusions we need to demystify simply by being here and now. If we can discover how much choice, control, presence and cognition we do not have, then we start to become aware of what is really causing all the suffering and how we hide from it.

We feel that if we can articulate some feeling or theory about what makes us suffer then we understand it, yet we continue to suffer.

This is the danger of assuming we know what is going on in the present moment.

We know we don't know past lives and we know we don't know the future, but we are absolutely convinced we don't need to know how to really be in the now.

If only there were some way to convey that the more we are in the now, the more we know about our past, present and the future.

With the experience of now, we can break the chain of perpetual abuse and alienation. We can unlock the code in our DNA. We can repair the suffering of lifetimes with the realization of the present and prepare everything to be of conscious choice in the future.

Experiencing the profundity of the present moment was called hyparxis by Mr. John Bennett: a place outside of the time space continuum where things can heal. This experience of hyparxis is where the unlock from patterns of the past occurs and propels us into a future of freedom.

With freedom, big freedom, comes the recognition of realms outside of time and space.

Who needs to work toward that when we can pay someone to tell us?

I have found that any notion or intuition of my past lives was more valuable when I saw it for myself. I definitely couldn't do that before I had done massive amounts of work in the present.

What good does it do to know we were a conquistador in Spain or a great painter or someone who died from childbirth or someone who drowned. It may explain present fears or desires, but what is wrong with accepting the fear and dealing with it in the here and now without knowing from whence it came. The fact that it is a result of another life or a long chain of ancestors passing it on through DNA makes no difference when we must deal with it karmically in this life. Only knowing it in our present moment will truly achieve the transformation we are seeking.

Does knowing past lives somehow give us license to feel and act a certain way? Does it really help us to understand why we do what we do or does it get in the way of understanding how to deal with it in this lifetime.

Let's look at knowing about the future. Does it taint our perspective? Does it help influence us to make better decisions? Again I have to ask what good is it to know what will potentially happen? (emphasis on potential because everything is in potentiality). Perhaps it is simply to satiate our curiosity and it's fun. Perhaps it takes the place of us having to discriminate for ourselves.

Now truthfully, I am fascinated by divination, crystal balls and messages from different mediums. I believe we all have guides and angels by our sides that we can access through presence. We can get information in so many ways, but without the clear understanding of presence within ourselves, we will have a hard time repairing the past and preparing the future.

FOURTH WAY RETREATS

Many profound and life changing moments of my life have occurred at meditation retreats centered around The Fourth Way. These methods spun out of the idea that we can work "in the world" as opposed to retreating from the world. It is called the Fourth Way because it is not just the way of the fakir, transformation through the body, nor of the monk who uses prayer and contemplation of the heart, nor of the Yogi who practices the stilling the mind.

The Fourth Way combines all three methods through various means to be done in everyday life.

"It has no specific forms or institutions and comes and goes controlled by some particular laws of its own."

–G. I. Gurdjieff

Learning attention by using three functions, the moving center, the emotional center, and the thinking center simultaneously is a primary tool of the Fourth Way. Separately these "brains" have their own way of behaving. Together they can allow me to gain perspective about myself that otherwise stays compartmentalized and unseen. I can begin to recognize the many "I"s in my life. One part of me will sabotage another part of me. This is what creates conflict and distress within me.

P. D. Ouspensky, a proponent of The Fourth Way and student of G.I. Gurdjieff, described our fragmented self as a house in which you could only turn on the lights in one room at a time. As my work progressed, more and more rooms could be lit at the same time. Having a true Observer meant the lights were on in all the rooms. This will give me separation from my ego's ridiculous reactions.

I acquire an Observer that can see these various parts.

When I have an Observer, it is more possible to laugh at my ego's antics. I have traction in non reaction. I have more choice. I begin to understand what causes my suffering.

If I am unaware of what causes my anxiety, fear, anger and stress, I will continue to treat the symptoms. No amount of anger expression will cure the anger source. I may have an idea intellectually of these causes but until I am in circumstances which allow me to truly see, I can change nothing.

Retreats based in Fourth Way practices can provide ways to experience the three centers while doing regular activities. How does that benefit me?

I can learn how to recognize and distinguish more precisely which of these functions, my body, my emotions or my thinking are in operation. This may seem simple but it isn't. What I think is my emotion may be my thinking and until I see that, I cannot understand why I am triggered or why I get aggravated and angry. Uncovering this can be the unlock to many of my reactions. I can recognize the crux of my problems: identification with my thoughts.

Self-study in an environment which intentionally sets up conditions for me to experience this makes it easier to recreate that when I get home.

When I can develop the capacities of each one of these centers simultaneously, another force comes into play. I access a clearer picture, seeing what causes the war within myself. I begin to have control over my actions and what affects me.

Doing meditation, the Gurdjieff Movements, zikr, and presence practices together for a time is the formula of The Fourth Way retreat. Each one of these methods refines one of the faculties. Meditation is for the Mind. The Movements require my physical attention but also my emotions and my thinking. Zikr or chanting opens my heart.

Consistent effort over a week with others will provide a more refined energy from which to see these three centers in action. It also accelerates the transformation of each individual.

I can experience discipline in a way that I may not be able to enforce for myself. When I get a taste of this specific kind of Work, I start to have a visceral, emotional, and mental understanding. This gives me a reference for how to work at home.

HERE COMES
THE JUDGE

My judgement of anything, be it my body, my actions, my situation, my status, my income, my partner are the way I separate myself from myself and others. It is the energy of thought always having to evaluate whether something is right or wrong in my eyes.

I am so conditioned to evaluate in this way that I am seemingly not affected by it. I no longer know it is happening. Even my slightest thought about how my body isn't in shape is the energy of separation. I am no longer in the now of my body and its experience.

Ironically, I use judgement as a safety mechanism from connection. I measure up how things are for what good reason? To see if things are good or bad in my book? I may call it "evaluation," but in disguise it is judgement even when I say something is great.

When things are relegated to being either good or bad, I have left my Being behind. No longer integrated, I must make accounts as to whether this fits into my picture of the way things should be.

By judging others, I separate myself from connection and love. I cannot accept the way things are and I become negative. I believe someone should not have acted in the way they did. Someone did not appreciate me enough. Someone has acted poorly and I must point that out even if only to myself.

This habitual capture of energy and attention from my "formatory apparatus" (a term used by G.I. Gurdjieff) keeps me from discrimination, an act involving empathy and connection to others and myself. With presence to this judgement, I can more clearly know what course of action to take.

When I sit with judgement and experience its energy, I gain a perspective of higher consciousness, I immediately sense the fear. I understand that my judgement is a strategy to separate myself out of fear of connection. That connection is ironically threatening and unfamiliar and so I make it so. I solidify my position of isolation as real.

It seems so counterintuitive that I am a slave to the mechanism that keeps me separate from my Being. I don't want to be separate. I want to think that I am so connected.

I believe I want to be connected, but my actions say and do otherwise without my knowledge of the habit to which they are accustomed.

Whether I was steeped in healthy doses of criticism as a child or not, I seem to take up the practice out of sheer necessity because of where I live in my thoughts. Only thought energy produces fear when it cannot control. When the energy of connection and love enter, the thinking is relegated to its proper place and it fears its loss of control.

The power of connection and acceptance breaks the barriers I have formed over a lifetime. It seems as if it is overwhelmingly powerful, like a mighty storm. When I surrender to this Love, I know God and I do not try to control that. It is a moment of holding attention and letting go at the same time.

I watch the judgement from all parts of me in a simultaneous convergence of curious questioning, and suddenly spiral into knowing it shouldn't be there. I realize that judgement of my judging has crept in again. I watch the whirlpool of struggle between accepting what is and judging the inability to do so until something gives way.

I know the resistance is too much to bear. I want to let go because I know it is wrong and yet I realize the desire to change the state and calling it wrong is a result of judging. If I can accept my judging and evaluating honestly, sincerely, and wholeheartedly, I begin to see the fear.

This is the fear of surrender to love and connection because it threatens my habitual home of separation. It feels like the eye of the hurricane and the seed of my discomfort and at the same time, my wish is to let go of this fear.

If I can sit with my judgement on every level, I can feel that deep resistance.

I remain confused and unknowing but with my attention placed on observing from a new awareness not possible from my thinking or my emotions or my body, I remember God.

I remember that I Am.

This newfound Presence leads to ultimate connection on a Being level and I let go.

I forgive.

I am able to accept what is.

THE LAW OF THREE

The Law of Three is represented by the triangle in sacred geometry and can help us understand process. We can use it effectively in any decision, manifestation, and means to self-transformation. In any given situation, we have 2 forces present, but for something to come to fruition, it must have three.

Looking at the triangle, we have a reciprocal relationship at either end of each of the lines and unification in regard to the three elements.

The enneagram displays the Law of Three in which the triangle represents the three forces.

When looking at the enneagram, the triangle inside of a circle represents intervals in a forward moving process where forces come into play from the outside. If those forces do not enter, the process veres in a different direction or fizzles out. This incoming force is what propels it forward and represents reception from something higher.

At these points of reception or conscious shock, the higher works on the lower to activate the middle. This is applied at certain intervals, and you can have an infinite number of inner triangles occurring as a process proceeds. (This is why I love the image of fractal triangles).

Within the Law of Three, the forces are known as the active force, the passive force and the reconciling force. We can work this into any situation to help us understand the need to take more action or the need to let go and receive, but the balance of both brings about the manifestation or the reconciliation of those two forces.

Working with this concept by trial and error is a great way to get to know how it works. Watching the struggle within ourselves and seeing how it resolves or doesn't is a way of noticing whether the third force is present.

If we are unable to hold the contradiction of yes and no (the two forces) within us through attention, we cannot experience the reconciliation known as the third force.

In staying with the yes and the no, we may find empathy where there was none. We may be able to follow through with our aim when there was no motivation before. We may be able to let go of some form of false control that kept us from accepting ourselves. Once these things occur, we are on the next segment of the process.

We can look at it as the alchemy which brings us to presence and self-remembering; certain almost inexplicable things happen at these special intervals.

Our ability to hold attention to our struggle will bring about the first shock (bottom right corner of triangle) and our ability to hold the attention much longer will bring about the second shock (bottom left corner of triangle). Without these shocks, we return to the beginning of the process and repeat.

One thing is certain, the meaning of conscious labor is the ability to hold attention to our struggle. Pushing away negative self-talk, for example, is not staying with the struggle of observing it in which we experience it in a new way. Our staying ability becomes the food by which we feed our consciousness. It is an opposing force.

We begin to experience what the third force really means when we can stay with the struggle.

We can also apply this law to stages of freedom.

There is an alchemical process that creates a secondary body to ground and house permanent development of our Being. When this body is formed, we begin work in a new octave from a higher center. This new octave is represented as a point on the triangle.

We strengthen our Being through presence and attention from all of our centers, the body, the emotions and the thinking simultaneously. Through attention, we develop self-observation. Through self-observation we develop Presence. Through Presence we develop our Being. Each one of these elements, Attention, Presence, and Being have a reciprocal relationship that could be represented by the triangle.

The author Red Hawk uses this example in his book Self-Remembering. In this case, he puts attention in the bottom right corner, presence in the bottom left which becomes a foundation for the higher aspects of consciousness housed in our Being. Our Being also simultaneously influences both attention and presence.

He also looks at the triangle in terms of me, other and a higher source. I have a relationship with God/Source/Unity and I have a relationship with other people. My relationship with other is my foundational bottom line of the triangle and through that we become the forces working together for something higher to come in. In this case, he puts "me" on the bottom right, "other" on the bottom left and God at the top of the triangle.

This triangle also represents a process of transformation in relation to connection.

We can experience a shock or the first point of resistance as we begin the work of self-observation on ourselves. This is the bottom right point of the triangle. We must persist and at the same time allow something else to come in, in order for us to see more about ourselves and how we function in the world. As we progress, there comes a secondary shock from the outside in which we begin to see another as ourselves.

This is a new tier or "octave' in our transformation and represented by the bottom left of the triangle.

Finally, we enter the unity of God where we experience no difference between self and God, the apex of the triangle.

When we can experience this new knowledge of ourselves, it gives us the chance to better understand others. From there, we begin a life of connection.

The struggle to find our way out of isolation and into connection will bring about the third force of reconciliation where we have all three elements absolutely present. True connection involves my authentic self as a touchpoint with the authenticity of another. This is an outer manifestation of Source.

The Christian Trinity of Father Son and Holy Ghost is another great representation of the Law of Three. It brings to my mind the relationship between God, the human and the spirit unified. In this way, we are God manifest in human form. The elements of source energy, we as humans with bodies, and the intersection of spirit become a whole picture of opposing forces reconciled. We can see how the notion of the higher working on the lower to activate the middle is so applicable.

We can consider our self-remembering and the development of our soul as the middle in this scenario. It is the liaison between heaven and earth. It is where we experience our God nature. To have that, we must be fully in our body, hearts and minds with full with presence in order for the forces of God to act upon us in a new way. Our Soul then develops accordingly.

The Law of Three works as we work to incarnate. When we are experiencing the body, we begin to feel what we have been avoiding. If we combine sensation of body with noticing our thoughts simultaneously, something miraculous comes about to enable experiencing our feelings.

We experience new impressions that were imperceptible before.

Continuing to work in this way of full integration, we start to understand connection to Source on another level. This is the development of the permanent awakening of our higher centers. This is how I am you and you are me and we are God.

For me, initially the effort was simply learning to stay present with a struggle and bringing sensation into the picture. Noticing how staying with the contradiction of my many "I"s brought about a new picture which then fed my consciousness.

This is how I became familiar with the Third Force and the Law of Three.

ABIDING WITH
THE UNWANTED

Abiding with an unwanted emotion is the only way to effectively dissolve it.

If we take our negative self-talk, our "inner considering," and send it away as unwanted or find ways to ignore it, we do not learn an important process by which we gain understanding. Our struggle to rest in an uncomfortable place and watch from a witness perspective, unified in body, heart and mind will bring about impressions of a higher nature. Those new impressions are what propel us forward in our understanding of unwanted emotions.

This is what developing attention is all about. Most think it is to be more peaceful and zen like and perhaps conjures the image of someone who never has negative states or irritability. It is true that the more we work with attention and presence, the more we are unaffected. In fact, there does come a turning point where our Essence is so truly fed by attention that we no longer get attached.

Through the practice of integrated presence and abiding with the unwanted, it is possible to have less reaction and live in the flow. However, the only road to that station is through watching our emotions and negative states.

The purpose of presence is to notice the self-talk in a new way without getting attached. We may go in and out of being able to do that. We may give way to anger, our bodies filled with adrenalin, and our minds racing, but with effort toward presence and maintaining sensation, we get to build the attention muscle. Developing that muscle is the way to see in. It is the way to observe the details of this negative state so we have understanding.

When we experience this anger, we feel it as "wrong" or undesirable, so we do one of several options. Either we suppress that anger at the command of ego who believes this is not an evolved way to act, or we unconsciously repress it or we express it uncontrollably.

None of these are an effective way to deal with anger, fear, irritability, elation or any other state of attachment simply because it does not deal with the attachment aspect of it.

Now we often come to the conclusion that to express the emotion is the best possible road to take so we justify our unskillful and misdirected anger, our frustration with tiny things that don't really matter, and our excuses for doing nothing about it.

There are also schools of thought that believe intentionally expressing it, like beating a pillow or punching bag are a healthy way of getting rid of this emotion.

In this way we feel the emotion. We hold nothing back. We believe having these things that trigger us is a completely normal part of life. We express and express wondering where all this is coming from. We justify our behavior in thousands of ways and we blame others constantly for the way we feel or the way we are dissatisfied.

I propose something very different in my school of transformation. It is a method I learned in a Fourth Way school that was so effective in dissipating these states and for seeing into what is actually causing them.

First of all, as long as we remain captured by the automatic functioning of emotion rather than consciously feeling, we will always be slave to these negative states. To be conscious is to have a choice not to react before it happens, but this takes a lot of practice. That developed practice leads to empathy with self and others.

The first line of defense is to stay in the negative state and simply watch it without trying to analyse why it is happening.

One problem with mindfulness and meditation and spirituality is that we often use it to not feel. We think being in the now is being able to push it away or have one part of us talk down another part of us. Our clever ego finds ways of convincing us that we are in fact observing these thoughts when in fact we are simply experiencing conflicting aspects of ourselves warring with each other.

We think mindfulness means not having states like this. We use meditation as a means to escape instead of facing the attachment.

I want to help us all understand that this is a slow road full of pitfalls. We will notice that our ups and downs often get bigger because we are working hard to get rid of the low state. I realize that there are many who have serious depression and could not push that away even if they wanted to. There is total consumption of the attention in these cases.

However, it is possible to begin practices that will develop attention so keenly that we can dismantle these negative states. We go through the madness instead of getting rid of it somehow.

When we find ourselves overcome with anger or anxiety, we must cook in it. We can acknowledge it and feel it, but we do not have to express it. This creates a conscious struggle within us. We build an observer by staying with the abusive self-talk and listening from a new perspective. By observing, we discover so much of it is the thinking analyzing, comparing, and retrieving memory. In other words, we have to observe from something else other than the very thinking which created it.

Not expressing it might look like not yelling at your mate, not complaining, not arguing to prove you are right and most especially bearing the unpleasant manifestations of others.

Allowing ourselves to watch the emotion while maintaining the awareness of body sensation, and listening to the thoughts and feeling the emotion is an effective strategy. We don't suppress or repress or express. We experience the state from a new perspective if we have practiced intentionally maintaining sensation of the body in easier situations.

I cannot tell you how many times I have been at a point inside where central command is yelling "Houston, we have a problem, but we don't know what it is or how to deal with it."

At this time, I watch it with utmost curiosity trying not to yell or react but acknowledge on the inside that I feel like doing that, that I am angry and that I am now taking in all details. Where is my body tight? What are my racing thoughts actually saying? What are the emotions I am actually feeling? The reaction feels justified. How can I struggle to stay with it without expressing it. This is being in the yes and the no.

It takes a tremendous amount of practice before the attention is developed enough to hold an impression objectively in the yes and the no. This is the beauty of practicing presence.

Presence, however, is also a very misunderstood thing. Many of us think we are being mindful if we are here and now with thought. We try to escape the negative state by sending it away through imagination or visualization. This is still in the thinking realm and will not allow us to understand and observe the state fully.

If we can learn to observe the state fully, it dissipates on its own. Our Essence is now watching it, not our attached personality, and we are able to feel. Each time we do this even for a glimpse, our attention feeds our Essence instead of the parts of us that are pulled all over the place. What we feed grows.

I encourage you to develop this specific kind of attention. The goal is not always to feel peaceful, though it is an end result down the line. The goal is to notice the negativity as a result of all kinds of unconscious shenanigans. To do that, you cannot push the negative state away. You must abide with the unwanted state to gain consciousness.

The more conscious you get, the more you see the whole attached automatic behavior in full gear. The more you do that, the more you can catch the wind up, instead of being jolted all over the place.

TEACHING

I have been performing and teaching piano for over 30 years.

I have also been teaching meditation for about half of that time and started my own meditation practice about the same time that I started teaching piano.

In other words, a good majority of my working life is sitting one on one with individuals either creating beautiful piano music or meditating and counselling.

Both entail lots of listening and connection.

It has been an incredible opportunity to develop discipline, courage, and passion in others and myself.

One of the ways I do this is by enrolling students in music festivals and competitions besides the usual studio recitals. Last week, the Seattle Young Artist Music Festival provided just such an opportunity. It's simply the extra added push to help achieve a high standard of playing.

Doing this every year affords me the possibility to help children experience challenge. Through their own choice, they commit to do what it takes to get ready. There is an aim in place and a limited time frame in which to get it done. This propels them forward and holds them to the task.

Deadlines are a Godsend.

My piano teaching often parallels my instruction of presence. It becomes the journey of struggling with egoism or at least holding it at bay and watching it. It is a way to help them realize states of identification. When they get distressed over something not being perfect or if they are nervous about performing, it is simply a lesson in seeing the attachment to an image of themselves. They can experience their attachment to how they think things should be and, most especially, to what other people think.

We only hold what other people think in high regard when it defines us.

The struggle to accept what goes wrong and not reflect in hindsight during a performance is also a mindfulness practice. Once a mistake occurs, if they don't keep their mind on the present notes at hand, more mistakes start happening. They begin to lose security and confidence, and then the nervous tension escalates. The secret to performing is accepting what is and then getting on with it.

Sounds a lot like life, doesn't it?

Of course, without persistent preparation and practice, performance is a disaster. If they are not prepared, they have to draw from faculties that are not yet set in their bodies or minds. Vice versa, if their fingers know the drill somewhat automatically without their theoretical intelligence behind it, it becomes a house of cards, a catastrophe waiting to happen. The fingers will play without their minds there, just like we can drive a car and be planning out our entire future without getting in a wreck. The minute the stress of people watching is in the picture, their fingers somehow lose their way and accidents ensue unless they have backup systems in place.

So my teaching is about learning to not care about what people think and to be so prepared that when we lose our nerve, there is something else to rely on.

Practicing performance will take care of most of this.

These qualities always transfer to other areas of life.

With this system, young pianists learn that there is always more to fix, more to improve, and more to perfect to secure a piece. The standard of excellence requires insight into what more can be done to make it failsafe while simultaneously knowing that perfection is rarely attained. It also allows them to look more closely at the genius of a composition and how it all fits together.

The next step is to accept where they are when it comes to show time. If they have done their best and are ready, they get to enjoy the music and let go of this notion of perfection.

This goes for any profession and even the practice of meditation.

As with meditation, there is one eye kept to the consistent practice. There is no cramming in music, just as there is no cramming in liberation. It all happens at a slow and steady pace with sparkling breakthroughs to inspire us on.

No one can beat down the doors of heaven.

In this role as teacher and mentor, I am the slave driver and the encourager; the listener, the supporter and the bad cop. If I want them to really learn, I must be diplomatically honest and frank. I must hold them to their word and show them what it takes. If they are any bit serious they take it in stride and know that I care. It's all in the delivery and, like parenting, they won't always like me but they'll appreciate me in the end.

It's not easy helping people reveal themselves to themselves.

With all this, I too learn more about myself and my connection to others. It's true that if you want to learn more about something, teach it.

GREEN WITH ENVY

The subject of envy has come up in my mastermind group, with my students and my clients, so it feels appropriate to address it.

Envy is a result of comparison. It is a desire for something else. It is a resentful discontent as a result of someone else's fortune or possessions. It comes from a perception of lack.

It also happens as a result of desiring the qualities or attributes of another person.

I think we can all agree that one of the ten commandments, "thou shalt not covet thy neighbor's goods" is about envy.

Let's compare envy to jealousy.

Jealousy comes as a result of losing, or the threat of losing, something you already have. It carries with it the feeling of being taken from or being abandoned, whereas envy comes from lacking the thing altogether.

Do we suffer from envy when friends, coworkers and family members are successful? Does it feel threatening to have success? Perhaps we had an envious sibling or parent who treated us terribly or ignored us when we achieved something important. This may have caused us to downplay or even hinder our own achievement in order to be loved and accepted.

Many people have learned to tone down their own success in order not to threaten a relationship. Their progress will threaten a codependent marriage because the only thing holding it together in the first place is an exchange of love for security. If that delicate balance of dependence is disturbed, they feel threatened that the other is gaining more independence and will no longer need them. This could be in terms of money, transformation, or even progress toward a more conscious way of living.

Conversely, there may also be envy that one person gets to slack while the other works harder than everyone else. Envy then morphs into blame and self-pity that someone else has it better than we do. Our lack of boundary and authentic voice gives way to resentment.

When looking at envy, we need look no further than the predominance of "lack mentality" and competition that has been instilled in us for centuries. The patriarchal model of dominion and power shows us someone's loss is another's gain. There is no desire to support or applaud another's success because it takes away from our own. We might congratulate someone outwardly but inwardly we are envious.

I am defining success here as happiness, abundance and fulfillment. With this lack mentality, there is not enough success, wealth, clients or goods to go around. This fear creates hoarding (money, love, support) in order to hold control and power over that exchange. We then feel compelled to compete for that power, wealth or happiness.

We hear lots of talk of "healthy competition" and I ask us to consider what that means in terms of systems. When there is enough to go around people can choose from several sources. If the wealth is held in the hands of the few, we are unable to have variety and diversity.

For example, if the way we receive information is held in the hands of the few, we no longer have numerous perspectives and freedom of speech but a propaganda machine controlled by those who own the airwaves.

Our democracy is also threatened if the politicians are bought to fulfill the interests of those who want to maintain wealth and power. It cannot thrive when dominion, greed, and power are the predominant themes.

A healthy environment in which we all thrive, where democracy and equality is respectfully fulfilled can only happen when goods and services flow through the hands of many. Many news outlets, many small businesses, many farmers, many people offering services that are promoted and supported by all. This creates healthy competition which doesn't feel like competition at all, but exchange of goods and services from many people. Less envy, more prosperity.

Poverty mentality is defined by the belief that there is not enough to go around - whether it's love, money, happiness or success. Certainly in these times in the USA when there is a great deal of wealth held by the few and a disappearing middle class, we feel this as reality in our economic systems. There is not a healthy exchange of goods amongst many people in order to sustain a middle class. When wealth is concentrated and does not flow amongst many people, greed and control comes strongly into the picture. The have-nots fear there is not enough, and the have's want to keep it that way. Even donating to poor countries rather than trading with them keeps things unequal.

There are also many of us who deliberately deprive ourselves of abundance believing this will make up for someone else's lack. This behavior displays lack mentality. Our identification with altruism, fairness and equality becomes the reason we deprive ourselves. This mentality believes that if we deprive ourselves, someone else will gain by it. It boosts our ego. It is as if our poverty is a noble cause and will solve the imbalance and provide for the have-nots.

What does this really have to do with envy? Why in our heart of hearts don't we celebrate the success of another but instead feel threatened or unsuccessful? We become filled with self-pity that we ourselves are not there too and judge those who are. It stems from a false perception of ourselves and our place in the world. We feel compelled to compete instead of help one another along the way in hopes that we get it and they don't. If we can understand the new paradigm shift, we will celebrate each other's strengths and offerings, knowing there is enough for everyone. There is room for many at the top because the top does not look like the tip of a triangle but a large pool of prosperity. This is a feminine principle.

In this large pool, our needs are met and we care for each other. We stand strong as fulfilled individuals able to trade and serve with dignity instead of control, whether that be love, resources or knowledge.

This is relationship between two on a solid foundation. Our attention can ascend to a higher order of existence.

When we feel insecure about ourselves, it is very hard to celebrate the success of another. We criticize how they got there, question their motives, and simply wish that they would stay with us in misery. They force us to look at our own patterns. It may exacerbate our feeling of inadequacy to the point that the only way to relieve it is to tear them down. Misery loves company.
There is no room for another's happiness because it simply accentuates the feeling of lack with which we have become conditionally identified. People who are not even competitors but simply successful/prosperous/happy become the enemy. We envy their freedom.

When we feel confident that we too can have that success in work and in relationships, we are able to support and celebrate each other's growth. When we feel threatened because we harbor fear, we tear them down to our level, keep them dependent, or in our control.

In fact, the way we do business, family and relationships is a direct reflection on how we view ourselves. If we need to control and dominate a situation or a relationship, for example, we actually are motivated to do so by our fear of lack. In this scenario, friends and family are in our lives not for love, but to serve our needs and fulfill something we cannot fulfill ourselves. Their freedom and happiness is a major threat. Their dependence keeps us feeling better.

When a crab has finally figured out how to get out of the pot, the others will always try to pull him back in.

ENVIRONMENT AND ENERGY

When traveling, I notice my environment more. Things are not so taken for granted when out of the usual routine. Environment and energy go hand in hand, so I begin to hone in on my energy tracking skills. This applies to environments and people.

My trip the last couple of weeks took me to the East Coast of the US which has a very different feel from the West Coast. It's oozing with the past and everywhere I went, there were many more people per square foot except perhaps Connecticut which had a spacious feel. Buildings were older, spaces held certain "vibes," the general public was much more racially mixed than Seattle and many areas I went through were depressed and dilapidated. I also saw the high end of every city I visited, all in dense urban scenarios.

My experience of energy goes from macro to micro so I pick up on the feel of the city. This comes to me as a "feel." For example, the area in Philadelphia I visited was not the greatest neighborhood and I felt jittery. Boston felt clean, fun, and easy. New York felt intense, slightly agitated and exciting.

Next, there were the homes in which I stayed and the energies were as varied as the people in them. Things would ebb and flow so I had to constantly assess what was mine and what was not mine. This is one of the plights of an empath. Learning boundary is essential to understanding how to tune out the radio stations and stay on one's "own channel."

I would sometimes find myself getting grumpy or wigged out and realize it was part of the person's home and their energy that I was experiencing.

Bringing sensation to my body and watching the feelings helped me sort out what was mine and what wasn't.

Sometimes I realized it was energy that belonged to the building or home itself from a cumulative collection of emotion and activity over a long period of time. Discerning this kind of thing takes practice so the first step was to realize what was mine. This can only be done through maintaining sensation in my body and observing. That takes a lot of effort. I must deeply experience sensation in my body. It never comes from "thinking" sensation.

Of course, if one has keen intuition, it will simply come in visions, smells, body sensations, feelings and auditory messages. There are many ways intuition works. Once I have established myself in my body, I sense how I am feeling. I get a clear sense of me from the me-not me practice in which I sense my energy boundary and then see if it is meeting other boundaries. This is most easily done with individuals.

When assessing energy, it is best to start with individuals. Sometimes I can be with someone and notice after I have been with them that I am totally drained. Since I don't experience extreme ups and downs from doing a consistent meditation practice for 25 years, I know that this could be the result of me not maintaining enough boundary (sensation in my body) while around a person who sucks the energy even without meaning to.

Sometimes I can experience a feeling of being invaded and these are people who project energy outward with no regard for others. They are simply invasive out of neediness and they don't know it. If I maintain enough sensation and awareness of my energetic boundary, they are unable to invade and they sometimes will feel slightly "dissed" because their energetic games aren't effective.

There is yet another type of energetic tendency in people to withdraw completely as if they have no edge whatsoever. They cannot meet me and so I feel almost as if they are not there.

These are just some types of energetic patterns in people. I have an energetic edge and the more I work with understanding where my edge meets others, the healthier my relationship is with people and environments. It is interesting to go about my day and look for this invisible phenomenon going on all around me.

Here are some questions to consider:

When you are with other people in small groups or one on one, how is the energy exchange happening? How do you feel while around this person? Do you get slightly scared, irritated, anxious for no reason? Bring sensation to your body and then reassess the type of energy the other person is putting forth. Of course, you can take in many impressions about a person or environment and glean a lot of information. Listen to their tone of voice, look at their body language and posture, watch their eye contact or lack thereof, try to sense an energy from them. They may be saying one thing and energetically do the opposite.

There is so much going on that we can't see so getting oriented to that will open up a whole new world.

It is easy to spot someone who is giving off so much negativity that I want to get away fast. Not only do they show it through their words and actions, but it can be felt. I ordered a coffee in Boston in a hip cafe and immediately was struck by a severe dose of this energy from the barista at the counter. He was not only miserable but really unfit to serve others in his state. No smiles, no connection, no cooperation with our needs or requests and thus... no tip. I pointed out to my daughter that maybe his mother died and she promptly pointed out that he would not be there if that had happened. More likely he just got ditched by a partner.

I walked into a jewelry/artisan shop in the east village in New York where many vendors had booths in one big brick room with tall ceilings. There was a lot of beautiful handcrafted merchandise. After looking at two or three booths, both my children and I were drawn to a particular booth. We all ended up buying things from a woman with whom I struck up an interesting conversation. She had a bubbly joyful energy. She connected on an energetic level that maybe people could not perceive, but they certainly felt like buying her stuff. It was remarkable to feel her vibe.

Now I hope you will go out and experiment with watching energy of environments and people. It can change a dynamic on a dime. It can explain whether you have healthy boundaries. It will help you understand what is really going on with you and others.

What is your experience with energy? How do you assess what is going on around you? Are you keenly oriented to the unseen? Can you feel others' energy distinctly from your own?

PERFECT HARMONY

Perfect harmony implies resonance generated from a fundamental tone. When we think of overtones in a harmonic series, the harmonics are frequencies doubled and incrementally raised so as to be a part of the whole and sound distinct but "matching." Harmonics are a part of the whole, like fractals of light in a prism and representative of the unity and diversity of all things.

Harmony is the result of the sympathetic movement of more than one thing. To have harmony, we need at least two things resonating. Resonance can be defined as the synchronous movement of neighboring objects.

Sound and light are resonant frequencies that we experience as separate and unto themselves yet they cannot exist without the fundamental. When we have a fundamental note, the harmonics stack up in a repeating series, just as light and color are part of a series.

The physical representation of sound can be seen in cymatics in which grains, particles or water form geometrical patterns when resonating with certain frequencies. They are manifest wave patterns, repetitive series of waves known as nodal lines of vibration. Even the old Chinese copper singing bowl demonstrates this phenomenon. When rubbing the handles, the bottom begins to vibrate.

To us, harmony represents a symmetrical aspect of sound. Harmonics are integers and multiples of the fundamental sound. They are divisions of the whole and still very much a part of the whole because that is the source from which they generate.

For us as humans, we are also resonating at certain frequencies. Our energy corresponds with gradations of consciousness, so the more refined our consciousness is, the more we resonate on multiple layers within the fundamental. We embody more "harmonics" and experience this by living in more than one world simultaneously. We do not escape the core fundamental and only live in the higher frequency as we progress. In fact, the more we progress the more important the fundamental. We can only experience the higher frequency by absorbing and embodying the fundamental at the same time. In other words, our higher frequencies cannot exist without the fundamental.

The fundamental can be seen as our grounding from which we splinter off into fractals of higher consciousness, yet we are always always always part of the fundamental. All of us are part of this fundamental. When we are separated from the fundamental that unites us all, we are off kilter. We are not able to resonate with God; namely our higher nature. We might be higher than a kite on all things in the etheric realms with no connection to how we act and move in regular life. We might be moving along in life but unable to connect to others. We may have huge insight and intuition into the spiritual realms, but no way to help ourselves. These are just some examples of being disconnected from the fundamental.

Our personal healing is the quest to resonate with the primary fundamental. Ironically, a broader perception of this phenomenon occurs when we can encompass and vibrate with the harmonics. This blends different tones creating harmony. We experience more of the fundamental whole when higher more rapid frequencies are resonating within us.

Our original fundamental is earth energy here on this planet and it too resonates with a larger fundamental within the Music of the Spheres. If we are to experience the perception of these unheard frequencies, we must find ways to align with it and heal. We can go nowhere without the mighty vibration of our mother planet. The force of Gaia is our way to ground in a greater fundamental presence within the Universe.

When we resonate on such levels, our experience becomes unified with the common energetics from which we all stem. Somehow we have become out of step with these frequencies. We experience dissonance and cannot resonate within the Universal Fundamental of Life.

For the ancient Egyptians, this was the purpose of the Great Pyramids of Giza among the many other surrounding pyramids which mimicked the formations of constellations. They pointed the way to resonance, to repetitive "series" of frequencies for us to pay attention to and they provided a means for sound resonant healing of earth energies with the corresponding human energy field. Certain times of the year marked by specific constellations in the sky offered an opening for resonance regulation. These pyramids served as markers for those times.

We are learning new ways to regulate sacred resonance for healing ourselves and the planet. Just as the ancients knew how important this aspect of harmonics was, as seen through their knowledge of Sacred Geometry, Sound/Resonance, Light, and the Heavens, we too are relearning what is needed for the transformation and recalibration of our energies. We must begin to resonate with the new Gaia fundamental that is changing to support our rise in consciousness.

What does this mean in terms of our present day practices of transformation and understanding of resonance. How do we come to experience how we are resonating?

When we can eliminate the static, the toxins, and the interference, we begin to experience our Gaia fundamental. This in turn generates a powerful platform for harmonics to begin to resonate to the level of the Divine Source. One can almost imagine a wave bouncing back and forth between the two. Without one, there is not the other.

We eliminate the static through genuine conscious labor, through the internal struggle to be here now in a way that is outside our usual realm of cognition. We must develop attention of steel to grasp the subtle imperceptible wave and surrender to it. The more out of sync the collective energies get, the more we easily sway with the mass frenetic frequency. We must be able to hold a certain higher frequency through attention.

Without work toward freedom and consciousness through maintaining stillness, we are pulled by the lowest common denominator of frequencies. Within this subtle stillness we learn to maintain, we find Presence. Presence grows the more we make this conscious effort. Those who are able to hold the higher frequency aid others in finding this place of resonance. Just by being together holding the higher frequency, we begin to create harmony and resonance. We begin to vibrate and hold the new resonant frequency of the Gaia fundamental. We begin to experience the dynamic present moment which connects to the all and everything.

Within the dynamic present moment, we are outside of time and space. We are able to heal the past and thus prepare the future forever and permanently. When in the present moment, we are in perfect resonance with all that is, so that we can see outside of the constricting paradigm in which we usually live. When we develop attention, we develop the ability to hold the frequency of presence and our life begins to change in ways we never thought possible. We begin to have empathy. We begin to connect. We begin to support one another. We begin to care. Each individual's transformation raises the frequency. So like the pyramids, we become conscious beacons of recalibration and synchronization. We are doing what the pyramids used to do. That synchronization rests in the unseen realm of consciousness where the Music of the Spheres clearly resonates.

Can you hear it?

EMBRACING THE FEMININE

What does it feel like to embrace the power of the Feminine for both men and women? What would our society look like if we experienced the balance of masculine and feminine forces?

What if you were accepting and kind to yourself knowing that each day you are doing the best you can? What if your creative juices were coursing through your veins with a deep need to be expressed? What if that was encouraged, supported, and revered?

Life could feel invigorating and full of deep satisfaction.

We are collectively feeling so far away from that. Our culture expresses violence, anger, and depression everywhere we look. If we are not careful and conscious of it, we can feed ourselves an endless stream of negativity. We are obsessed with production, perfection, competition and consumption.

The drive to be more, do more, have more, and achieve more is creating an impossible standard for our lives. We "beat ourselves up" over anything and everything. It is ego driven and it reeks of the shadow side of masculine energy.

Right away, I want to clarify that masculine energy in itself is not a bad thing. It is the affirming force, directed and intended, and necessary in our lives. However, whilst lacking the presence of the feminine force of receptivity, things have become very imbalanced.

We are transitioning away from a world in which the masculine qualities of logic, doing and thinking are prioritised over the feminine qualities of being, creating, nurturing and feeling.

The crumbling of the Patriarchy is at hand and with that, the decline of archaic systems: societal, economical, and political. We as individuals can embrace the unity of Nature, taking its cue for collaboration instead of competition.

Exciting times to be alive.

We have been focused on directed effort and achieving and profit at the expense of our planet. We have learned to ignore our innate heart wisdom. Life has become a driven frenzy of uphill battle: something that creates overwhelm. It is impossible to keep up and it is making us sick.

We recognize the pain of the situation in the arts, economics, environment, business, agriculture,and the media. The more we shut out the strength of the Feminine, the more angry, violent and isolated we will get.

When closed off from this wild feminine force, our masculine force of control predominates. There is no regard for the whole; no sharing of resources for the good of the many; no letting ourselves off the hook; no allowing. No wild expression of self just for the sake of experiencing that empowerment.

It is the acceptance of the Sacred Feminine, the Receptive Force and the opening of a collective Heart Center to meet the Masculine that will remedy the situation.

From our hearts, we can embrace our shadow. We will crack open and access the deep dark places within us that have been pushed back, crusted over and hard baked to endure a life that threatens our vulnerability. We will come to love and care for ourselves on a deeper level. We will learn to listen inside to the terrible tyrant guarding dominion over our soul with its shoulds and shouldn'ts to make way for forgiveness and acceptance.

Only from this higher self-acknowledgment can spring the genuine caring for others and our planet. We will stop the desecration of our own life source: planet Earth, because we will have come to understand how to nurture ourselves. We will participate in the flow of abundance available to all. We will embrace an untamed source of creative energy.

This is not because the Feminine does this. It is the presence of both forces creating a Third Force that makes it all happen. Afterall, the Third Force is the catalyst for creating human life, the blending of the masculine and the feminine. Men send forth a directive seed, activating and initiating a process. Women birth from their bodies and represent a gestative creative energy which gives rise to the ultimate creation, life. We can use this as a metaphor for our lives and all that we do.

With both forces present, things become easier and more satisfying. Money, love and resources become available where it seemed there were none. When we embody the understanding that we deserve this, the gifts of the Universe abound. When we work toward our goal and willingly receive, a higher vibration is created. We blend the yes and the no, the doing and the receiving, the give and the take. This applies to life and all matters spiritual. We feel the effervescent spark of surrender.

This is Mind in conjunction with Heart.

It is living the Magic.

We will find The Way.

HOW TO UPGRADE YOUR FREQUENCY

When looking at energies and how to upgrade your frequency, we can measure several things.

First of all, we can look at the kind of energy most people talk about. It refers to whether we are tired or more full of "energy."

But what does this actually mean?

We can describe our state as vibrant, full, not tired, focused, and not dispersed when we consider how we are feeling when we have energy.

We can feel drained, tired, lethargic, distracted and unmotivated when our "energy" is down and uncollected.

This is mainly looking at one gradation of energy that we feel on a coarse level.

When we are physically ill, we know we have fallen below a certain threshold of vitality that ordinarily keeps us functioning properly.

When looking at personal transformation and living at a higher frequency, there is much to understand about energy and how it acts within us and upon us.

Energy is a property of all things that can transform and uplevel in frequency but it never disappears. In other words, it can be converted but never destroyed.

Here is the classic definition from wikipedia which I cannot say better:

"Common energy forms include the kinetic energy of a moving object, the potential energy stored by an object's position in a force field (gravitational, electric or magnetic), the elastic energy stored by stretching solid objects, the chemical energy released when a fuel burns, the radiant energy carried by light, and the thermal energy due to an object's temperature. All of the many forms of energy are convertible to other kinds of energy. In Newtonian physics, there is a universal law of conservation of energy which says that energy can be neither created nor be destroyed; however, it can change from one form to another."

This can all be applied to our conscious transformation as humans.

In my line of spiritual teaching, we often refer to energy as force and pay close attention to loss or gain of it. John Bennett, author and my teacher's teacher, created a classification of energies when looking at spiritual development. He divided twelve energies into three categories: material, vital and cosmic. The material energies are somewhat natural and under our "control"; the vital energies require our participation; and cosmic energies are beyond our power to direct. We as humans are apparati for the cosmic transformation of these energies from one form to another.

In a nutshell, Bennett classifies energy in terms of our ability to do spiritual work and enhance our psychic functions (if you want to know the whole system, please read his book entitled Energies). Each level of inner work requires corresponding levels of energy. For our understanding and consciousness to become more refined, the energy working upon us and within us must be of a higher and higher frequency. There is a particular quality of energy that enables our ability to see more sensitively than is possible from habit or sleep mode (a place where we live most of the time). In sleep mode, our sensitivity remains in a state directed by thinking.

Not only does Bennett consider the quality of energy but also the quantity and the intensity. These factors can create a perfect storm for our own personal growth and ability to observe. For example, we may be working on the practice of "presence," where thought energy, feeling energy and sensation of the body come together in perfect harmony. A certain amount of energy is required just to remember to try to be present.

However, the intensity and quantity of the energies that we can apply in this practice may not be enough to achieve presence, due to leakage. Our pool of energy is leaked by constant low grade worrying or inner considering, so there is never enough to make that present moment happen. Effort alone will create an upgrade whether we feel successful or not about the result, but the quantity and intensity needs to be there too.

We live a serious catch 22 as far as energy is concerned. When we want to become more conscious, we make efforts through intentional friction (intensity). In order for that energy to upgrade, however, there has to be a certain amount of that type of energy in our bucket to reach a tipping point. We are usually running on automatic energy which allows us to function quite comfortably (or not) without any consciousness. We are not aware that negative emotions and reactions are seated in habitual mechanisms requiring a higher level of energy to see them in action. As we meditate or do vigilant mindfulness practices to integrate our thinking, feeling and sensation, we begin to collect and operate with sensitive energy. If, however, we leak that energy by various means like worrying, anger, alcohol, drugs and even malnutrition, we are unable to gather enough (quantity) to make something tip the scale. So... what we are trying to see leaks the energy we are trying to see with.

If we can maintain conscious effort often enough (frequency), we begin to gather more of the kind of energy it takes to see within (quantity). The intensity of efforts will then raise the quality of energy so that we begin to have huge aha moments that go well beyond insight. These are moments of clarity beyond a shadow of a doubt and feel like something outside of thought, outside of time, and outside of our habitual range of seeing.

The important thing to know here is that effort applied often creates the upgrade. Trying to observe our negative states creates friction. Most of us believe we know how to observe our negative states simply because we are experiencing them. When we are caught up like this, we are not observing them. Our attention is completely captured and we find ourselves hopelessly unable to extract ourselves from our identification with being who we think we are (insert whatever role you wish here, dutiful daughter, soulful leader, the fraud, not enough, being successful, being mindful, or being perfect). We are relegated to a certain prison when lower grade energy is at play (aka automatic energy in Bennett's terms).

Luckily striving to wriggle free and truly observe will produce something. No effort goes unrewarded. Once that upgrade to sensitive energy occurs, we suddenly see with some modicum of separation from our thoughts. We begin to notice things about ourselves previously imperceptible. We wake up. Our work then has a new particular quality of striving to break through.

If there is enough sensitive energy in supply, our full capacity blossoms and develops when a higher creative energy (a universal cosmic energy) acts upon us, producing conscious energy. With this new energy, we can truly remember. The world of psychic function is in its grounded form and the opening of our heart center is attainable.

In short, there is so much to learn through experience in terms of energy upgrades. The science of how energy works within us can help us understand what to do next, how to work and how to gain the right amount of force to then sit back and surrender. It makes the difference between us simply surviving and living a conscious life of choice.

LIVING A
RESONANT LIFE

Living a resonant life has everything to do with surrendering to a larger universal vibration. It can help us learn to let go of the control we exert over our lives. We discover a new mode of working consciously in the world. In addition, we experience harmony in all that we do. Miracles seem to come out of nowhere and life gets a lot more magical.

Resonance of this caliber requires respect and acknowledgement of a higher vibration. There are cosmic forces at play that we can come into contact with when we are open and prepared to work with them. We understand that there are many possibilities or outcomes to any given situation. We live in a quantum arena whereby listening and choosing consciously, we participate with a higher force. We connect with our conscience by resisting the filters that keep us from playing in concert with these higher forces. We start to dance with the Universe.

What am I really talking about here?

Life can be easy or it can be very very difficult if we ignore the flow of higher forces. We have opportunities coming our way everyday. We have people come into our lives for reasons we may not know of until further down the line. We have synchronicities occurring at rapid fire succession that we may not even see. We have a chance to connect with the Divine at any moment of the day. Attention to what comes our way and surrendering to it instead of fighting with fear, often leads to amazing results.

We may be asked to do something we really don't like, but because the Universe has offered it up and we surrender to it, we find something kicks into gear. We start to learn that our likes and dislikes form a barrier around us that keep us out of the dance. If we are willing to surrender to what is calling, we might find that something changes the course of our lives. It is a feeling of not being totally in control but at the mercy of what comes our way and accepting it.

A business opportunity may appear that has nothing to do with what we had in our plans. If we ignore it, we may head down the slow road. Taking it may suddenly turn a corner where we were once stuck. We are resistant to change. We are resistant to taking risks. We are resistant to being open to what was not in the plan.

Someone may ask us to go to an event and we go even if we don't feel like it. We become inspired by our experience. It is like a game of surrender. We often override the flow by getting our "will" involved.

Take health and fatigue for example. We may be so identified with being successful that go go go feels like the only way to get to that success. We may ignore how fatigued we are or we may work when our body is sick. We don't like that it can't go as fast as we want it to. This is living in dissonance and will catch up with us.

We may have careers that are making good money but we are miserable. We are not doing what would make our heart sing, but instead doing what we think is the right thing; the thing that will make the most money. We limit ourselves and live in fear of doing what we really want.

We might be trying to advance in a career that part of us thinks we should do, but nothing is really taking off. It may feel laborious and slow. When it is resonant, it does not feel like work!!!

Also, our message may not "resonate" with what is authentically us and so no one is attracted to it though we do all the "right" things.

We may be in a relationship that deep in our hearts we know is not right, but we keep going because of what people may think, or because of the guilt we generate from having a "failed" marriage, or the juggle the kids may have to sustain. Staying in the dissonant relationship can be felt throughout the family and the children get imprinted with a scenario that perpetuates dysfunction.

We may even stay in it as a compensation for the pain we felt as children in divorced families, swearing we will never do that to our children.

All of these motivations behind not allowing resonance in career, health and relationships comes from a deeply developed sense of like and dislike, shoulds and should nots, insecurity and fear. We stifle our ability to surrender to greater possibility for fear it may be a mistake. We may refuse an offer that has come our way because it was not in our plan. We may not leave a toxic situation out of pride, guilt, or shame.

In some sense, living a resonant life means taking the risk to listen to something greater than oneself. This takes effort of a certain sort which will upgrade the quality of energy working within us. This effort often feels like going against what we like or what we think should be.

For many years, I participated in a business that was absolutely not me. I surrendered to what life was offering at the time it showed up, even though it did not "resonate" with me. Little did I know that that business would propel me into understanding how to reach a greater audience with my most valuable message. I could more easily share a precious teaching that transformed my life. That short lived career taught me how to run an efficient business as a musician as well. It brought me full circle to doing exactly what I love in a way that could support me. Once I returned to my passion, it went into full bloom and has steadily grown and prospered. I would never have had the perspective I have now if I had not done the "wrong" endeavor.

As we begin to re-evaluate our lives, we can ask the question, "Does this really resonate?" We can surrender to things that come our way even if we feel we weren't supposed to have this happen. We can take cues from chance occurrences as nudges from the Universe. We can sit, watch and wait instead of immediately saying yes or no.

It is not easy discriminating between our likes and dislikes and going with the flow. It takes tapping into something much greater than ourselves. It feels risky and uncomfortable sometimes and that may not "feel" like resonance as we know it. We often have a false sense of resonance as our fear holds us back in "safety." I ask you to look around at the circumstances in your life and really honestly evaluate if things are resonating.

I would never have had the amazing experience of living in Paris for seven years if I had not agreed to put a hold on my college degree and gone on a whim with my sister on a 3 month sabbatical that she had orchestrated. I may not have had my French son who completely steered my life in another direction. My life would not be what it is spiritually today. For me, something in the adventure my sister invited me on, resonated even though it felt disruptive to my studies.

Can we be willing to be pliable, swaying and bending to the call? Can we question when our lives really feel out of whack, when we are tired constantly, when we are pulled down by the everyday, when we are tolerating an abusive or dysfunctional relationship? We must question the motivation behind staying in that state. If we look closely, it's often our ego wanting to take "the high road" and stick it out. Our ego may also be completely identified with being the martyr as well.

When we are living a resonant life, things flow. Things feel easy. I am not saying that life does not offer challenges, but those challenges come as welcome beacons of change that herald transformation. We listen to something that sits just outside of our comfort zone and we resist the urge to get in the way.

In what ways has surrender turned your life around?

How have you resisted change for the better?

What is your experience with synchronicity?

THE POWER OF GROUPS

When seeking transformation, the power of a group cannot be underestimated. Let's face it, we are more effective together than competing or working on our own. We live in an ever growing atmosphere of isolation and fear. We don't go out as much to do anything and we are not connecting face to face. It is important for us to remember the beauty of coming together.

From small organizations and businesses to women's gatherings and spiritual groups, we have the chance to experience what it means to work together. When we gather toward a common goal, intent on allowing each to contribute to the whole, we gain more force than our own individual efforts can produce.

I have experienced the extraordinary phenomenon of accelerated transformation through participation in and facilitation of group retreats over the last 20 years. One of the purposes of the Awareness School retreats is to allow people to understand what happens when people gather to meditate and work mindfully together. Something more happens to all of us simply because of the group. If a magnetic center is formed in a group that has been together for a while, a distinct momentum affects everyone.

My motivation for writing this piece is to speak about the magic that happens when women gather. This can happen in something as informal as a Mom's group or a book club.

I have just finished an extraordinary long weekend with my mastermind women's group: a set of powerful women leaders coming together for support, transformation and healing.

We are diverse yet hold a common thread of spiritual women in business for themselves: each involved in sacred commerce, a term I learned from the book, Sacred Commerce.

Their definition of this term is: the party-cipation of the community in the exchange of products, information, and services that contribute to the revealing of the Divine (i.e. beauty, goodness, and truth) in all, and where spirituality — the return to the Self — is the bottom line.

Along with this common aim of sacred commerce, we understand the bottom line to our success is through mutual support. This not only refers to business, but also personal transformation. Healing the bond between women that has been fractured by the Patriarchy is also an important aspect our time together.

When women gather, there is a magical feel to it and some women even gather for the purpose of magic itself. Our culture has long condemned this ancient ritual connected with nature and the rhythm of the moon. The practice of women gathering holds the power of healing the wounds of history when women were burned at the stake for being midwives, healers and psychics. We were taught that it was dangerous to practice ancient arts in circle. We were taught to compete. We were taught that to be successful we must do it at the expense of others. We were taught to go underground.

Mostly we were taught that it is unsafe to heed the call to gather. Something inherent in our nature. We began to sow the seeds of dysfunction between mothers and daughters.

We forgot to trust one another.

The power of women gathering at this time is to sever our connection with a dark past. Through support and love in circle, we rectify the mother wounds and the sister wounds. As one of us accepts and sees the pain of the past, we all face what is locked in our deepest selves.

What we do for the one, we do for all.

Many years ago I was in circle with women to celebrate the spiritual wheel of the year. We studied the significance of nature on our psyche and our connection to it. We made things together, sang songs, and created family gatherings that pertained to the seasons. The mere fact that we would meet monthly, listen to each other's stories of birth, death, and relationship, created a strong bond. Moreover, this little family, like my new mastermind today, was able to bring back important elements of what women have done for centuries.

We are now reclaiming our power to sit at the table equally with our brothers who are also learning a new way. The patriarchy is crumbling and our men need only hold the door in protection and love to support this in happening. We will walk through the door with ease and grace to take our place at that table.

We are all learning to hold each other up, to see the gifts of the other and to hold each other in reverence and acceptance rather than competing. This is not the rise of women into power over men. This is the emancipation of women all over the world to stand equally with men, so that together we are co-creators of a new world where war and dominion are a thing of the past.

BEARING THE PAIN
OF SUICIDE

The tragic suicide of my daughter's classmate at school last week has gotten me to reflect on inner issues that go unseen. I may never know why someone is driven to end their life, so I develop possible scenarios. There was no note and it was not a drug overdose. Was it a snap decision? This boy seemed joyful and pleasant with his peers, a great athlete and a good writer. He was going to be the editor of the school paper with my daughter next year. We are all still reeling from the shock of this occurrence.

The school had counselors available and lots of information for parents about kids behavior in light of this event. They were worried about a copycat phenomenon. All events, like the Ultimate Frisbee party, proceeded like normal, but everyone had this tragedy lingering in the back of their minds. We didn't say too much to each other, but the coach told us how much a team is like a family. In fact, the whole school community felt closer because of this.

Death brings people together, making our friendships and family even closer. I have spent three days now comforting and holding my daughter at various times of the day and night as she grieves the end of this precious life. She is realizing the way a candle can be snuffed out so quickly and unexpectedly and how loss is a part of life. Her thoughts have pondered the darkest places knowing it was not an accident, but an intentional act. We acknowledge that there are unspokens that need to be spoken.

Though our family may not have known this child well, he has brought us together in a unique way; one that makes us appreciate each other. I find myself feeling grateful for the health of my family and each person in it.

I try to imagine the loss his parents must feel and I hold them deeply in my prayers. I am sure at this time there are many families in our community that feel the same way.

A child's suicide makes us question what goes on behind the scenes of such a positive façade. How much do they hide from their family and friends, hoping it will go away. How easy is it for them to seek help? Perhaps they don't want to burden anyone with an incessant wish to end their lives which lingers just below the surface. Be it unchecked depression, bipolar disorder, anxiety around sexual preference or cyber bullying, we must learn to catch the subtle signs of distress in our youth.

I am no expert in this arena, but I do help people see and understand subterranean stress, anxiety, and negativity that can eat them alive. I was once plagued with this, so I know it is possible to uncover what makes us feel and behave the way we do. We push on in stoic silence until the dam breaks, but we don't have to. We may be compelled to keep up the act of being OK while we are suffering from a mechanism that has been in us since childhood. We may not even be aware that we actually need help.

We may not realize that there is a way out.

There has always been suicide, but this death makes me wonder about the current state of our society with an increasing trend that has been steadily rising since 2007. Boys are four times as likely to commit this act than girls. An NBC article on CDC findings states, "Suicide is the second-leading cause of death among children and young adults aged 10 to 24. In 2012, more than 5,000 teens and young adults died by suicide."

These are troubling statistics and more current information may reveal that suicide amongst all ages is on the rise. Things feel somewhat hopeless for many. We suffer silently not having the tools to understand how to alleviate it. There are many wonderful therapies out there today, but I recommend something that encompasses somatic experience and embodiment. Traditional psychotherapy helps and is necessary for so many, but we can go beyond analysis by working with awareness, intentional sensation of the body, and meditation. Analysis often keeps us exactly in the realm that created the issues... in our heads.

Combining psychotherapy with expanding our consciousness may be the key to unlock so much of our anxiety and suffering.

We may never understand what was exactly behind this boy's suicide, but it makes us question our own children's resources and support systems. Are we listening to them?

This suicide has had a widespread effect. He has reminded us that we can take nothing for granted; that life could end tomorrow and that what we have today is precious. When we approach life cognizant of death, everything becomes more precious. He has given us that gift.

RIP dear one.

HUMAN SUFFERING AND THE DARK NIGHT OF THE SOUL

I was recently inspired by an interview with Marianne Williamson who spoke about depression, human suffering and the Dark Night of The Soul. There is so much to say about the collective suffering to which she alluded. If we are at all sensitive, we will feel the pain of terrorism, destruction of our ecosystem, hate crimes, and mass shootings. If we are feeling that pain and turning our heads, we are indeed becoming immune to the darkness around us.

"When a storm is coming, buffaloes don't run away from a storm, they run directly into it" Williamson states. This struck me. In the work I do with people, this is a given. We must enter the madness to get through it.

We are a culture that avoids pain and suffering and yet we are prisoners of our own suffering. We learn to suppress it, mask it, or numb it with substance abuse, pharmaceuticals, eating disorders, self-inflicted pain, and overworking. Ms. Williamson talked a lot about our inability to tolerate and feel the shadow side. In this present culture, we are encouraged to be positive and think good thoughts. Popular culture teaches us that these positive thoughts will attract the good things. We are taught that getting these "things" will make us happier.

She also points out that we are being diagnosed with depression for things that are a natural part of living. We are not given a blood test or brain scan but a questionnaire to determine whether we are depressed. Being sad or having dark times is part of life.

"Demons come out at night and they must be stared down. They must be transformed or they will find subconscious ways to punish you," says Williamson.

So true! Self-observation is a means to stare this stuff down. What we see in staring it down is our attachment and identification with progress, success, or needing completion from an outer source. We are identified with what we think should be and this causes immense suffering. It makes us depressed. In fact, depression is one big state of identification that with care and vigilance can be worked out.

"The dark days are part of the natural order," says Williamson. We cannot go through life without them. The more we avoid them, the more it seeps out in horrible acts within our culture.

I believe we are experiencing a collective Dark Night of The Soul at the end of a long swing of the pendulum toward the decline of civilization. We see inequality due to greed, mass shootings and climate change as part of that manifestation. We see a rise in suicide and bold acts of self-loathing. This can be seen as a natural shift that occurs throughout history. If you read The History of Civilization by Arnold Toynbee, you will note that these times very much resemble a period of decline.

The good news is the phoenix arises out of the ashes and a New Era emerges. We will swing from this most material of times to a more spiritual enlightened age, which is clearly in the works.

We can also look at the Hindu records of ages or Yugas. These times would be known as the Iron Age or Age of Kali.

Wikipedia states: "Kali Yuga (Devanāgarī: [kəli jugə], lit. "age of [the demon] Kali," or "age of vice") is the last of the four stages the world goes through as part of the cycle of yugas described in the Sanskrit scriptures, within the present Mahayuga. The other ages are called Satya Yuga, Treta Yuga, and Dvapara Yuga.

Kali Yuga is associated with the apocalyptic demon Kali (who is not to be confused with the goddess Kālī. The "Kali" of Kali Yuga means "strife," "discord," "quarrel" or "contention."

It is a cycle and we will be reborn, but we must feel and acknowledge the pain in ourselves in order to transubstantiate the collective suffering. Our spiritual work of transformation is so key.

It involves going through the fire of that pain as an alchemical process. We work to presence that pain through attention and vigilance, through the path of the heart, not the head. We work and ask to be worked upon, not to be changed, but to accept. We ask not to have it taken away but to be understood.

"What you place on the altar will be altered" is a most brilliant idea from Williamson's latest book Tears to Triumph. She directly refers to putting our suffering before us and lifting it up to God so that we may see and understand it in a way we did not before. We ask that our eyes be opened to allow us to feel it in ways we could not have before.

Part of the importance of experiencing our pain and understanding our depression, both individually and collectively, is so that we understand the suffering of others. When we ourselves have gone through that kind of suffering, we gain empathy. We become more sensitive to those around us.

"Not experiencing enough of our own pain, not being sensitive to our own pain makes us less sensitive to others' pain"

–MW

So, in summary, we must acknowledge that what we are feeling is a normal part of life instead of trying to push it down or medicate it. We can begin to distinguish what is necessary suffering and what is accidental suffering that arises from the identification of our own ego. We must discriminate what is ours and what is not ours, while at the same time understanding that we will feel the collective if we are any bit sensitive. We must know that part of the dark night of the soul is a spiritual initiation that one must go through in order to get to the other side.

As we experience it, we start to understand forgiveness of self and others, plus the importance of grief. Perhaps seeing it as remorse of conscience is another way of deeply processing it.

"If you allow your grief, when it ends... it ends, and if you don't allow it or suppress it, it's going to bite you." says Ms. Williamson.

I am convinced that we are suffering from stuffed emotions and the avoidance of pain.

In The Work, we are encouraged to intentionally suffer to create friction, to rub up against our likes and dislikes, to observe our own suffering in order to understand the source of that suffering. Much of that suffering is illusion, created from states of identification, but that is part of life. It exists as a mechanism to protect ourselves from ourselves and must be dealt with delicately. Seeing our own suffering can get depressing. The "terror of the situation" is revealed and we realize the world around us is one big manifestation of the human predicament.

When we vow to intentionally suffer, it means we are willing to face the unnecessary suffering.

We are willing to stare down the demons that keep us awake at night. We are willing to look at how we avoid feeling. We take measures that may seem wholeheartedly unpleasant, but we know that in the end, there will be emancipation from our own private prison of suffering.

That individual emancipation is the answer for the collective.

BEING PRODUCTIVE: THE NEW AFFLICTION

I used to think being productive was my personal affliction but I now realize more and more, it is the disease of today in our fast paced goal oriented society. I am no anthropologist and so do not know how it is affecting the plains of Africa, but in our postmodern world, most of us suffer from working too hard.

We are compelled to fill every moment with productive activities, forgetting that we must have the balance of restoration, inspiration and space.

I had a rather large personal struggle recently that spurred on this reflection. It is not some brilliant eureka discovery. My personal experience with it has been an ongoing struggle and perhaps it can help you understand your own relationship with being busy.

Whether you are an energetic person or slow and methodical, you have a relationship with being productive, being successful, being useful, having a plan, taking action, being driven toward a goal and discomfort with idle time.

A couple of weeks ago, I found myself unable to move forward with specific action items. Strangely, I walked around wondering what I should be doing next concerning my classes, offerings, concerts and CD's. I am perpetually filled to the brim with ideas and projects. Even a few weeks ago, I was swimming in "what next" not knowing which thing to choose because there were so many. I could not for the life of me prioritize the many balls I was juggling.

I then began to wonder why am I trying to juggle so many balls? In my holistic and mindful self, I know there is divine timing and all will get done. There is infinite space for all to manifest.

All is well.

But something had gotten under my skin that needed observation.

If I slowed down and experienced the pause, I started getting antsy. There aren't enough hours in the day to get done what I need to get done.

If I am not being productive, a subterranean feeling of inadequacy emerges from the depths.

Taking much needed time to reflect and vision... to pause... can start to feel like "I'm not getting anything done" for many of us. We start to question and evaluate our performance. We spin out of control if we don't have a plan. We feel guilty for taking a much needed rest.

 What were my money making activities yesterday? Am I achieving my goals? What if the money doesn't come in? Oh no, people are having so much success around me, but I am not. They are getting ahead and I am not. I have to work harder. I can't take time off.

This is the load of bullshit we feed ourselves.

We suffer from comparisonitis. We suffer from lack of stillness. We live only for the future which will never be the present. We skirt feelings of inadequacy by keeping busy. We believe we have to work really hard. We don't listen to our bodies. We aren't in sync with nature. We lose sleep.

Part of this is built into our culture. Being productive has been hard wired into us.

Most of us believe in order to be productive, we must drive ourselves hard. More is better... in every sense of the word.

We work hard to have more stuff as if more stuff will make us happy.

We work hard to have more prestige or fame as if this recognition will validate us.

We work hard to prove ourselves worthy.

We work hard to get to the top and be the best.

We work hard because we are afraid of losing our jobs to someone else who is willing to work harder.

We participate in an imaginary race in which there is no real winner.

We continue to run toward that ideal future where things will be better.

Boundaries compromised. Self ignored.

Stop. Just stop.

There is no end to this kind of cycle until we bring consciousness to living a fulfilling life in the present. It requires getting our priorities straight and not constantly living for the future.

A great article on this subject is *An Antidote to the Age of Anxiety: Alan Watts on Happiness and How to Live with Presence.*

British philosopher and writer, Alan Watts has wonderful insight on living in the present.

He writes, "If to enjoy even an enjoyable present we must have the assurance of a happy future, we are "crying for the moon." We have no such assurance. The best predictions are still matters of probability rather than certainty, and to the best of our knowledge every one of us is going to suffer and die. If, then, we cannot live happily without an assured future, we are certainly not adapted to living in a finite world where, despite the best plans, accidents will happen, and where death comes at the end."

As I pondered this article and my own predicament of feeling uneasy about not being productive, I began to feel something move inside that has been deep seated in my belief system, things like not being worthy if I am not successful. I realized that my definition of success in itself is askew. I began to understand that things can come easily without having to work so very hard all of the time.

I understood that my priorities are to not work so hard (though I enjoy the work) and do things with rest, work, and play in balance.

How do you reconcile this need to fill every second up with productivity?

Do you feel guilty for taking an hour to do nothing?

Is it hard for you to take a vacation?

Do you regularly schedule self-care and time for yourself?

DANCING IN THE NOW

"Dare to see that grace is right here, not as a destination that you will reach one day by means of a weary journey – not after you get "enlightened," heal your past, meet your next partner, or "raise your vibration." But as a lover for you to dance, play, and explore with, in the unfolding, eternal now."

—Matt Licata

I loved this quote from Matt Licata. It is completely in sync with my latest series on being driven.

Daring to experience grace in the now is quite a challenge for most of us. Accepting "what is" is the ultimate zen teaching and used by so many modern day teachers from Byron Katie to Eckhart Tolle. We know this is the way. We feel we work toward this end, but we don't really know how.

Our personality, that mechanistic outer shell built to function in this world out of the need for protection and acceptance, will go to great lengths to make us believe we have it together. We may believe we are accepting but deep down we continue to judge ourselves in the most harsh way. We keep impossible standards. We set ourselves up for defeat and failure.

We may appear alright when actually below the surface there is a deep dissatisfaction of self.

We navigate fear like a familiar route, avoiding the pitfalls of pain and grief.

How can we work to be able to accept what is?

I have 3 steps that will build a bridge to learning this dance.

1) Attention

The basis for all our personal transformation is attention. By this, I do not mean focus... I mean expanded awareness. We are there in the background of any given activity. We are aware of our awareness. I use several tried and true tools to develop this special kind of attention.

2) Self-observation

With expanded awareness, one is able to begin the difficult task of Self-observation. Most will think that they already know how to observe, when actually it is the thinking center observing itself. This will never bring about objectivity, so our work is to understand what it means to be integrated in thought, feeling and body to bring about a real observation. An observation must remain neutral with no impetus to change or improve what is seen. (That is the hard part.)

3) Recognizing Identification

When we are identified with a role or a belief, our attention is captured and no longer objective. There is no observer present and thus we get mired in feelings of discontentment, inadequacy, and fear which then dictate our behavior. Developing steps one and two allow us to recognize our states of identification and accept what we are seeing.

When that part of us which is identified feels compelled to make matters better, or belittles ourselves and others for not being perfect, we suffer. Our identified self acts according to our like or dislike. When we are constantly attached to what we think should be (identified state) , we are stuck in a prison of non acceptance. The effort here is to rest in the yes and the no of the situation until we break through.

Another force comes in from the outside when we stay with this yes and no. We struggle to accept what is and in comes the third force.

In states of identification, we may not feel things are going fast enough or well enough. We may find we are unable to get motivated in a way that is "productive." We may find we cannot connect with others in the way we want to. We may feel life can only be good if we have the right partner. We may compulsively need to make more and more money at the expense of our down time and our family time. We may feel that sense of dread each day. We may know that something is not quite right, but we can't put our finger on it.

All of these scenarios involve what we think "should be." The more we see how our lives are dictated by our likes and dislikes, the more free we become. Working with like and dislike is one of the most important practices to catch ourselves in a state of identification. When we do things we "don't like," we start to see what is behind needing to drive ourselves so vehemently. When we strive to put the discipline of acceptance in the place of avoidance, we experience an opening.

Every one of these instances requires us to accept what is, instead of judging whether something is bad or good. Every judgement stems from our identification with like and dislike. Every identification with like or dislike creates frustration and "lack of control."

We cannot change someone else's actions, beliefs or influence. We cannot stop someone's hate from manifesting in this world. We cannot win when we hold perfection as a standard for ourselves or others.

What we can do is stay right in the yes and no of what "it" wants and notice from a place of integration where dots are connected between past and future in the glorious dance of now. In that place, we understand on an infinitely deeper level something about ourselves. We allow it to be, by watching it and not changing it. Our effort to watch this struggle with how we think things should be and how they are not that way, is the way to be here now. We learn to accept by recognizing ourselves in a state of identification and watching it with expanded awareness.

The dance of now is a special place and once we get good at it, life gets a whole lot more enjoyable. We react less. We feel balanced and whole.

We see more grace in every gesture at every turn. We actually feel gratitude. We shift. We twirl. We dance instead of going through the motions.

These writings reflect an entire system of learning presence through expanded awareness. Presence allows us to catch ourselves in the state of identification.

We have a chance then to really dance.

STILLING THE MIND

The most basic and necessary spiritual practice is stilling the mind. Even a short practice of sitting each day and bringing your attention back to breath is as meaningful a practice as any. There are many paths to God, but underlying all of them is stillness of mind. This entails the development of attention both on and off the cushion. It is easier to begin this practice on the cushion so one can focus simply on that task.

When this practice accumulates momentum, miracles occur.

As a practitioner of meditation for 30 years in which I rarely miss a day of sitting, I can attest to these miracles. At this point, I can settle into a deep place of no thought and union with God within minutes. That presence and strength accompany me as I go about my day. Even at times of great duress in relationship or stressful circumstances, I am usually able to find the resources to resist reaction and to make incredible effort.

Everything in my life has been affected by this practice of stilling the mind.

I have overcome incredible obstacles that have kept me from loving. I am much more quick to forgive myself and others. I can find myself able to choose not speaking when my greatest urge is to state my opinion about something. I can resist the urge to be right. I can listen much more easily when it has never been my natural tendency.

If I can do this, so can anyone. It starts with this practice of stilling the mind even if at first it feels not at all possible. There must be many many days of feeling like one has failed: failed to still the mind, failed to break though, failed to see results, failed to not react and much more. I cannot tell you how many times I have sat with my mind whirring at an insane pace wondering why I continue to try. I wondered if the mind was capable of utter stillness. I observed how associative thought would ride every wave that comes its way.

The secret is to keep trying and to keep failing. That is what builds up the strength.

I may experience this in exercise. I fail to achieve the right number of reps. I give up just before hitting my new distance. My muscles ache and I just can't do one more sit up. All of this failure still builds up the muscles.

A spiritual practice builds strength of the zen mind. One can then pray with the heart. One can act according to conscience more easily. One can resist speaking when it is best to do so. One can listen to God from deep within.

I cannot know this truly without stillness of mind.

If I have a tendency to want to be right, this practice of stilling the mind helps me to accept what someone else is saying even if I may think they are wrong.

If I have a tendency to want to put forth my two cents because it shows I know more, stillness of mind will stop me from saying anything.

When I feel that every particle in my body is reacting in pain or sorrow, I can remember that this too shall pass.

I can recognize the ego's power to convince me of my own self-pity.

I can begin to have empathy where there was none. In so doing, I learn to not take things personally and to realize from whence someone else's words are generated.

With stillness of mind, I can connect the past to the present in a vortex outside of the time space continuum: the place where true healing occurs.

I can bear the pain of difficult relationships in which I have staying power to learn, instead of running away or cutting myself off emotionally or numbing myself in drugs, alcohol, or medication.

With stillness of mind, I can learn to accept myself and the mistakes I make, instead of adhering to the ridiculous standards of perfectionism my ego creates.

I am able to wriggle free from being identified with my ego's ridiculous standards which allows me to beat myself up to the point of feeling hopeless or even suicidal.

It all starts with a practice which grows to a necessity which then evolves into living by conscience.

My stillness of mind is as necessary to me as my oxygen. It has saved my life. It has brought me close to people and I am truly grateful. Every time I stop, I am immediately connected with the Infinite Source of Wisdom in which I can surrender to love. I can bypass my need to figure things out for the future in that moment and sigh a sigh of relief that nothing is necessary at this sacred time except to be.

I push aside the wish to resolve matters or ask for more, and each time I do so, I am rewarded ten fold with a point of grace in which I am forgiven and I am loved.

As I sit and find my mind wanting to race, I remind myself that there is time for that later. For now, I can simply keep bringing myself back to breath. Even if I fail to do this one hundred times in a meditation, it is a very good meditation. It is the effort that counts and beats not sitting at all because I think it isn't working.

Over the years, as my discipline has created stillness, I use it as a resource when faced with the alluring desire to react. It strengthens my ability to let go. In fact, it is the only way I could have ever let go.

It guides me to know what is right in my heart.

OPENING OUR HEARTS

The opening of our hearts is tricky business.

We must first learn how to work through daily practices that help still the mind and develop attention. I believe that without that, we never move toward real choice in our lives. Without attention and the development of expanded awareness in which we can see ourselves more objectively, we remain under the spell of our ego and its likes and dislikes.

We may think we have choice but as long as we live under this misconception, we will not discover just how little choice we have in life.

We may be cognizant of how much we sabotage our lives. We may see how frustrated we get when faced with difficulties in life. We may notice in times of great strife how much we beat ourselves up or compare ourselves to others. We may feel like failures even when life's accomplishments are apparent. However, without this more subtle awareness, we cannot see what makes us do that. We do not notice how constantly our actions are influenced by micro states of identification.

Without strength of attention, we are always under the influence of our ego.

With more awareness comes the phenomenon of watching ourselves fall prey to the mechanical and habitual mode we live in most of the time. This is the mode that makes us believe what others are saying when they are tearing us down. This is what allows us to forget who we really are as divine beings of God and only see what we don't have. This is what perpetuates the battle of the many "I"s within us that allows us to praise ourselves one minute and beat ourselves up the next. This is what makes us hold ourselves responsible for other people's happiness.

Under these circumstances, there is no steady constant by which we can navigate our course. When someone lights into us or blames us, we take it personally instead of seeing them with empathy and understanding their situation.

Contrastly, we may be unable to look within with strength and humility at the truth of what someone might be saying.

Once we develop this steady constant though relentless effort of attention and self-observation, we can stand back and catch ourselves just at the moment of "weakness." The attention allows us to see the automatic thoughts that usually go unnoticed. Self-observation in this context is not the thinking observing itself. It is a developed observer that is integrated in thought, feeling and body to bring about something we normally would not see. Self-observation is very misunderstood and is considered easy, but I am referring to something very different that takes the discipline of attention.

Each true self-observation we experience begins to create a composite experience of solidity of essence. We build our ability to be authentic to ourselves. We hold to our own truth instead of the standards of what people expect of us. We begin to free ourselves from being a slave to our identification with being loved. We start to experience our own strength and self-acceptance every time we catch ourselves in this state of entrapment. This allows us to deeply understand our own wholeness thus freeing us from the need to be loved. We stop looking for it outside of our own God source.

Once this daily practice of self-observation and the maintaining of attention is strong, we can turn to a different force. This is the receptive force in which we are strong enough to ask for mercy.

Here's the difference. If we don't develop a means of working to free ourselves and take responsibility for our actions, then we are constantly asking God to fix things without being involved. Most of us have been taught that when we pray, we ask for God's assistance to change things.

We neglect to ask God to show us what is, so we can learn.

We try to take ourselves out of the equation so that an external force alone will change things. This is the ego's trickery.

God is not going to help if we don't try to help ourselves. A more appropriate request in prayer might be asking to allow us to see our part in a messy situation. We can ask for strength, but continue to be our disillusioned selves without trying to resist that part of us. We then blame God for things not working out. We can continue to make the excuse that we are "sinners" and are forgiven as a justification to continue our bad behavior.

We can neither do it ourselves, driving toward enlightenment as if it was just another goal to achieve, nor can we just ask God to do it for us. There must be both!

With the reconciliation of these two forces, we have the opening of the heart.

From my perspective and from experience of working with others for 20 years, this opening comes most effectively after one has learned how to do daily activities of effort to build a container. This container is the development and recognition of one's own essence and spiritual strength even in the shadow of difficulty. This container then allows us to open up and feel without breaking down. It is a subtle process that needs encouragement and support.

This is the kind of process that creates permanent change. Once we are actually able to open to love, we fill what was once mechanism with choice. We experience forgiveness on levels beyond comprehension. We acknowledge the pain of others because we have faced our own pain. This is how empathy works. This is how we no longer act out of need but out of understanding.

This container can be seen as a new spiritual body, that we have developed through the very right kind of effort. With this in place, we move from practical technique to receiving on a profound level. Of course, we make efforts in a new way which encompasses asking and surrender in sheer faith.

This is trust in something much higher than ourselves, plus our own effort, but it does not exclude our effort.

We cannot run around in confusion simply asking for it to be fixed, but we ask that it be relieved as we make effort at the same time.

This is the ultimate experience of the two forces coming together in reconciliation.

It is the perfect storm.

In that storm, we find self-acceptance, forgiveness and love.

DOORWAYS TO OUR EXPERIENTIAL WORLD

Our senses are the doorway to our experiential world.

If I isolate my attention to focus on one sense, I begin to notice that much of my experience is the result of a combination of senses. Even my imagination will fill in the blanks as if watching a magician doing sleight of hand.

The difficulty of isolating a sense comes from being human with sensual experience that uses the combination of those senses all the time. With a combination of senses, we see more or imagine that we do. My perception of hearing the leaves rustle is enhanced by seeing them flicker in the wind. If I close my eyes just to listen, I get a different experience but my imagination may fill in the blank of seeing that flickering because it has been seen so many times before in association with the sound.

When I hear a babbling brook, my mind may picture the pattern of water on the rocks or the width and depth of that body of water before I even see it. Observing exactly how my senses collaborate and conversely how my mind fills in what I don't actually perceive, gives me a clue as to how I don't see objectively.

The exercise of trying to isolate my attention to one sense only, without filling in the blanks, tells me a lot about my world and how present I am.

If I sit out in the woods with the intent of listening, I hear a multitude of bird calls, a dog barking, an airplane, and a truck far off in the distance. I recognize these sounds and try to track the different bird sounds and how they repeat their pattern.

Suddenly my mind starts to think about the impact of humans on the environment because of the airplane which has now blocked the sounds of the birds. I begin to reflect on the infringement of technology on nature and wonder whether we have really made any progress at all. Suddenly, I bring myself back to listening and realize that while I was deep in thought, I heard nothing of my environment.

My perception completely changed. I lost the focus of listening even though my ears were most likely still hearing the birds, but my attention became captured by thought. I was no longer aware of my surroundings or the sounds I was hearing.

I decided to make this a practice on a daily basis: simply to listen to my environment for a fixed period of time. I think this most certainly could be done with any of the senses. In the past, I have set out to truly experience taste during a meal with increased awareness, knowing that I take in thousands of impressions simultaneously like texture, chewing, sensation in my mouth etc. I strove to notice this aspect of taste without losing myself in thought.

In conclusion, I could not do it while immersed in thought.

Of course, while focusing just on sound, my mind was putting things together. This involved thought of some sort, but my attention remained on listening. The mind would interpret, so to speak, what I was hearing. There would be thought trying to analyse which sound was which bird, whether one bird was calling in response to another, which bird seemed to have a dominant piercing sound compared to the light warble of another bird in the background.

As my exercise continued over the week, I noticed the stark contrast of being lost in thought more and more. The exercise of maintaining my focus on listening made me much more aware of when I wasn't.

I am asleep to my environment when I am lost in thought though I can continue walking down the street or drive the car to work. I am asleep and captured by association, inner considering, and analysis instead of objectively taking in impressions.

My awareness of environment keeps me alive and safe, but I have learned to manage in sleep. As my attention strengthens, so does the subtle nuance of seeing beyond the visible or hearing the barely audible.

As my consciousness expands through attention, I am opened to a world that remains closed if I am lost in thought. If I am habituated in being lost in thought I am unaware that I am lost in thought until I do something to make me aware of that.

As I become free, I experience increased perception beyond the five senses and through the senses. I am able to be there in the background, present and aware.

Meditation can bring about similar realizations, but working with the senses through isolated attention will reveal things in a different way.

Once I got good at this listening exercise, I brought in intentional awareness of sensation in my body at the same time to produce yet deeper impressions. Simply to watch how my perception changed gave me a clue as to what I do as I go about daily life and where it is much more difficult with the myriad distractions of industry and technology.

All of this translates to learning to wake up and observe what we do in our minds. We begin to hear things we never heard before that have been going on automatically an entire lifetime. When we notice something with our consciousness, it is no longer automatic. It is perceived outside of trance. A tool develops in which we are there, present, watching the thoughts with a remembrance of Self.

When we can actually see objectively or hear objectively, we have choice and freedom.

Just in doing the listening exercise, I became aware of how impossible it was to hear while in thought.

Through work with attention, we realize just how asleep we have been and how it is impossible to make choice. How can we choose when we are unaware of what actually hinders the choice?

How can we choose not to react when we cannot see the automatic behavior that has already hijacked the emotions to produce anger or resentment?

As my consciousness expands, I become free of automatic behavior. I can listen to my heart which was previously drowned out by constant thought and inner reaction. I can compare my experience to listening to nature only now it is my authentic voice. My essence becomes stronger than all of the personality traits designed for my ego's survival as the dominatrix of my existence.

As I develop my ability to maintain awareness, a kind of strength grows in me. The more strength I gain, the more I am able to struggle to maintain the attention. I suddenly find myself hearing what I have never heard before. I wake up to my own self. I realize how much noise I make on the inside that has drowned out the sounds of tranquility, reassurance and love.

SACRED LAWS

When I return from retreats, my heart is more open, my eyes are keen to things around me and I am quiet. I want to hold onto the experience and the feeling that was created by that particular group of people. The beautiful process which occurs in the short amount of time we were together feels like weeks. Time is condensed and expanded in ways that seem miraculous to me. We as facilitators and students enter into it, not knowing the outcome.

I plan and organize, choose different movements, meditations, and chants according to our theme. There are those that run the kitchen and the practical work in a similar process. I create a structure, and must watch daily what is happening with the group, where to step on the gas as far as the schedule is concerned and when to let up.

I also let go and surrender to the efforts of the participants. I don't make anything happen. We as a group create the event.

Just like the kitchen organizer, I can provide ingredients, but I don't know how the soup will turn out because it is not just me cooking.

Each retreat has a different flavor and different outcome.

I am in awe every time.

If the right conditions are put in place, something is set in motion and the process takes its course. We as a group are able to start our octave on an active "do." We don't know if we will pass the mi-fa interval which requires a certain concentrated effort from us and a receptive force from the outside. This interval is represented by point 3 on the triangle in the Enneagram figure. Once this interval is passed, a New Octave is ignited on a different level and things begin to happen in yet another dimension.

For a retreat, that new level happens in the Being World in which a distinct and different part of us is now participating. The jump in this interval is palpable and indicative of a more refined unification and a new energy coming in to propel things forward. Participants may not know exactly what it is, but they know something has occurred. Spontaneous silence in which we are connected can be one beautiful example of this. A Movement coming together like never before in which everyone is completely synchronized with their parts, each other, and the music is another.

This process is known as The Law of Sevenfoldness, or the Law of Octaves and is in activation in all that we do. Ouspensky wrote, "every process, no matter upon what scale it takes place, is completely determined in its gradual development by the law of the structure of the seven tone scale." Learning about this enables us to understand more of our world and how we function within it.

We begin to see that at some points in any process, a new energy needs to enter to accelerate things forward. Awareness of this helps us to know when we need to push against an opposing force, incorporate and accept hazard, and learn to participate in the Natural Laws of Occurrence.

I first learned of these sacred Laws when my teacher explained the Enneagram to me in a Movements class. No one would deny that it is a Sacred Symbol filled with mystery to be pondered and experienced. There have been countless things applied to the Enneagram including the personality types which most people associate with it.

Gurdjieff is known for bringing this symbol out of hiding and into Western Culture. It is claimed that he discovered its true meaning from a Secret Brotherhood in Central Asia. No one really knows the truth about the origin, but it is certain that one must experience its True Living Nature to understand it.

When I tell people that part of the lineage from which I teach is based in the ideas of Gurdjieff, they often ask me what number I am on the personality enneagram.

Gurdjieff had no idea about a personality enneagram and did not develop it. Studying personality types and types of coping mechanisms where one pegs themselves as a certain thing can be a very slippery slope. I have no idea what number I am, hopefully all of them.

The Enneagram represents two Laws that are in constant play in the Universe from the smallest atoms and sub particles to our own transformation. When the Higher blends with the Lower to activate the Middle, it is called the Sacred Law of Three and requires an Affirming Force, a Denying Force and a Reconciling Force. This can be seen in our daily lives on a constant basis and is represented by the triangle in the symbol.

The Law of Sevenfoldness is a more complicated process and is brilliantly explained by John Bennett by an example of cooking a meal in the book, Enneagram Studies. This Law is represented by the lines which connect 142857 on the Enneagram. There are many books written about this and I suggest reading Steffan Soule's *Accomplish The Impossible* or A.G.E. Blake's *The Intelligent Enneagram* for a more detailed explanation of how both of these laws work in our daily lives. Another great reference book about the ideas of Gurdjieff is *Gurdjieff's Transformational Psychology* by Russell Schreiber.

Each of us can come to know our process and how to participate in it. Surrendering to a process or a teaching, and reception of a Higher Power is part of that. I must learn when to quit driving and receive. I must learn when to push forward in the light of setbacks and resistance, known as the Second Force. Keeping an eye on this during a retreat enhances everyone's experience. In this way, our world becomes bigger, dynamic and full.

BOUNDARIES AND
THE ME/NOT ME

Every student, no matter what the motivation behind their mystical search, must confront the issue of boundary sooner or later. It is certainly true from my experience with my own search for freedom and transformation, and true of the experiences of my students. In order to thrive more fully, each one of us must understand what boundaries are.

When we think of boundaries, we think of borders and walls, limits of an area or dividing lines. Presently, most of us consider personal boundaries to be limits we set on the way others behave toward us. When a certain line is crossed, we are violated in some way.

For us to understand boundary fully from a transformational sense, we might consider what is me and what is not me. We work with sensation to understand what we are experiencing within ourselves and discern what is someone else's energy and what is our own energy.

Empaths are constantly blurring boundaries and unable to tell "what is me and what is not me." They are rather porous, like sponges, taking on other people's emotional states and energy patterns. HSP's (highly sensitive people) are also prey to other people's and other place's energies because they have no protective membrane, so to speak.

We don't have to be empaths or HSP's to experience lack of boundary. In fact, it is a predominant aspect of lack of freedom and choice.

When we are constantly basing our decisions on what other people think and how they will view us, we have lack of boundary. When we are unable to say no, we have lack of boundary.

When we are unable to use the power of our own voice to speak our mind, we have no boundary. When we are chronically doubtful, shaky or blocked, we have lack of boundary.

There are so many ways that having no boundary can manifest, from constantly needing to please others to being abused to not giving ourselves room for proper self-care. The myriad of symptoms is apparent in so many of us today.

So why is there such a preponderance of lack of boundary with each other and even within ourselves? Before we go into what it looks like to have no boundaries, we must look at what is the seed cause of such a prevalent phenomenon amongst so many people.

When we have no sense of authentic self and we operate from automatic patterns, we generally have no capacity to set boundaries or understand our actual needs. We act out of necessity to fulfill those false ideas of what should be even if it doesn't feel right. We sacrifice our needs in order to fulfill the illusion that if we please someone else, they will like us more, or respect us more or see us as kind, caring, thoughtful, good, or dutiful. This illusion is carried out so often that we do not see it within ourselves, yet we do feel the consequences often.

We are also taught as children about boundaries directly from our parents. When they exhibit clear and healthy boundaries with us, we learn to exert those boundaries for ourselves later in life. If we are not taught about healthy boundaries or not shown a good behavior model, we have no reference. We have no security. We are not free to be ourselves. This can often look like parents with no boundaries of their own!

The fact that most of us have been loved conditionally in some way or another means we have learned that to be loved we must conform to that person's likes and dislikes. We get unconsciously trained very early in life and we act under the influence of that training with most everyone until we wake up to what is really going on.

When we are not awake, we suffer in so many ways and instead of taking responsibility for that suffering, we blame it on others. This keeps us from having to confront our own lack of boundary, our own actions, and the dichotomy within us that keeps us from our essence.

We beat ourselves up and feel guilty when we don't have boundaries. We suffer, not because someone demanded something from us, but because we gave in to their demands when we really didn't want to.

Another hallmark of boundarylessness is resentment. We project the reasons for our suffering onto the other person. We blame them for being pushy, demanding, needy, or manipulative, when in fact it is our inability to say no and hold a boundary.

Being a victim (self-pity) is also a hallmark of having no boundary. Let's face it, people are never going to be how we want them to be. People are never perfect and often their actions are unconscious and unintentional. However, we most often see their actions as intentional and directed at us. They may be acting out their own unconscious automatic patterns that have little to do with us, but without insight, empathy, and boundary, we take it all personally.

Coming away feeling drained, both physically or energetically from an encounter with someone leaves us unable to spend time with them or to have healthy relationships. In fact, we may come away feeling "bad" often, which puts a huge strain on the ability to have a relationship.

Giving away too many services for free, going overtime and not allowing yourself to be compensated properly is yet another sign of lack of boundary.

Notice how your lack of boundary plays out. Be on the lookout for times when you feel resentful toward someone. Ask yourself how you are not presenting healthy boundaries in this scenario.

Notice in ways you put everyone else first at your own expense, disguising it as "being considerate."

How do you accommodate other people when you really want to say no?

How often do you tolerate being treated poorly without leaving or communicating your feelings about it?

THE MESS OF ENABLING AND RESENTING

Imagine how many times we have been disappointed with someone's behavior. They are always late. They continue to break some household rules. They are abusive. They are our children who do not act responsibly or who continually do not do their part. They are friends who never call. They are lovers who don't want to have sex. They are neighbors who don't cut the dandelions.

You name it. There are always people who do not do what we feel is the right thing, but we are expecting this of them. If we are still waiting for them for dinner, taking out the trash because they didn't, still calling when they won't, and miserable, then we do not have healthy boundaries.

When we stay with an alcoholic who is wreaking havoc on themselves and the family, and do not set clear boundaries regarding to rehab, we enable the behavior to continue. Because we are ashamed of their behavior as well as our inability to leave or take a stand, we make excuses for them. This is how they do not feel the consequences of their actions.

If we rob someone of feeling consequences, we rob them of taking responsibility for their actions. This is the classic enabler who displays no boundary.

If we do the dishes when we have set clear expectations that it is our child's turn, we give the message that it is not necessary for them to carry their weight. Someone will pick up after them. If we ask our small children to clean up their room and then clean up after them when they don't, we send the very message that they do not have to do it.

If we have not taught them how to clean up by doing it with them in the beginning, they may really not know how, yet we blame them.

If we make up lost time for someone who is late, we give the very message that it doesn't matter if they are late. If we wait to serve dinner to accommodate a chronically late family member, we do not allow them to feel what they are missing when they don't eat with the family. They may not even care like we care. This is when we must evaluate what is right for us, not what is right for them.

If we worry about our children's success, constantly helping them, we rob them of learning how to do the homework/work/practice themselves. We create extremely codependent people who do not know how to fail.

But what if we don't want dirty dishes everywhere, while we wait for the kid to do them? What if we have house guests coming and everything is a mess? What if we really want to see the person and eat dinner with them even if they are always late?

In these cases, we have to be OK with things and people being the way they are and not what we think they should be and do.

There has to be a clear decision within ourselves that accepts the behavior for what it is without the expectation of it changing. We then have to decide whether we want to tolerate it or not. In many cases, it is often that we are lazy about allowing consequences that they will actually feel, often known as tough love.

For example, if someone doesn't do the dishes, but we like the kitchen clean, then we cannot keep blaming them for not adhering to our cleanliness standards. They obviously don't care if the dishes are done. We impose a certain picture of how we like things on others and expect them to comply. Now we may want to teach our children that everyone contributes in the family and an orderly kitchen is more hygienic and more efficient to run. When we are hungry and pots are not available or worse, we have to scrape days old macaroni stuck to the bottom, we cannot get right to the cooking. They have to learn this through experience and consequence to know its truth. Some people just don't care if they have to wash it right before they use it.

They don't care if the place is messy. Go look in any college household.

So what is proper boundary here?

Either we have to give up our expectation of how we want others to comply to our likes and desires about keeping the kitchen clean and do it ourselves, or we let a little chaos happen with dirty dishes piling up and let the kid scrub the pan the next time he wants to make macaroni.

It is hard when it affects others in the house, but the collective will start experiencing the consequences of someone's actions. It will eventually be learned that all things go better when each individual takes responsibility for his/her actions.

If we do wash the pot, whilst resenting the kid/wife/husband who did not do it, then our boundaries are not in order. Perhaps we will devise some way for that person to feel the consequences, but the issue is enabling and resenting.

Understanding our own needs/standards/desires without putting the expectation on others to fill those needs is a healthy boundary. We learn to accept what is and decide if that is right for us. We teach our children in a way that they feel the consequences, instead of nagging and punishing. Shaming and condemning never goes very far with anyone.

Now that we have the picture of what it means to be an enabler, the real work comes in struggling to not be one. We may find ourselves powerless to leave an abusive relationship. We may be afraid of saying no. We may pick up the pieces over and over in order to make things right. We may tolerate unskillful behavior under the guise of being tolerant and "bigger than that," when in fact we are miserable.

The work of three centered awareness is a surefire way of discovering what really lies beneath our enabling. This allows us to see in a present moment how we are put together from the inside. It will show us the why. It will shed light on our own sense of unworthiness, our fears of not being accepted, or being alone, or our desire for power. It takes practice in attention to get this kind of perspective of our inner self. That practice will counteract the enabling because we start to directly see the cause of our actions in a new way.

The first step is to notice that we enable. The second step is to catch ourselves in the moment of enabling. We then implement a form of inner struggle with not doing it. What are the feelings going through us at that moment? Are we able to observe our thoughts? What makes us give in?

Are we enabling someone by keeping them from feeling the consequences of their actions?

In the case of children or parents, do we continue to blame them for not being, having, or doing what we want?

Do we give away our power and the right to be satisfied and at peace by blaming and resenting someone with whom we continue to enable?

Lots of questions for us to ponder as we go forth.

Blessed Are The Enablers, For They Shall See The Hard Way.

DEPTH OF PEACE

Through waves of breath
Reminding me
Of the eternal thread
That connects me
To an endlessness
Security
Slow stillness
Full of weight
And broad expanse
Through a gate
That stays open
No fear, really no fear
Just what is
And nothing can replace
This remembrance
From which I have
Always been and
Always will be.

POST RETREAT
KITTEN THERAPY

Sometimes it is not possible to carry out what my agenda asks for.

I have not felt like burning the candle at both ends to fulfill what I set out to do and that is fine with me.

I really feel like sitting around with my new kitten and just being.

This does not mean I have stopped doing everything. It means I respect when my life needs balance. Returning from the retreat where I experienced not one iota of stress about the future, where I turned off all social media, email and contact with the outside world except the kid left at home, I could not pick up the pace that permeates our culture.

I am grateful that I don't run around with my head cut off like I used to, having to fill every moment with something productive.

I have slowly let the wheels start turning even though I am preparing to record a professional speaker demo video, preparing for a Fall piano tour and launching the Ecourse for an October 1st start. That is a tremendous amount of things to put on top of regular family life, plus teaching and running the group.

I have been preparing for those things in advance so it is a daily disciplined rotation in which I trust all will get done.

My work involves so much creativity that it is a joy. However, putting pressure on myself can easily creep in, so it is my time to work and intentionally struggle.

Honestly, I have learned after doing so many retreats that re-entry can be difficult. The most important thing is to keep up a solid practice to maintain what was acquired. In that way, it not only lingers but remains fixed in my Being forever.

This particular group was a scrumptious soup of seekers. Every retreat is different according to the group dynamic. Those lucky enough to attend this one did not go untouched. There were individual moments of transformation that then rippled through each one of us.

It was a cascade effect.

The higher energies were palpable. We unlocked a code together in the Trembling Dervish Movement. Raw tender places accessed through poetry along with lots of hesitation and reluctance to let go in this art form.

We unleashed our blocks in as many ways as there were people and I stand in awe of the experience.

In fact, tears come to my eyes when I think about the power we accessed as a group; a power that unleashed itself so profoundly that we are all feeling the re-entry.

I watched myself from a teacher's perspective and a student's perspective. I learn every time even if this was about the 27th one I have facilitated. I shared some of the teaching space with a visiting colleague and so it offered me a chance to step out of the teaching light and sometimes exert boundaries which has been a steep learning curve for me.

I feel like every time I write about a retreat, I cannot help but refer to the fact that time stands still and connects all of them outside of time and space.

There is a feeling of endlessness and connection to a living teaching.

We do not practice mandatory silence. It falls over us like a blanket of knowing. We feel the bond of that silence that evolves over the week. To those who have never practiced stopping, it starts out awkwardly and squirmy, while seasoned members drop in quickly to hold the line.

I am forever moved when we drop in together and there is often a distinct moment in the week when that happens. Something new has entered the energy of the group, even if there are a few who are still thinking away.

All I can say this week upon returning is that getting my priorities straight is not very hard. Everything feels in perspective and I walk slowly.

I have to sit with this new kitten.

If the blog is late... oh well.

I drink from a deep well of peace.

The chaos whirls around me and I am unaffected.

I am not going to push, override, or lose sleep.

I will dive deep in this place of self-remembering.

I will hold fast when the winds start to blow.

Most of all, I bow my head with hands to heart in gratitude beyond measure for this incredible work available to those who are willing to go home... I mean really home.

Alhamdulillah.

THE PLIGHT OF THE EMPATH

The proverbial empath has the difficulty of distinguishing between the me and the not me on a regular basis. Sometimes they are known as Highly Sensitive People or HSP's but there is something more about the empath than simply being sensitive. Both must work hard to understand boundary.

The empath has an innate ability to see, feel, and intuit energies of others quite easily. They often absorb those energies unbeknownst to them.

An empath often experiences things like the emotional climate of a room, the negativity of someone they are with, or the psychic overload of someone else's thoughts. By definition, the empathic person will pick up aspects of other people and things like tuning into radio stations.

Conversely, they may also learn to blame other people's states for their own automatic behavior and negativity.

The biggest task for the empath is to understand what belongs to them and what doesn't when it comes to energies and negative emotions. They can leave an encounter feeling completely drained. However, it is not just empaths who suffer from coming away feeling drained after an encounter.

Many of us who are unaware of how people use energy may be oblivious to the needy people who suck the energetic blood of others without even knowing they are doing it.

It is up to each one of us to sense and observe our own energy in regard to others. As skill is acquired, we may notice exactly what other people do energetically. This is the way to understand boundary in a way we perhaps have not realized.

Often when we think of putting up boundaries, we imagine a large force field or bubble around us. Doing this uses imagination and visualization and is a one centered activity, namely the thinking center, and will not produce effective results for very long. How many times have we created this kind of imaginal barrier and found that it has not worked very well?

We then look to the outside for relief in terms of clearing this energy out.

There must be an understanding of the use of more than one center synchronistically to bring about actual results. For the empath, it is especially important to learn how to be in the body with a sense of self when with others and in difficult environments. Without this, they morph into similar resonant frequencies in which there is no distinction of self. They meld into the energies like a chameleon.

Healers, body workers and psychics must also become very skilled at this distinction of self through simultaneous activation of centers so they also do not come out drained of force. While working with clients and maintaining attention on sensation in their own body at the same time, they acquire a practice that is founded on healing techniques in which they not only serve as medium but also a catalyst.

Having a sense of self by practicing intentional attention maintained on sensation is the answer to so many of our problems. It provides literal grounding. No visualization here. It takes a degree of attention that must be built up through practice. Many people think they are experiencing sensation when in fact they are only thinking about sensation. It takes true effort to build this awareness.

Once this muscle is established, all of us, including empaths, can begin to sense more of the environment than ever before. With a physical sense of our own body, we can start to understand the being aspects of energy and the separation of self from others.

This can be a dramatic discovery for an empath who has been unduly suffering for much of his/her life. They may even know they need some kind of protection but have not had the right resources to understand the Me/ Not Me on this level. The search for remedy has been from the outside instead of an inner practice.

The Me/ Not Me phenomenon can begin to be understood on such a deep level with practice. It is possible to clearly see what other people are doing energetically in regard to us. We do not mesh with them to find that out, but sense it on an entirely different level without danger, without drain, without having to "clear' the energy of others from us.

We create a real boundary when we are able to maintain sensation in our body which is sometimes very hard for empaths and HSP's because one of their coping methods is to leave their body. When things become too much, they relegate themselves to a place where they do not have to experience such sensitivity. People who suffer from chronic pain may also know this pattern.

This is how the empath gets into trouble in the first place: the meld.

The first practice I teach is how to have attention to sensation in the body. Now when someone comes back to me and says they had sensation all day or for an entire hour then I know they are not experiencing sensation. Attention must be built up.

This subtle awareness brings new light to the way we take in all impressions. Our thinking and feeling changes with sensation present and we know it. For an empath, maintaining sensation or bringing oneself back to sensation over and over as they forget is the exact solution for what they are suffering from.

If they can maintain attention in this way, they will begin to understand the Me/Not Me like never before.

BOUNDARIES WITH FAMILY AND SELF

I have been asked several times in the last week about what to do when you aren't comfortable being around a family member and yet you don't really want to cut off relations completely.

This is definitely a boundary issue which falls right in line with my series. I want to address this question fully from the practical standpoint and I want to answer it in terms of our own inner boundaries.

We don't choose our family but in a way we really do. I believe somewhere back there before we are born, we actually do choose what we need to learn in this life. All of our hardships and traumas contribute to that soul education, so that we can move closer to connection and love. Most of the trauma we experience in childhood tends to make us want to close off from others. We find ways of justifying that later in life so we don't have to face our own inner demons.

It provides us with so much to work with!

Because history builds up with family, it is extremely hard to be objective. Patterns form and we identify with certain roles. Perhaps we have always been the fixer and the hero. We might be the victim of someone's abuse or someone's blame. We may learn to protect our vulnerability at all costs because of the pain we have suffered.

At some point, if there is work on oneself, we come to the realization that we no longer want to be in that role. The game has always been played with more than just us and probably for many many years. So what starts to happen when someone drops out of the game?

The first question becomes how does one drop out of the game? This is how we exert a healthy boundary. In the beginning, we will not be skilled at doing this, so it might look like withdrawal or even no contact. With more skill, it is learning to cook in our own reactions, bringing sensation to our bodies and giving full attention to watching the phenomenon going on inside of us while we are with the other person.

This takes a LOT of practice and can be more easily achieved if there has been a steady practice of maintaining attention in other less demanding situations. When we start to do it in highly charged environments, where a family member is really pushing our buttons or triggering an automatic response, we begin the work of understanding how we are identified with our own suffering.

This may sound extremely harsh to those of you who feel persecuted or misunderstood and those of you who feel invalidated or not respected. This brings me back to the age old quote, "we don't choose our family." We love those who have not treated us well and we know that they probably had no ill intention. They more than likely couldn't help their own behavior, so what do we do about what we will put up with and what we won't?

Usually when we are able to see the phenomenon behind our own reaction, it affects the other person' actions. Understanding ourselves and tempering our own actions is all we can do. We cannot change other people, nor should we try.

If we are in an abusive relationship, it is up to us to walk away and that can be very sad when it is a spouse, a parent or a sibling. We gain enough self-respect to extract ourselves from such denigration, and establish parameters around which we will interact with this person.

If it isn't physical or psychological abuse, but simply a bad dynamic, then it is worth trying to establish a boundary within ourself. This is a boundary we must establish with our own ego, so everything has to be put into question.

Are we being triggered by a distorted perception that has been tainted by the past? Do we drag the past into every encounter with that person like it is a ball and chain around our leg?

Are we wanting to be treated more respectfully and yet find ourselves blaming the other person for the entire bad relationship? Are we projecting our actions onto the other person?

It is terribly difficult to have objectivity in relationship, especially with family. We have to start with ourselves because that is all we have to work with. Our own personal work will affect the relationship.

In order to see objectively, we must watch ourselves like a hawk and keep our actions in check. When we are tempted to speak unkindly or do something we really don't want to do, we must work inside to not react, speak, or do that very thing we know is in complete pattern. When we do this, we start to discover what is happening to us on the inside.

When we do act mechanically/in pattern/without choice, it is usually based in some need that is camouflaged and unmet. These desires run the gamut from needing to be loved, accepted, and heard, to the need to accept and love oneself. We may understand that conceptually, but we will continue our mechanical behavior until we understand it in our Being. We have to feel and see it in a way that acknowledges this need on a deep level; on a level of intense vulnerability.

When we reach that place, we can begin to grieve this needy place in us. With consciousness of this, we can begin to heal. We feel a new kind of peace in this self-recognition. When we heal, we will see ourselves in others. Our empathy will free us from the confines of the conflict. We find ourselves able to be in the presence of the person who could not show us the love. We understand that they couldn't love us because we couldn't love us.

We start to see them as us and then we can dive into forgiveness like never before.

When that cracks open, love is possible. The other person will feel it. They may begin to melt and your new found boundary that comes from self-respect and love does not project need onto them. We don't feel the need to react when they aren't giving us what we want because we don't need to have them give this to us. Their actions begin to change because of our lack of reaction.

The game is over and they quit blaming us or picking us apart.

It is worth it to find your way through to acceptance and forgiveness, even if this person has deeply hurt you.

Without it, we will continue to act out the pattern unconsciously in frustration and deep unhappiness. We continue to stay connected to our suffering. We continue to blame someone else for our own unhappiness.

Game on.

WORK, STRUGGLE, AND COMMITMENT

When you think about those three words, what feelings or associations come to you? I imagine not the most pleasant things. For you workaholics, it may sound like heaven.

In a world where everyone is overworked, stressed, and experiencing time poverty, imagine trying to conduct and promote courses and meditation retreats based on The Fourth Way practices involving practical inner effort out in daily life, sacred dances that create struggle in oneself, and commitment on all levels as part of the program.

How distinctly unorthodox in this day and age!

Most of the retreats and courses I know of offer a buffet of practices or classes, relaxation techniques and many chances to slither out from under our ego. That ego does not want to be discovered for what it is. It will have us convinced that going the extra mile or getting up early or getting out of our comfort zone is just not on our required agenda.

It will convince us that we can start tomorrow.

It will justify wriggling out of commitments when something more shiny, easy, or sexy tempts us.

It will tell us to get up and give up just when the alchemical shift is about to happen.

Complacency, apathy, avoidance behavior and self-indulgence are prevalent everywhere we look. Many times it is shrouded in the term "desire."

A seminar that can create conditions for us to experience what it feels like to struggle through those tendencies will deliver results. From struggle, a more refined energy comes into play. We can learn to draw from a strength that was previously unavailable and discover a power that will grow from this conscious labor. We become more equipped to vanquish the foe.

That foe will go to great lengths to hide from us.

That foe creates negative emotion, anxiety, paranoia, worry and distress among a plethora of other states. To struggle against our normal tendency, our conditioned pattern, our preferences and our comfort zone, will provide the food necessary for our own transformation.

Countless examples abound:

What about holding an asana to the point that we surrender to it? - where effort becomes non effort, where our ego lets go of achieving.

Remember when first learning to sit in meditation and the absolute agony, the pain in the legs, the desire to move, the rampant racing of thought, the feeling that this will make us crazy if we continue another minute, the desire to run far, far away?

How about reaching new strides in exercise where we dread the upcoming hill on our bike because our quads ache but something in us continues ahead.

-the push just before the breakthrough on a run.

-falling off the horse and getting back in the saddle

-redoing an experiment again and again knowing intuitively that our hypothesis holds water

-the impetus that pushes us to jump off the high dive, cross the suspension bridge or round the bend on a very precipitous cliff when we are afraid of heights.

-having faith that we can love again... or even at all.

If we don't struggle with our full effort, an effort that pushes against our comfort zone, our conditioned beliefs, and our identification with who we think we are, we will not know the freedom beyond it. This means pushing against our story of being a failure, or of not being good enough, or of being the best, or of being successful and all the rest of it.

If we cannot commit to ourselves and be trustworthy and honest, what makes us think we are going to do it with others? Integrity is created from this kind of struggle and sacrifice. Commitment means following through no matter what comes up. It requires the sacrifice of instant gratification.

Ultimately, this kind of effort must commence from an active "do" (as in do re mi). It has to come from a place inside that spurs us to action. This starts an affirming octave in which we initiate the struggle from our own conscience, and not from someone else's push.
We thus own it in every way.

There are two kinds of effort. Struggle derived from ego simply fulfills our desire to fix, to be better than, to do well, to achieve, and to win. That type of effort always compares its results to others.

Struggle from the right place needs no recognition. It comes from within. It is born of an inner humility and a sincere aim. The reward of deep transformation will spur us on to great things. We begin to manifest because we are part of the flow of the Universe.

No need to prove anything to anyone.

ACTIONS DON'T LIE

How true am I to my word?

Do I make idle promises? Do I do what I say I am going to do? Do I say yes when I know I am thinking no?

When I think of actions in relation to my words, many things come to my mind:

Integrity, trustworthiness, honesty, commitment.

It seems that a lot streams out of our mouths with no regard for what we are actually feeling.

Broken ceasefires and ending wars have been weighing heavy on my mind. Press conferences in which our government says they don't condone such awful inhumane actions while sending "support" and weapons are baffling to me. There is surely something else behind all of that.

Friends also come to mind. I am a faithful friend, though sometimes I don't call enough, but I do not wait for someone to call me. I call them. I once waited for a friend to call because I thought the relationship was lopsided. I was making it happen. Four years later, I am not really waiting for the call anymore. Her actions have spoken louder than her words "Let's get together soon" when we cross paths in the grocery store.

My children come to mind, especially the ones who have already left home. I no longer have the chance to give them a random big hug or stop my all important tasks to listen to what they have to say in a time of need.

I think of some dear people in my life who have passed away, knowing that I could have done more or been there for them in their dying days.

For me, actions sculpt the concept "Carpe Diem". I never know what tomorrow may bring. If an idea comes to my head, or a feeling in my heart, or gratitude for someone or something, I take action.

I make a plan and implement. I express creative impulses through music, writing, or connection. I initiate sex. I let someone know how much I appreciate them. I call.

I stand by my word no matter how much I don't want to do it.

When I can match my actions to my words, I learn accomplishment. I become someone of integrity.

I am also very careful now about what I say and what I commit to...

ATTENTION, SENSATION, AND WHY IT MATTERS

When I first came across the notion of attention and sensation, I thought I understood all there was to know about sensation. Sensation to me meant being able to "feel" my arm or be aware of my beating heart when I was about to walk out on stage. I knew it as pain in my throat when I was sick or a tight muscle after too much exercise.

To feel my body seemed just so... obvious. Not until I immersed myself in the ways of zen, awareness, self-observation and then self-mastery did I begin to understand the importance it would have on my life. I basically learned that sensation used as an awareness tool is the foundation for self-knowledge and freedom.

Like everyone else, I lived my life from the head up. I also suffered from prolonged sexual abuse, so it was hard for me to be in my body most of the time. Not only did I learn to leave my body in most intimate situations, I basically wasn't there most of the time to check in on my physical needs and basic self-care. I could run my body into the ground with hard work, cigarettes, coffee and stress. Let's not mention all the alcohol and drugs that inundated my system.

I was not in my body to experience any emotional pain. I learned to block out feeling in the most mysterious ways. I often thought I am "above" that, more evolved, and so completely stuffed the emotion. I found ways to dissociate from my body.

To be in my body meant that I had to start to feel, but even after meditating in a zen dojo for 6 years, I was simply stilling the mind.

I could see a massive improvement in my daily life in regard to reactions and fear, but I still had all of the ramifications of living out of my body.

Studying the Fourth Way would open my eyes to a new world: one in which I learned that to have moments of expanded awareness often was the key to opening my heart. Expanded awareness is a loaded experience and now I teach it in courses, on retreats and in meditation groups. It allowed me to experience all of me in a unified whole package. From that perspective, everything changed. In fact, I realized there was nothing to change and everything to see and accept.

I was taught that sensation is the first tool of awareness to master. It was not just so I could be in my body (although that is what it did), but it was to learn to divide my attention. It was not just for getting grounded (although that is what it did), but to experience what was me and what was not me. It was not just to take me out of my thinking (although that is just what it did), but to integrate the three brains, moving, feeling and thinking as a unified field from which to observe myself.

It is rarely taught in this way.

When I ask my students to begin to practice sensation, they usually notice their aches and pains more. They notice what their bodies need. They start to notice more tension. These are all positive steps toward understanding sensation, but it does not yet entail the use of sensation as a tool to expand their awareness.

They notice their attention being pulled to different physical phenomenon when they are in a negative state, racing heart, tight throat, upset stomach, but many of us notice that anyway under those circumstances. That is when the physical is so loud that we can't help but experience it.

Once the practice is underway, something magical starts to happen. When we start to use attention to maintain sensation in the body while we do other things, our awareness expands beyond what we could have known without it. With the body there and our awareness of it and other things too, we are given the chance to see so much more.

We can take in impressions from the outside at the same time as taking in impressions on the inside. Our intentional awareness of sensation gets easier and easier the more we try to do it. It is our preparation for self-acceptance and healing trauma.

You might wonder how I just made that leap.

If we are able to maintain this expanded awareness, we are prepared to see our age old habits that have literally been set in us over many many years. Our habits range from leaving our bodies, to overriding self-harm, to nefarious distraction games we play with ourselves. They are made of stock emotional reactions and identification with what is right and wrong, good and bad. These habits are limitless and we don't think they are habits. We think we are aware.

That is the scary part.

I thought I had so much knowledge about my own trauma and my own suffering, but to see it in this new way is to instantly heal. I saw how attached I was to my suffering. It took a lot of practice to maintain sensation and experience the things I had been avoiding feeling and seeing most of my life. When I started seeing it from this new perspective without judging it, I could stay there. I could ride the wave of pain or shame and begin to understand it in my body, my feeling and my mind all at once.

Doing this not so simple practice lead me to see that from which I hid most of my life. I became more prepared when things got difficult, when all the gremlins came running out in gangs within me, ready to tear me apart at the seams. I started to see how I sought love in all the wrong places. I could fight the urge to say yes when I really wanted to say no. I was equipped with a resource I had never had before and I could begin to see all of the automatic functioning that I had previously assumed was conscious.

An accumulation of presence began to pool within me. I gained strength where I had none before. I began to gather bits of me that were scattered all over the place. It all started with this practice of sensation to expand my awareness.

When I have sensation, I am present.

When I am present, I can watch within.

When I can watch within, I can accept.

When I accept, I heal.

THE ELEPHANT IN
THE ROOM

Post election Day 2.

We have all been reflecting on how this has happened. It has happened just like it happens every time. In the US, we elect someone into the highest office of the land. It wasn't rigged in the way Trump professed. It may be due to archaic laws still in place regarding the electoral college.

It in every way is a reflection of our inner selves.

With media playing a key role, we see how large swaths of people can be influenced. In the beginning, Trump was often featured for the sake of ratings. NBC made him into a celebrity as The Apprentice and knew he would keep money flowing in during the election season. The Clinton campaign's leaked documents showed its own interest in that coverage, thinking there was everything to gain by having such an easy opponent.

Trump began to sing the song of so many Americans who are truly hurting with no jobs and low wages. People who have to work two jobs and very long hours, and still are not able to make ends meet. I don't think they are all bigots and misogynists. They are people who are suffering and very angry. They are not the enemy.

He spoke to an activated voter base who are the very product of our system. A system which does not support infrastructure, education, healthcare, and has suppressed the right to assemble in the form of unions and otherwise. It is a system which promulgates inequality, sexism, racism and fear. It is a country that has focused on profit through unregulated banking, insurance and large multi national corporations who operate as humans under the constitution.

While Trump was getting all the media coverage, Bernie Sanders was talking to thousands and thousands with a sometimes similar message with no media coverage whatsoever. His message was one of hope for many in the shadow of a strengthening oligarchy. He recognized that one of our main concerns should be climate change and the importance of dismantling our dependence on fossil fuel. One wonders if Sanders had been the nominee, would he have been able to carry the weight that Clinton could not.

Once Trump did get the nomination, the media took a bias against him, which then made it look like all of the institutions that had cheated so many Americans, the elites, the "system" were against him too. This bolstered his position and he was championed as a hero to those who have lost faith in the system. No matter how much bigotry, hate and misogyny is embedded in his personality, it could be ignored by the very large part of the country that is suffering so much.

Some of the same people who voted for Obama then turned around and put their hopes in Trump, from rust belt workers to small Ohio business owners. His concurrent message of anger and hate spoke to their collective shadow and let it grow to epic proportion.

Trump represents the shadow we are not dealing with.

This is the elephant in the room.

I don't believe someone so narcissistic as Trump really has people's interests at heart. He spewed off at the mouth to win the game.

But that is what we do with our own inner transformation.

I could go on and on with why and how this all happened.

We all have opinions and theories to support our blame.

The important thing for us all is that we have come to a turning point in, not only American history, but the history of the world; a point in which we must now listen to our conscience, and focus on individual transformation as an agent of change in the coming Age.

We do not recognize how grave things are until the darkest hour is upon us.

We do not see that it is all of our own doing.

We now perhaps can begin to consider that there is an elephant in the room.

We are in the bottom pit of the Kaliyuga, the Age of Iron, in which the delusional world plays out and manifests on an extraordinary level. It is now as individuals gather together in full force- in the name of love and preservation of spirit- in the name of our relationship with nature and God- in the name of solidarity of human dignity, that we must begin to act.

This can only happen if we recognize our own capacity to be the change and embody the foundational elements that encompass freedom. If we do not start with our own selves, we will continue to manifest the shadow side in greater and greater proportions.

The elephant will simply get bigger.

We need this collective shock. It is not just happening in our country. It is happening worldwide but because of that, a positive counter force will begin to grow. There is a movement and it is happening from the bottom up with each tiny individual.

Things never change from the top down.
Things never change from this religion or that religion, this ism or that ism, this political party or that political party.

It only happens from the metamorphosis that occurs within us. One in which we embrace our shadow. One in which we accept who we are and observe the war that is happening within us. That war within that beats us down everyday.

The one that criticizes every move we make.

The one that latches onto hate, blame and alienation of self and others.

The one that pushes back insecurity through dominion of others.

The one that finds any fix it can to numb the pain.

We have remained in a sleeping trance for so long that when the outer shock occurs, it appears as a monster rearing its ugly head.

We didn't see it coming and we want to blame someone else for it.

We are flabbergasted and again filled with fear.

We still don't see that it is of our own doing.

"We can neither hope for an Obama nor fear a Trump." - Edward Snowden said in an interview last night.

We could not see that it has been creeping in for ever so long, right under our complacent noses, from leaders of all political parties.

What we must do now is wake up and recognize that our own transformation is what generates the change we are seeking. There is no savior to guide the masses. The only savior is each of us taking responsibility for our own actions and our own inner process.

We think the way to change it is from the outside.

We must be brave warriors who pick up the sword of Christ, of Zarathustra, of Mohammed, of Joan of Arc, of Nakano Takeko, of Archangel Michael and all the many others whose sword represents the courage to see within.

This sword is not the sword of war and hate and killing. It is the symbol of courage that initiates our greatest inner struggle to embrace our darkest parts.

Every act of love is courageous.

Every act of forgiveness is the process of self-acceptance.

Every individual choice that helps our environment is the recognition that we are part of a moving whole and not dominators of destruction.

Every attempt at true connection is an act of healing.

Every time we reach out to help another feeds the necessary counterforce.

We elected Donald Trump through our own doing, our fear and our lack of inner understanding.

Yes all of us.

Let us now take responsibility for what is deep inside of us in order to manifest the world we want to have.

This is the only way we will address the elephant in the room.

A DIFFERENT GRATITUDE

A few days ago I had to travel to find internet and yesterday I simply went without it. Perfect for my Thanksgiving article. Even if many of my readers are from other countries, I am sure they will appreciate my theme of the blessings of contrast.

We take a lot for granted and losing the internet will drive that right home. I also gained a fresh perspective of gratitude this weekend from a day seminar I hosted.

Both cases were a direct result of lack.

A little perspective here:

For many years, I have been hosting retreats and seminars of an esoteric nature. The teaching is subtle and the practices demand an attention to which most are unaccustomed. After a couple of movements sessions, people are tired in a new way and they may realize that they don't often utilize this special kind of attention.

Maintaining expanded awareness is a skill we have to practice in order to build a stronger "attention muscle." That new muscle brings about extraordinary transformation in our lives because we start to notice the automatic in ourselves. When things are automatic, we take them for granted, we recognize them as things we have labeled; there is no inquiry; there is no consciousness. There is no freedom and we constantly suffer the consequences.

We may be somewhat aware of our "self-talk" but we are not aware of its consistent presence in our lives or how it is created in the first place. We are not aware of how it consumes our attention. We are not aware of the energy it costs us. We may not understand loss of force until we see it manifesting in our reactions and our negativity, blame and guilt.

Creating circumstances and conditions for us to be able to notice what we take for granted is what The Movements (a term now used to refer to the Sacred Dances of Gurdjieff) are all about. This is what we practiced at the seminars this weekend.

It is never a very comfortable situation to observe what we take for granted within ourselves. It is never easy to lose what we take for granted in any circumstance.

This is the beauty of loss and struggle, for it takes us into a new zone and reveals the perspective we were looking for all along.

One of the wonderful and most satisfying things about the seminar last weekend was the number of attendees. It has taken a certain effort in the form of consistent offerings over the years to gain that kind of attendance. People don't just come out of the woodwork. They must have a certain curiosity and trust to be motivated enough to come to something where they know it might be difficult.

My husband always jokes that we would have hundreds at our retreats at this point, if we were offering catered relaxation yoga retreats. But we aren't. We are working to help people get uncomfortable enough to see within, and that entails discipline, self-honesty, self-acceptance, self-observation, and loss of the very things that keep us from ourselves.

My point is that I would not have this more poignant joy in my heart about the number of attendees if I had not experienced the contrast in the form of lack of attendees in years past. To have faith and be persistent in the face of "perceived failure" yields this kind of gratitude. It cannot exist without it.

Meditating again and again in utter frustration and being at the point of quitting have produced the tearful breakthroughs of gratitude in my past.

Defeat, loss, and failure after failure result in deeper, more heartfelt gratitude.

It's skin in the game.

It's how things work.

I learned this not only through my life of meditation, but also in the competitive world of professional performance as a musician. Each "bad performance" got me closer to how I perform today with clear presence and connection with my audience.

Lack is everywhere for us to experience, right down to losing the internet, running out of toilet paper, making do with what is in the cupboard, losing a lover, or stepping out of our comfort zone.

The contrast produces keen appreciation for what we have gained. It is in the recovery from sickness that we learn to never take our health for granted again. It is when our life is saved whether that be spiritual or literal, that we come to wake up with joy in our hearts daily.

It is the relief we feel for a new job or a new home after having searched for months.

Let's try to have gratitude for our lack whether that be attention, presence, joy, energy, health, family, lovers, money, help, peace, or safety, for this darkness will assuredly increase the light.

The acceptance of where we are in the process will ease the pain.

Many of us in the United States will enjoy big meals and family gatherings today. Let us remember those who are in serious need of shelter and food and appreciate the difficult times we ourselves have had, for they make today all that much better.

May we find the blessings in our lack and give thanks.

HIGHER INFLUENCES

When I was first exposed to The Work over 20 years ago, I was intrigued by the idea of A, B, and C influences. That is all I could be at that time... intrigued by ideas. None of it meant what I have come to understand about it today. That is the nature of a living teaching working into our bones over time.

Dharma must have vehicles through which it can channel. It is transmitted through people, sacred texts, art, music, nature, and even places. The vibrations from highest sources must have some way of reaching us and activating something within us.

A Influences are things that come from regular life. They help us to build careers and families. They are present in maintaining relationships and communities. They have everything to do with money and earning a living. They keep us under the illusion that we are making progress in this material world. They will definitely keep our will sublimated to the group, where individual thought is ditched for the group opinion in order to belong.

A influences are present if we approach this Work from the standpoint of regular life, switching our identification from one belief to another as if that were taking care of our limiting beliefs. It is doing this work for a limited reward that only rearranges our personality in terms of business, money making, politics. We start to believe our buying and selling is sacred in some way. We believe our side is the right side.

When we approach any method of transformation from a perspective of everyday life, we remain "outside of the teaching."

Yet, we must bring our spiritual practice into everyday life.

I have seen many people come into our groups and never recognize the presence of an inner sanctum. They fully believe they are taking part in something and they do to the extent that their level of Being will allow. We cannot expect everyone to enter the inner sanctum so to speak. For them, the teachings of this school remain A influences.

B Influences have existed outside of time, reaching us in different forms according to the needs of people and their level of Being or their depth of sleep. They are like the secret treasures that can have no value put on them. They are the mystical web that weaves throughout an inner force that has been generated outside of regular life.

B influences are the vehicle for C influences; the highest emanations from the Sun Absolute. These B Influences hold the power for the direct absorption of C influences, a living truth that comes through if the energetic container is powerful enough.

When we approach The Work from the perspective of opening to B influences, something has ignited our emotional center. When this happens, something has quickened for us and everything we say and do takes on greater meaning. Our efforts change in quality. They broaden into realms we cannot understand but begin to taste.

B influences can be experienced in certain holy or sacred places if we are open to their subtlety, like the pyramids, great cathedrals and ancient stone circles. The activated energy has been collected over time and we can feel that force.

Certainly many sacred texts carry the energy of God and codes of higher laws, like The Gospels, The Quran, the Upanishads, the Tao te Ching, but we can read them and totally miss the transmission because of our particular station in our spiritual life. The teaching can go right over our heads.

In occult traditions, one way wisdom traditions are transmitted is through a form that appears to be intended for an entirely different purpose and is called a legominism. The word may be nonsensical but the meaning is clear.

These were texts or symbols carrying hidden meaning and can only be received if we are in a certain place in our transformation.

The enneagram could be considered one of these symbols.

We become subject to B influences when our level of Being is ready to receive them. Nothing changes for humankind if we cannot absorb these influences. We then repeat history, continue our wars and our hate, our "self-improvement" and our crusades.

For things to change, our level of Being needs to attract something higher. When our work takes on an emotional component in which our heart is being opened, we are affected by the higher energies entering us from a new magnetic center. We become keenly aware that something is a B influence, something outside the confines of regular life. With our Being, we can perceive that something better does not mean something in the future, but simply an exchange of energies resulting in a permanent shift outside of time, the place of Now.

Everything that we do in this work from struggling with negative emotion to noticing how we keep accounts to making efforts to observe ourselves is for the purpose of understanding what it is to be in a true dynamic present moment. This is the understanding of Being, something that is all encompassing and outside of time. We must have a cohesive and integrated functional life to raise our level of Being.

When we are affected by B influences, things begin to change drastically and permanently. We will not have to keep dealing with the same ridiculous aspects of our personality, because we will understand from a very new and upgraded perspective. It is corrected permanently.

C influences come directly from the masters, Jesus, Buddha, Mohammed and the like. We come in direct contact without an intermediary.

By doing work in an esoteric system, we create a magnetic center that allows us to see and attract higher influences. These influences are already existent, but we simply become aware of them and affected by them.

We must ask ourselves if we are approaching our own personal transformation from A influences only.

Is there something deep within us being magically stirred?

Are we able to ease our grip on the material world and trust in something much more eternal?

Are our eyes open to the profound forces that can affect all of our worlds including the material?

THE INNER DILEMMA

Our Inner Dilemma stems from a dramatic feedback loop between our heads and our emotions.

It is a direct result of identification with our learned belief system. We have all grown up with a certain set of beliefs instilled in us through our parents, our education, our religion, and our environment. It is more or less imprinted on us as young vulnerable people and was reiterated over the years through a system of rewards and punishments.

We learned that certain behaviors resulted in praise and others in punishment and shame via conditional love. Depending on the outlook and the philosophy of our parents, we adapted a certain belief structure that we carried forward and implemented within ourselves as the Inner Critic or The Inner Victim.

There are certain parameters in which we learn "right and wrong" but this is at the discretion of someone else. They create the "shoulds" of our Inner Critic. Of course, there are certain absolute values to which we must all adhere, for instance, not hurting someone else or ourselves. These are outlined in all religions as Sacred Law. When we are not able to easily act within these values, we could be identified with our Inner Critic or our Inner Victim. We are unable to live by conscience and automatically fall back to regressed patterns.

Noticing when our Inner Critic or Inner Victim comes alive within our own thoughts is a good first defense. These thoughts offer a glimpse into how identified we are with the imposed beliefs.

When our performance does not match up to our expectations, our Inner Critic does the job of assessing and making us feel bad. We should have done this; for the Inner Victim, they should have done that. This causes negative emotions like anger, sadness, and frustration.

We would not have these negative reactive emotions if we could release ourselves from the state of identification. This Critic is the seat of judgement and our attachment to it creates the belief system. We become overly concerned with the outcome of our actions because we are trying to match up to the impossible standards of this self-imposed critic.

If we are unable to accept the way things are, then we are slaves to our Inner Critic. It creates strife and discontent which then gets reinforced by the Inner Critic saying "I told you so." If there are lots of feelings of anger, disgust, inadequacy, unhappiness, and unfulfillment, then one can be sure that The Inner Critic rules.

When we start to question this Inner Critic and notice how we unduly judge ourselves, we can unravel the feedback loop. This is the bulk of daily Work on ourselves. Negative emotion is our first red flag. Finding enough presence to observe the state of identification with The inner Critic is the practice. With consistent effort, life can become less judgemental because we have dismantled the feedback loop. We suddenly realize we are accepting the way things are, imperfect and all. We allow ourselves to be in the moment stepping outside of the influences of the past.

IMPRESSIONS

Taking in an objective impression of ourselves is a game changer.

We take in thousands of impressions a second, but it may be surprising to know that most are not objective. We move through the world through a series of associations. Most of what we take in is analysed and then associated with a retrieved memory. G.I. Gurdjieff referred to this system as the formatory apparatus and it works faster than lightning. Before we know it, we see something, associate it with memory and then react.

We rarely take in new impressions and so are unable to be very objective about ourselves or the environment in which we live.

For this reason, it is important to develop skills that will allow us to see things more objectively. With developed attention in our minds, paired with sensation in our bodies simultaneously, we start to stand in the present moment, free of judgement and analysis. In that presence, we have the opportunity to see something we have never seen before about ourselves.

Our transformation doesn't come from us labeling something as a limiting belief or coming up with reasons for why we do what we do. New impressions are an objective snapshot of us as it is happening, not an analysis afterward. Once we gather many of those snapshots, we begin to understand what actually creates our negative emotion. We start to see how these emotions like anger, fear, frustration or insecurity are built on associations that are highly subjective and untrue. We get a snapshot of how we are *identified* and *attached* to illusions of all sorts.

If we get good at taking in new impressions of ourselves, we may see how our sideways anger is unfounded. We may begin to not take things so personally and start to see how we have associated something someone has said with something negative or personal in our past. We start to see how we have been blaming others for what we could not see in ourselves.

New impressions are life changing.

INTERNAL AND EXTERNAL CONSIDERING

Here's the conundrum of internal and external considering.

We can get very very tricked by our own ego.

The terms internal and external considering were first introduced by Gurdjieff and the subsequent movement known as The Fourth Way.

First let's look at the definition of each term:

"Inner considering is a form of identification. External considering needs a certain amount of self-remembering. External considering takes into account other people's weaknesses, putting oneself in their place. External considering means control. Inner considering is when we feel that people do not give us enough, do not appreciate us enough."

—P.D. Ouspensky

I have known the definition of inner considering to simply be putting importance on what other people think of me. It is always and unequivocally a result of a state of identification with what someone else thinks. Our work is to recognize how our attention is captured and identified.

When first introduced to these ideas, I found it more accessible to recognize how my attention was captured by being on the lookout for internal considering. That showed me how hopelessly I was identified with thought. It often felt like someone was not treating me right or someone owed me something, even respect.

As I became more proficient at self-observation and not just thinking I was observing something, I began to get an emotional flavor of what this feels like. Once I could recognize this "flavor," I could catch myself more easily before it blew up into a state of negativity that grew a life and strength of its own.

As a survivor of sexual abuse, I was determined not to be identified with being a victim. I became hopelessly lost in the notion that I was invincible. Nothing could break me down to a place of vulnerability. I experienced my own inner considering in the form of worrying if people thought I was weak, smart enough, or successful enough. Weakness and vulnerability were signs that I did not have it together, but that "strength" kept me from feeling.

This created in me a way of deflecting my own needs and my own transformation.

We all identify to one degree or another. How big the mountains we make of molehills reveals how identified we are. How long does it takes us to let go?

We may be very identified with being a good person, a considerate person, a person who serves and thinks of others first. Many of our actions will be geared toward fulfilling that picture of ourselves, but if others do not appreciate it and our actions go unnoticed, then we find ourselves in an extremely negative state. We start to take accounts about how others' actions do not match up to our own. We feel we deserve to be appreciated and recognized for our efforts. We feel our good deeds should be reciprocated.

Another example would be to care about what someone thought about some action we took, for example, a class we gave, a speech we presented, or a dinner we made. What they think feeds a certain need that we ourselves are unable to fill. Putting importance on what others think completes the false picture we have of ourselves and when it doesn't sync up, negative states of extraordinary proportion ensue.

When we can catch ourselves acting out of the necessity to gain someone else's approval or love, we may be able to hear the thoughts that go along with the scenario.

By the time we are in the negative state concerning what other people think or how they have reacted, we have already gone through many stages of identification that we can learn to recognize. We have to do the work of observing ourselves.

Inner considering, always rooted in the past or future, can sound like this:

"Maybe if I had done/said/been more like this, he wouldn't feel this way."

"What if I am not being effective enough in my performance/teaching/ research?"

"Oh no, they might fire me because I just can't pay attention well enough"

"Why can't they appreciate what I have done for them?"

"Maybe I should have left well enough alone."

"What if I get fired for saying that?"

"Why can't they treat me better?"

"After what I have done/been through, he owes me big time."

"They are going to think I don't know what I am talking about."

"Maybe if I had been a better parent/lover/boss/student/worker, this would not have happened"

These statements are filled with shoulds, what if's, and regret of past actions and fear of what might happen in the future. These statements always involve what others think in regard to us.

Notice how much time you spend caring about what other people think in regard to yourself. It can clue you into the false illusions that create your suffering.

LIKES AND DISLIKES

When we try to discover more about suffering and its inherent causes, we will always find ourselves winding back to likes and dislikes.

Our suffering stems from identifying with what we have labeled as good or bad and here's why.

We are quick to judge and wish that someone else would change. We find fault in others so we don't see it in ourselves. We have preconceived notions about what should be for our lives, what is right and what is wrong, the success or failure of things, the black and white of it all.

Our mechanical nature, the lower self as master, will forever lead us to make either-or assessments of matters. The very function of our ego is to assess whether something is good or bad, right or wrong, proper or improper, but where did this judge get its ideas about which is which?

How does this judge run the show?

We get very upset when things are not the way we think they should be.

Every person has a different idea about what should or should not be. We will never all agree. There are absolute values to which we can aspire to live by as guidelines, but something is distorted in the way we impose what we think is right or wrong onto others.

Because our ego resides in the conceptual mind, it has no way of understanding what lies outside of dualism. It is constantly assessing either or, this or that, good or bad.

379

When we identify with the dualistic nature of our ego, things simply become impossible to resolve. We will always be unhappy because things are not "as they should be." As long as there is a notion of "should," we are victims of our likes and dislikes.

When we put ourselves in a situation that "we do not like," we force ourselves to see how identified we are. We begin to realize that the thing we do not like is not us but has to do with some belief from our personality. It is an identification with something that "should be."

If we allow ourselves to do the thing we dislike, we confront different parts of ourselves.

By using an intentional effort to tolerate what we don't like, we are able to pinpoint certain things with which we are identified. We put our lower nature to the test. When we engage in something "we do not like," we start to realize where this dislike comes from. If we continually stay in the comfort zone of doing what we like, we don't get the chance to discover how we are trapped and we continue to suffer.

Through the years, I have engaged in practices that help facilitate this struggle. Giving things up for Lent is a perfect example of that kind of intentional struggle. Fasting is a part of every religion for this very purpose. In our group, we use themes that will help us understand what happens when we push against our likes and dislikes.

One of the key results that crops up is negative emotion, i.e suffering. Look at times when you are irritated with the way things are going or with someone's behavior. Where does the irritation come from? More often than not, it comes from the notion that things are not as they should be.

If we can accept the way things are without believing they should be another way, we eliminate this suffering.

What creates the shoulds? We have come to believe that things are bad when it doesn't go the way we want things to go. We identify with the judgement call of our ego.

We also take other people's actions personally as a result of this identification.

Take, for example, when someone is late. We become irritated because we feel slighted. We feel it is inconsiderate of the other person to make us wait. The late person, in our mind, has no regard for us and our time. The negative emotion stems from what we think others are doing to us.

There is absolutely no empathy occurring in this situation.

The late person may have had any number of reasons for their tardiness but it was not aimed at the waiting person. They may have a problem of being chronically late. In fact, they probably feel terrible and apologize.

The negative emotion which ensues in the waiting person is the result of identification with being a victim. They deem the late person's behavior as bad because it has made them feel bad.

When we imagine people's actions as centering around us and how it make us feel, we are victims. Our emotions and feelings are the result of someone else's actions. We have no boundaries. We are taken in whatever direction the wind blows.

People rarely behave the way you want them to! People rarely have that much malice in mind, but rather are oblivious of their own actions and the consequences that result.

When we judge people's behavior, or feel that we ourselves have failed in some way, we are adhering to a certain set of beliefs that have formed about what is good and what is bad. Our work toward transformation is to shed light on these likes and dislikes. We are then able to "break the spell" of the conditioning and allow our Being to become free.

We will no longer take things personally.

When we are able to see our attachment and aversion to things as illusion, our Essence gains strength. We starve the personality. This comes from a place of non identification with what is bad or good, right or wrong, pleasant or unpleasant. It requires practice in being present, outside of the place of judgement.

If we can put ourselves to the test, the struggle creates just the right energy to feed our Essence.

SELF-SABOTAGE, THE MANY I'S, AND IDENTIFICATION

We all know the phenomenon of self-sabotage. It comes sneaking in when we least expect it and it is definitely something we have no control over. We lack consciousness around it, but realize it is from our own doing. We don't know how to stop ourselves.

A worse case scenario is knowing we self-sabotage and not making efforts to do something about it; the ultimate self-sabotage.

First let's talk about why self sabotage exists in the first place.

Many have heard me talk about the battle of the "I"s within us. When we set out to do something noble, like eat properly, quit smoking or drinking, get up in the morning and meditate, we are often faced with another part of ourselves that wants nothing to do with this decision. These parts are fully distinct and unaware of the others when we are operating and fully identified with one of them. This is the nature of identification in which we believe that the part of us that wants the diet is all of us. By the very definition, when we are identified, our identity is wrapped up in the ideas of self put forth by that part of us.

The one that wants to go on a diet wants to appear better to others. The one that wants go on a diet wants to be a healthy person and doesn't want to get sick or be in bad health. The one that wants the diet knows that eating better would make them feel better. The one on the diet might feel if they look better, people will like them more, or they can find a good partner, or be more accepted in society. There is a lot wrapped up in the one identified with eating more healthily.

There are other parts of us, however, that cannot resist emotional eating and have upheld that self-comfort process since childhood. There may be sugar addictions that have stemmed from a form of self-medicating once drugs and alcohol were no longer an option. There may be associations with food in regard to rebellion and control. We may sabotage the diet because we are afraid of attracting a partner. We become identified with the neediness for comfort, control, rebellion etc.

When these two opposing parts of us come head to head, we experience it as shame and guilt around our actions.This may be the underlying cause of the self-sabotage. We are used to living in an environment that was first been established by our parents, teachers, friends and other authority figures, so we learn to carry that forward. If we have been shamed over and over for anything from sexuality to shining brightly, we ourselves find subversive ways to sabotage our good intentions in order to carry forth that environment of shame and guilt. Only now it is us doing it to ourselves.

If we can realize through true self-observation that our actions are a result of needing to promulgate an environment of shame and guilt, we can start to understand self-sabotage and what it is really about. I often call this part B of an observation. We can get to the back story of our sabotage when we sit with our need to feel shame and guilt.
We have learned to shame ourselves in order to carry out what was conditioned in us. We learn to do things that make us feel guilty because that is our norm.

Therefore, the first step in correcting self-sabotage is to listen and observe consciously in a present moment of integration to the pattern playing out in our head. We know we do it, but we probably do it a million times more than we think we do. Every time we can catch ourselves in the act of believing how horrible we are, how unsuccessful we are, how inadequate we are, how ugly our body is, how miserable our life has become, we step outside of the conditioning and develop the group of "I"s that wants to solve this.

There may grow a consciousness around this self-bashing. We know we feel it. We hear the voices. We may be totally asleep through the eating of the chocolate cake, simply living in the comfort zone. We may also be suffering greatly in the act, knowing we "shouldn't be doing it."

Any addict will tell you that experience of doing the thing they have no control over and thinking right then and there, I don't want this anymore but they can't stop themselves.

The addiction may be the need for consequent feelings of shame, guilt, and self-pity. These are buffers to help us not to see the "I"s bumping into each other. We live in these states of self-pity and self-bashing. It is the norm until we begin to strengthen our more spiritual and self-loving "I"s. Each time we can catch ourselves identifying with these feelings of self-disgust and shame, we strengthen something within that can do something about it.

A new magnetic center begins to develop and a magnetic center gains force and momentum through attraction. As the magnetic center grows, it becomes easier to loosen our grip on this identification. A new part of us is able to see more easily and accept what we see. We start to have compassion and understanding toward these parts of us that just didn't know any better. We start to feel the pain we have held back for so long. We soon will start to forgive ourselves for carrying the nonsense of our conditioning which we had no control over.. We can forgive ourselves for being helpless to the machine that was us until we found a way.

So the next time you find yourself in the middle of an act of sabotage, start getting very curious around what is actually going on. Always bring in sensation to your body to get a more rounded and objective view of self. If you have gotten to phase B without any awareness of your own sabotage, get curious and watchful about this habitual state of self-bashing. Notice again that this is where you are living. It is a habit. You don't want to replace it with another habit because that is just as unconscious as the first habit.

We want to consciously dismantle it by seeing it for what it is outside of a state of identification. The only way to do that is to develop attention and watch ourselves with new growing perspective.

RECIPROCAL MAINTENANCE

We don't know our role here on planet earth.

We don't know our purpose.

We do not see ourselves as part of a whole system and thus we suffer tremendously and continue to destroy our own resources. Whether it is a result of some catastrophe not according to law as Gurdjieff put it or something else, it is clear that something is afoot.

We eat live things not dead things and so, in order to survive we destroy part of life on earth. As we feed off of life on earth, we also must pay a price for the debt of our existence. We believe we are at the top of the food chain with no regard to the evolution of a sustaining system.

Surely there is something more for us to understand about our place in the Universe.

In the cosmology of Gurdjieff, our evolution as humans provides a reciprocal maintenance with the substance of earth. We are able to transform energies because of our consciousness and free will. It is our role to evolve enough to contribute to an ever sustaining planet. This comes in the form of advancing and upleveling our consciousness in order to feed the Earth and replenish what we have taken from it. Our energetic transformation is part of the necessary maintenance, otherwise, we produce food for the moon.

(More on that later.)

He presents a three fold value system, namely:
1) Human's concern with their own welfare in light of their mortality
2) Humans place in nature and the obligation that entails
3) Our supernatural obligation to fulfill the purpose for which we exist

Let's explore further.

Everything is connected and systems support one another. How could we be outside of that loop? Our self-importance keeps us blind to this connection and purpose in the scheme of this maintenance. When we destroy the elements of nature, we must "energetically pick up the slack" that that element served. As animals go extinct, we involve and sink lower in the chain. We become animal like in our behavior and in our emotions.

Everything has a purpose including humans. We are three brained beings capable of transforming energy, unlike animals and plants. When we work consciously, transforming energies, we feed the system and contribute to our own self-transformation. This is the goal and purpose of the grand experiment of Earth in Mr. G's eyes.

Our sense of entitlement is our downfall. We believe that the earth was made for us but in fact the opposite is true. We are three brained beings with a moving center, an emotional center, and a thinking center. We feed off of the two and one brained beings below us in the chain. Each strata of energetic sophistication encompasses the previous ones. We may feel we are at the top of the food chain, but the Law of Reciprocal Maintenance says otherwise.

"The sting of the doctrine consists in the inclusion of man as a class of beings 'whose lives also serve for maintaining something great or small in the world'."

–J. Bennett

Our transformation of energy serves as a catalyst. We can choose to live and die without making any effort toward our evolution. In this case, we simply die and involuntarily give off energy for the planet. We can, however, voluntarily produce a finer energy while we are alive to feed a larger system. In doing so, we also contribute to our own eternal life.

That eternal life is not a given as professed in all religious dogma. That dogma in a way let's us off the hook.

When we extract minerals from the earth with no regard for the consequences, we destroy a necessary balance in the ecosystem. When we cut trees down and pollute the waters, we are destroying life in its delicate balance. We live with no respect for this balance, but we must consume in order to survive.

How could we think that we can feed off and destroy certain elements in the balance and not think that there is nothing for us to serve? How can we so easily ignore our own self-destruction?

"Under the primary law of conservation of matter, the conditioned universe manifests loss of order and final dissolution with the passage of time; but Gurdjieff taught that high level energy is generated at an unconditioned level of Being as a corrective to the process of entropy, and this energy makes evolution possible."

- J. Bennett

The fact that our inner work toward higher consciousness could contribute to the regeneration of the planet may seem like a far reach, but if we look at ourselves as transformers capable of involution and evolution of energies, we can see that we humans play a part in the system. Our evolution creates a higher frequency that will sustain the planet instead of destroying it. Otherwise, we too will experience a mass extinction in order to involuntarily feed a system out of balance.

A FINER SUBSTANCE

One of the divine gifts we have for our inner work is our breath. At any moment we have the possibility to breathe consciously. When we do so, when we remember our breath, we are brought into the present moment.

Our attention to this breath and what it can transmute can make all the difference in our lives. With each conscious breath comes distribution of light throughout our system. If we are aware of the finer substance that exists in the air, a refined essence that we all share, we can realize that we all have instant access to it. The more attention we pay to this aspect of elements in the air, the more purified our breath becomes and we are fed.

This is the secret to divine alchemy.

In trying to create a mindful sacred daily practice, we come up with excuse after excuse. We are extremely skilled at making excuses for ourselves. We will come up with anything to excuse ourselves from being here now.

Why?

Because if we begin the work of attaining light consciousness, our reality as we know it may turn upside down. Everything we know as us may be proven false. All security systems hacked. All foundations crumbled.

We may know somewhere deep inside that everything we have built our daily life around is a false pretense for living; the way we do our jobs, the way we search for love, and the way we remain dependent on things that don't serve.

We know we are unhappy and longing for meaning but continue to reinforce the deep grooves of automatic behavior. If we seek our true purpose and listen to our heart, we risk losing everything we have built up for years and years. It means our life has been a sham.

If we get a taste of this divine light and get even a little traction, it can sometimes send us running toward feel good new age fluff. We search for anything to fill the newly found void that keeps us from actually facing the scary shadow stuff.

Yes, the part of us that identifies strongly with good and bad will cling to self-improvement like a bulldog.

We also run to easy listening and smooth jazz types of spirituality with pretty riffs and lots of sappy emotional melodies. The sentimental journey substitutes our chance of feeling what we are really hiding from.

It's a patch. It's a fix.

It makes us feel really good about ourselves until we don't and go back for more, but it isn't expanding our consciousness one iota.

The litmus test is how we live our daily lives, how happy we really are, how capably we experience acceptance and love through right action. That is how we can assess our level of Being and how our practice is working or not.

Are we connecting, thriving (uh that includes making money), creating, rejoicing, relaxing and partaking of an inner force that permeates everything we do?

It's the thing that can make even collecting garbage a soulful expansion of our God Consciousness.

We have a chance any second of the day to raise our level of Being.

We have a choice at any juncture to remember to breathe consciously.

Those moments add up to a very big deal.

ABOUT THE AUTHOR: MOLLY KNIGHT FORDE

Molly Knight Forde, professional classical pianist, international transformation mentor, inspirational speaker and author leads people to personal freedom using wisdom teachings and unique awareness methods practiced out in the world, not just on the cushion. As founder of the Awareness School, she teaches the Art of Self-observation and has been facilitating global retreats, on and offline courses, women's groups as well as one on one mentoring for over 15 years.

She is trained in Zen Buddhism, Fourth Way Wisdom, Sufism, Reiki Healing, energy work and is a certified coach with the Gaia Project for Women's Leadership.

Her greatest wish is to contribute to the New Epoch by assisting individual transformation through expanded awareness, meditation, Sacred Dance and music.

Her book *The Abundance Mindset,* and CD's *The Art Of Dance* and *French* can be purchased on Amazon.

ABOUT THE ARTIST:
VANESSA COUTO

Vanessa Couto is an astrological coach and artist. She is also considered by her clients their 'cosmic travel guide and mentor'. Through her coaching work, she helps her clients get a better understanding of who they are, what is their life's purpose, and how to navigate the threshold of birthing a more aligned life. In her coaching and teaching she weaves astrology, storytelling, art and depth psychology. The motto she lives by is that we are all midwives to each others' dreams.

Find out more about her work at www.vanessacouto.com

ACKNOWLEDGEMENTS

There are many to whom I have gratitude for providing me the opportunity to work, especially my family.

I am also in deep appreciation for those who have helped me make this book possible.

I cannot get very far without acknowledging first and foremost my primary spiritual teachers, Raymond Kotai Lambert and John MacPherson who taught me the ways of the fakir, the monk and the yogi. Their dedication to all matters spiritual, and their devotion to my progress has made life not just bearable but beautiful.

To all of my students over the years who have attended retreats, weekly meetings, and private sessions, I give many thanks. You have enabled me to learn how to clarify these ideas for all of us. You have shown me that it is possible to carry a living transmission forward. Your dedication has meant so much.

To my women's groups, I give a most sincere shout out, for you dear sisters are the vehicle for the collective healing of women everywhere. May we come to see the balance of Sacred Masculine and Divine Feminine restored.

Thank you to Dawn and Sean for all of the proof reading and countless corrections.

Thank you to Jason Storey for his beautiful design work and unending patience with me.

Thank you to Vanessa Couto for being the amazing artist that she is and contributing so greatly to the look and feel of this book.

Thank you to Russell and Tony for reading this manuscript and providing your candid input. I am in deep gratitude for this.

Finally to my immediate family, Sean, Alexander and Zoe, Schuyler and Lila. You are my rock, my joy, my everything, not to mention lots of grist for the mill. I love each one of you dearly.